T0329703

PEN AND SWORD

MARY S. MANDER

Pen and Sword

AMERICAN WAR CORRESPONDENTS, 1898–1975

UNIVERSITY OF ILLINOIS PRESS

URBANA, CHICAGO, AND SPRINGFIELD

Library of Congress Cataloging-in-Publication Data
Mander, Mary S.
Pen and sword : American war correspondents,
1898–1975 / Mary S. Mander.
p. cm.
Includes bibliographical references and index.
ISBN 978-0-252-03556-2 (cloth : alk. paper)
1. War—Press coverage—United States—History—
20th century. 2. War correspondents—United States—
History—20th century. 3. Freedom of the press—United
States—History—20th century. 4. Censorship—
United States.
I. Title.
PN4888.W37M36   2010
070.4'33309730904—dc22   2010007689

*This book is gratefully dedicated to
Dr. Alycia Chambers, who is truly made of gold.*

Contents

Acknowledgments

Most of this book relies on unpublished manuscripts and military records. I want to thank the many librarians from Boston to California who helped out. Librarians are often the unsung heroes in our information age.

I would also like to thank Rebecca McNulty and Joan Catapano for their great patience and professionalism throughout the review period. Two blind readers gave my text a thorough reading and made excellent suggestions for revision. Terri Hudoba did a stellar job of copyediting. This book is much better for all their work.

My friends have heard about this book for several years. They were supportive—tirelessly so. They include Mary McGuire, Cynthia Finch, and Carolyn Marvin.

The late Jim Carey would have liked this book, I think.

I also must thank the Pennsylvania State University for supporting my work. Many thanks go to my deans Stanley Paulson, Brian Winston, Terry Brooks, and Doug Anderson. There's a special place in my heart for Doug's help because he made it possible to finish this project.

Abbreviations

This list of abbreviations was compiled with the younger reader in mind. Younger generations no longer are necessarily informed about what the Boomer Generation would instantly recognize. Common, widespread abbreviations such as U.S. or CBS are not included here.

AGDF   Adjutant General's Document File (not to be confused with AGO records)

AEF   American Expeditionary Force

AG   Adjutant General

AGO   Records of the Adjutant General's Office (not to be confused with AGDF)

AGWAR   Adjutant General, War Department

CPI   Committee on Public Information

FSB   Fire Station Base

G-2-d   Press Censorship Division, Intelligence Section of the Army

GHQ   General Headquarters

GI   General enlistees in the Army in WWII and sometimes in Vietnam

GVN   Government of (South) Vietnam

INS   International News Service

MACOI   Military Assistance Command, Office of Information

MACV   Military Assistance Command, Vietnam

MACVOI   Military Assistance Command Vietnam, Office of Information

MP	Military Police
MPC	Military Payment Certificates
NCO	Noncommissioned officer
NEA	Newspaper Enterprise Association
ONI	Office of Naval Intelligence
PACEX	Pacific Exchange
PIO	Public information officer
PRO	Public relations officer
RG	Records Group
SHAEF	Supreme Headquarters, Allied Expeditionary Force
UPI	United Press International
USO	United Services Organization

PEN AND SWORD

Introduction

In the war in Iraq, many journalists are described as embedded. Being embedded means news reporters are attached to military units engaged in armed conflict. This is not a new development in the history of American war correspondence. In every war discussed in this book (from 1898 through Vietnam) reporters accompanied soldiers into battle. The term "embedded" was first used during the U.S. invasion of Iraq in 2003, largely because the military was responding to pressure from news organizations that had had only limited access in the 1999 conflicts. Furthermore, in every war save the one in Cuba against Spain, journalists signed agreements to qualify for accreditation.

The term "embedded" provoked criticism, largely by armchair pundits, of the arrangements worked out between the military and the news media because critics thought such arrangements amounted to a propaganda campaign.[1] There are many good reasons to embed journalists. Chief of them is survival. Of the 123 reporters killed in Iraq at this writing, only seven were embedded. It is true some reporters sent a few pieces of inaccurate information—but that has occurred in every war studied here. There is no perfect information universe.

Journalists bring their own supplies to the front. What they don't bring is paid for by their news organizations. Of course, journalists depend on the military for transportation to areas of battle and use of transmission lines to send their stories home. But where else would you want to report the war other than alongside the soldier? Being embedded gives journalists a front row seat and makes it possible for them to be the walking advertisement of the nation-state.

The view that journalists are puppets of the military is insulting to the intelligence of news reporters, and it is unmindful of the history and practices of modern American war correspondence. This book provides an introduction to this important aspect of journalism in the United States: the history and development of modern war correspondence. It is a synoptic account in the sense that the text situates its subject within the history of Western civilization as well as the history of modern warfare. It also provides an account of the war reporter and his search for meaning in a landscape where annihilation is a daily reality and where his very existence is put on the line.[2] It takes a great deal of courage to be a war reporter and an acute intelligence to find the words to convey his experience to his public.

In the following chapters I place American war correspondence in the larger panorama of the history of the printed press because doing so allows us to understand journalism in a much broader way than if we simply recounted the facts of the matter. That is, the institution of the press developed as a source of organized dissent and it is in dissent that the modern practices of censorship have their origins.

The ties between journalism and the state rest historically, then, in organized dissent, the hallmark of modernity and the reason why nation-states were formed. During war, the journalist's role in the life of the nation becomes more explicit than his role in peacetime. At the same time, censorship also becomes more explicit. I found such patterns of explicit censorship in archival records revealing of, among other things, the relationship between the First Amendment and other amendments to the Constitution of the United States—especially the Fourth Amendment. During war journalists often invoke the Fourth Amendment when their freedom to report on the war is being curtailed.

The period of time covered here stretches from 1898 through the Vietnam era. As such it showcases the evolution of the war correspondent from the beau ideal of the Spanish-Cuban-American War to the kind of postmodern war correspondent that emerged in Vietnam. This evolution must be understood if we are to understand the current war correspondent in the Middle East wars.

One cannot speak about war correspondents without speaking about the First Amendment. I have tried to avoid the pieties resorted to from time to time, the kind found in movies where a CIA officer aware of rogue agents chooses to go to the *New York Times* with his story rather than to his superiors or to Congress. This portrayal of the free press often raises the First Amendment to the level of a sacrament. A sacrament bestows grace. It is sacred; it dwells in the land of the unquestioned. The trouble with treating the First Amendment this way is that it can mask what is really happening. The outward sign of a sacrament is a ritual, a rite, whereas the outward sign of a free press is reasoned debate. A law is not a sacrament, it is a rule governing our public conduct. It is a guide helping our community to live according to our most basic values—those we all hold in common. The Constitution of the United States and the Bill of Rights are not calls to worship. They are parts of our common wealth. I have found that when journalists start to talk about the First Amendment as if it were sacred, they have stopped talking to their public and are talking to one another. And when the press is not communicating with the public, it is not safeguarding the integrity of the nation-state.

This is not to say that these national documents cannot or should not sacramentalize a journalist's experience. It is simply to note that scholars writing about journalism should bracket sacramentalized experience to explore it more fully.[3] This kind of journalistic experience is evoked by any challenge being made to any aspect of the founding documents.

The overall argument of this book is that the war reporter is a walking advertisement for the nation-state. By "walking advertisement" I refer to those early forms of advertisement found in the nineteenth century when a person was hired to walk around U.S. cities wearing sandwich boards looped over his shoulders that advertised something "not to be missed" by those, say, with discerning palates. I also mean to suggest that the war reporter carries around with him certain assumptions about his importance to the nation in living out the ideals embodied in the Constitution and the Bill of Rights.

This theme is developed in each chapter. Chapter 1 concerns the historical context needed to fully understand the evolution of war correspondence. Here I examine nationalism and its relation to journalism: the origins of journalism are rooted in the nation-state, particularly as it was framed in America. From there I plot the rise of conscription. If it were not for conscription, there would have been no Ernie Pyle. An Ernie Pyle only makes sense in the context of a universal or near-universal draft. Finally, chapter 1 explores military practice and praxis. By praxis I mean what passes for common sense among soldiers and journalists alike. Understanding military praxis is as important as understanding journalistic praxis because military praxis influences how a journalist experiences wartime conditions.

Chapters 2, 3, and 4 explore the evolving nature of censorship as it was administered by the nation-state over a period of about seventy-five years. These chapters examine how the military and the press interacted in each of four national wars: the war of 1898, the two world wars, and

Vietnam. I did not include the Korean War because it was the first war of the United Nations. By the time of the Vietnam war the army and navy had developed well beyond their World War II counterparts. Though it is true that Vietnam was the last war of the Cold War era, I refer to it as the nation's first postmodern war. It was postmodern for several reasons, but mostly because popular culture had pervaded the military and the press in ways that altered what each of these groups of players would do in carrying out their assigned duties, whether as soldiers or reporters, in the drama of world history. It was also postmodern because the mass media play an important part in how reporters in Vietnam understood themselves. (The clearest example of this is *Dispatches*, Michael Herr's book on Vietnam. There comes a moment when he recognizes that his own actions seem to follow the outline of a Hollywood script, where the reporter dashes from one building to another and crouches to avoid enemy fire.) Finally, Vietnam was postmodern because the military, like other institutions, was operating in an economy that since 1952 had been dominated by information and services.

In chapter 5 I redefine censorship, making it a medium or a particular kind of culture. Instead of looking at press censorship in wartime as a set of restrictions regulating what was publicly known, I redefine censorship as a particular kind of occupational culture.[4] Doing so allows us to see aspects of the press in wartime that we might otherwise not recognize or that we might discount. Hence I am asking the reader to set aside notions of censorship as prior restraint or any other mode of restricting what is published.

Nowhere do I suggest that reporters have been or are mouthpieces of the government. Rather, they dance with their partners in concert. One moves back, the other forward. Both avert their faces in a Janus-like posture of the directed glance. Truth be told, neither is really comfortable with the relationship the dance imposes on its partners. And when it comes to war correspondents, the partnership showcases not only the role of violence in our society—war—but also the journalist's ardor, his passion. At the same time the stance of the dance partners reveals their actual solitude and separateness. Chapter 5 describes this tango by examining the seven general patterns of behavior I found in the history of American war correspondence.

Having sketched out the role of censorship in the history of the press in wartime, chapter 6 then turns to the experience reporters had covering war. Early on in my studies of the press in wartime, I began to notice certain generic patterns in reporters' private and published accounts. The traces of genre found in journalistic experience surfaced like dolphins from the sea: the romantic dimensions of the epic, surrealism, irony, common sense, and tragedy. The most overtly nationalistic trope is the one of epic dimensions I found in the Spanish-Cuban-American War and in the opening weeks of America's entrance into World War I.

During the early days of my research I was uneasy about finding these traces because I knew that history is a jumble of things. The things I wanted to explain were messy, partial, misleading sometimes, and often ambiguous. Nobody went to bed in the middle ages and woke up in the Renaissance, as Isaiah Berlin noted. However, I could not deny the slices of surrealism or irony I found. I saw in the material I was looking at a set of binding elements that fell into place over the course of several years. That is, it seemed to me that the data—these tropes—suggested that the journalist was bound to something. My uneasiness led me to seek a deeper understanding of trope or genre in the literature on literary forms. Chapter 6 iterates the resolutions of these dilemmas.

When a journalist is situated in the scene of battle, his experience of violence and its aftermath quickly melt into conscious and unconscious meaning. The process of meaning-making is intrinsically an act of interpretation. The war correspondent's work, even in its most objective form, is an act of critical interpretation. There would be no point to journalism if reporters did not exercise their critical intelligence.

What is more, a report on TV or in the newspapers is also an evaluation. Whether the journalist became a professional through a college degree or through the school of hard knocks, he will seek erasure of himself from the scene he is writing about. He becomes invisible, but no less there than if he had taken a photo of himself for inclusion with the story. He does this disappearing act because he seeks an unmediated encounter with truth. His report tells us how to see this death, this battle, this war.

War correspondents compose stories rather than essays or chronicles because narrative allows them to speak of the horrific. As they wade through bloody battle sites, they seek the words they need to apprise the country of the day's successes and failures. Narrative is the most suitable of mediums because it is the simplest (and oldest) of speech structures. It is organized by time, a category of understanding simple enough for even a traumatized person to use. This happened, then this happened, and finally this happened. This compositional medium allows all of us to speak the unspeakable.

When a journalist uses these tropes he becomes an embodied ethos.[5] By "embodiment of ethos" I simply mean that his person represents far more than his own individuality. It represents the relationships we all have to one another and to ourselves as a democratic, American body. This is so because in accounting for his experience, the reporter assumes an obligation—to the soldier and the public—that he and only he can execute. His editor, especially, is not in a position to do this. And when editors intervene in a reporter's work, when they tell a reporter to change the story, or when they ask him to compromise on his autonomy, the true journalist will balk. And the reason he does so is because he is an embodied ethos. In his lexicon, he *owes* it to the citizen-soldier and the public to "tell it like it is."

Following Adam Newton's lead, I use "narrative" and "ethics" as reciprocal terms. Ethics are not treated here as a priori ideas or prescriptives. Ethics are relationships. They exist only *in* relationships. The deep-focus research a journalist does, the questions he asks, and the sources he both cultivates and protects—all of these are tools ensuring his objectivity, his fairness. Being fair is more than an occupational requirement. Being fair is part of being ethical. When editors and politicians tamper with a journalist's work, they encroach upon more than his job, they encroach upon who he is. He feels it in his gut, in his heart, and in his mind.

Chapter 6, then, documents the war correspondent's experience. It notes the tropic dimensions of his experience and it comes to a conclusion about their significance.

Chapter 7 details the occupational culture of American war correspondents based on everything the text has documented and developed up to this point. It is done in broad strokes to clearly portray the kind of occupational culture war reporting is. This chapter is not so much a summary of previous chapters as it is a sketch of the everyday world of the American war correspondent, a picture meant to convey his occupational culture. It is not an "ideal type." It is a narrative account.

The Conclusion sums up the main findings of the study. I also indicate the degree to which these findings are applicable to the wars in Iraq and Afghanistan. There are certain constants in battlefield conditions that both soldiers and reporters have to take into account as they do their work. For example, every battle is mediated by its terrain. A mountainous area will present problems that a flat desert terrain will not, and vice versa. This is as true of postmodern warfare as it was of any previous war, even though in some instances the soldier is sitting at a base in America and directing strikes through satellite connections against an enemy thousands of miles away. He still has to know the enemy terrain and how the enemy thinks about it.

This book was written in the spirit of the late Jim Carey's call to reinvent the field of journalism history.[6] It involves the telling of events from the point of view of the actors in the drama, rather than from a bird's-eye view. However, it goes beyond cultural studies because it rests on the research paradigm called hermeneutics. It privileges experience rather than certainty (as statistical social sciences do) or commitment (as critical scholars in general and British cultural-critical studies in particular do).[7] To avoid misreadings of my work, I want to itemize how this study departs from those traditions.

In the sense used here, "culture" does not refer to a way of life or an anthropological interpretation of a subculture. It also does not refer to or examine the traits of "high," "low," or "commercial" culture. Instead it treats culture as "webs of significance" with which we come to understand our lives.

Clifford Geertz was to the last half of the twentieth century what Freud was to the first half. Geertz's seminal work, *The Interpretation of Cultures*, influences many areas of study beyond his own field. In it he writes, "One of the most significant facts about us may finally be that we all begin with the natural equipment to live a thousand kinds of life but end in the end having lived only one."[8] The reason: we are encultured animals. We do not live by bread alone, but also by the meaning-making we practice. We are born, we grow, we experience, we mature, we decline, we die. In each of these stages our search for the meaningful turns who we might have been, our potential, into who we actually are.

While most cultural studies of this kind accept Kenneth Burke's definition of humankind as "animal symbolicum," I do not. I prefer the term "the historied being" because it more correctly sees not language as central to the development of humankind, but experience. Experience covers more areas than language because in all stages of life we know more than we can say. Experience is the primary datum of this study— the American war correspondent's experience, that is. I do not mean to suggest that American experience is paradigmatic of all journalists. But I do hope that this study will lead other scholars to study the wartime press in other political units.

Experience precedes language and sometimes, for example, in violence, language fails to materialize. The lack of language to get at the experience does not limit the effects of the violence on each person involved. If it did we would have no need for psychotherapy.

Hence, this book assumes that humans are in essence "historied." As such "human nature" is too generalized and universal a term to really tell us much about human beings, as Geertz so eloquently tells us. Consequently I focus not on rationality or essence in the philosophical understanding of the term but on the person, or the historied entity. In this way, this is a history of meanings disclosed in a range of evidence that includes press practices (e.g., interviewing sources, corroborating facts), and a reporter's attitudes (toward his editor, the soldier, his sources, the public, his audience), perceptions, published reports and columns, opinion pieces, and even personal bearing (clothing, posture, gestures).

The value of approaching historical events by recapturing the experience of a bygone day is that it allows those who were present at the time to speak for themselves, again. Many histories virtually remove the past from their accounts because they reconstruct them from the point of view of another era (their own). These histories are translations that appropriate empirical instances for their own ends. Often they are intent on showing how history has shaped the present moment. And there are justifications for doing so. A book like this one can and does build itself on these foundations. Moreover, society needs these kinds of histories. As Joan Didion wrote in *The White Album*, we do tell ourselves stories in order to live.

When I say history is what we are, rather than what happened, I mean to indicate the recursivity at the center of our lives. By recursivity I refer to the experience of bringing our past into the present moment, usually unconsciously. I also mean to showcase the significant differences between mainstream historical works and this one. Most historians ask the reader to look through the page to see social events, that is, a particular battle during the American Revolution. This history asks the reader to look through the page to see the experience of the actors in the drama, that is, what a particular journalist is going through as he reports the war.

Finally, a word about method. This study involved grounded-theory research—that is, the historical method of archival research, and the evidence gathered therefrom, relied on certain tools of interpretation. This entailed a constant process of triangulation. The study did not proceed from a set of hypotheses to a conclusion. Nor did it involve the discursive examinations of the cultural critical school. Hence it would be a misreading to see an ideal type in these pages. It would also be a misreading to introduce ideology as a fitting heuristic concept into the mix.

I am saying that ideology cannot be found in the experience of journalists—in other words, ideology is a legitimate concern for contemporary scholars. However, in this particular study it would be a mistake to think *I* am talking about ideology. When David Halberstam was diving for cover in Vietnam, he was not thinking, "I am (or am not) subject to ideology." This, even though scholars of another era could demonstrate the truth that he and the American press corps in general never questioned the ideology of the Cold War. He was experiencing fear and doubt. It is this sort of thing my study seeks to understand.

At the same time, I think a study of this sort can be mined for material supporting the work of these scholars. If nothing else, this book indicates that the process of ideology formation is influenced by trope formation. By this I mean to open up communications study in general and journalism study in particular to the influence of reading and absorbing the tropical understanding of experience found especially in literature.

This study proceeded by collecting evidence from many public and private archives where the papers of the war correspondents are lodged. It included military records in the National Archives of the wars under study: the war of 1898, both world wars, and Vietnam. I also included the archival records of Pershing's punitive expedition into Mexico because of the role it played in establishing the legal limits of the state's right to censor the news. These and all the articles and books written by journalists comprise the primary evidence here.

Theory is the recognition of patterns. The process of theory making and data collection were reciprocal in this study from the get-go. This is important to understand because this process goes to the question of validity of interpretation. In other words, I did not anticipate the categories or tropes found in the evidence. The evidence—largely the views of war correspondents—constructed the recognition of patterns for me. If you are studying and then writing about experiencing, you cannot predetermine what you will find. You must allow your subject to reveal that. This means that a scholar does well to be open to what he or she doesn't want to hear, as much as it means to respect the research subject.

For readers who must be convinced that the subject matter of this book is important, or that there is something new to know about journalism, let me reassure you. The nation-state is a community that rests on dissent. Dissent provided the hallmark of modernity and named the reporter as its detail man. War correspondence is testimony to this process. Added to that, studying the press in war allows us to see how violence disenfranchises us all. By including the Vietnam war in this mix, we can begin to formulate an answer to the question, What is the relationship of the nation-state in postmodernity to the free press and to the public? Although America has fought many wars since Vietnam, we have not yet reflected on, much less fully articulated, our role in world affairs now that modernity has passed away. This book ultimately can contribute to those kinds of reflections.

1 The Historical Context for Understanding American War Correspondents

In America, the institution of journalism shelters the nation-state. Even the most local story in a small-town newspaper or on its newscast is national, because the assumptions guiding its construction are grounded in our understanding of the nation-state. Every newspaper article, every newscast, and every documentary affirms and legitimizes the democratic community. No matter where a report appears—in the *Detroit Free Press*, the *New York Times*, the Springfield *Journal-Register*, on NPR, CNN, CBS, or a local radio station—wherever a news report is found, a national public is always present in it.

I say "in America" because each nation carves out a different set of practices governing its people and institutions, depending on its heritage and culture. In Europe, centralized monarchial states preceded democratic ones. From the very beginning, our national identity never supported a centralized state.[1] The features found in European states that were not part of the American scene in the eighteenth century include common ethnicity, common historical traditions, a national church, and centralized administrative machinery having the authority to act for the public.[2]

In the course of human affairs a principled conception of national identity emerged in America, inscribed in the Monroe Doctrine of noninterference. To early generations of the new republic, being neutral was not isolationism, as some have argued. Rather neutrality defined the nation as an entity beyond the sphere of Europe, that is, beyond its institutions as well as its influence. The doctrine was couched in terms of a "more perfect union." The new republic, unlike any other, provided the kind of environment where citizens could imagine themselves anew.[3]

Moreover, the relationship between the fourth estate and the government apparatus in Europe was different from the situation in the United States. In America, the press provided the nation-state its structural and procedural validity and has done so from the beginning, from the early days of the advocacy press to the commercial press. This resulted in a relationship that was consciously couched in adversarial terms.[4] Furthermore, public culture—not to say popular culture—its production and its consumption, became an ongoing political act. Consequently, even when done in the privacy of one's own home, reading newspapers and watching the news is an engagement in public life. This public life is not static and inorganic.[5] Abstractions like a priori and a posteriori are meaningless terms in public culture. Rather, it is ever emergent, daily being made and remade, shaped and reshaped, structured and transfigured. At the center of this public culture is the journalist.

This chapter examines the fundamental historical trends that were especially pertinent to the history and evolution of war correspondence. First, it situates the press in the larger history of the nation-state. From there it examines trends related to nationalism: censorship and conscription practices. The latter is especially pertinent to the development of someone like Ernie Pyle, whose stories were about G.I. Joe. Finally this chapter reviews changes in the military that professionalized the ranks in two distinct stages: those that culminated in World War II and those that were in place in Vietnam.

Journalism and Nationalism

The nation-state is of central importance in understanding journalism. The mythos of the nation-state in America is embedded in the mythos of the fourth estate and vice versa. It is set forth in documents like the Constitution of the United States and the Bill of Rights. These documents lend a greater degree of consensus to the events and values of 1776 than was really the case.[6] Such are their powers. In the 1970s, two hundred years later, the dissent and division of our society over the war in Vietnam seemed a troubling schism, one not seen since the Civil War. In truth, dissent has always been a defining trait of our republic.

Dissent as a hallmark of the modern nation-state has its roots in the eighteenth century. It became a social practice when newly emergent

European nations engaged in the struggle for self-definition, as well as the expansion, of their territorial possessions. In this struggle freedom of expression was often the center of debate. Hence the modern practices of the nation-state and, in America, journalism are both rooted in censorship. And it is censorship that gives these institutions meaning.

Originally journalism had been embedded in literature, which, with science, formed the first kind of modern public sphere. At the same time, the Protestant Reformation rendered all aspects of national and international discourse a problem because at this time religion was a political as well as a spiritual practice in the West. Furthermore, because religion was part of most everyone's daily life in a way that science and letters were not, much more was at stake in the debates concerning orthodox spiritual practices than in those debates about orthodox scientific practices. Consequently, censorship played a central role in the evolution of both the state and the fourth estate.

Furthermore, in the United States nationalism is tied to fighting for independence. Our nation came into existence as an act of breaking away that was based on social solidarity. Those who fashioned the new state were rebels with a collective identity. At the same time, recalling our beginnings this way casts into eclipse the considerable differences of opinion within the founding communities. Few people realize the degree to which colonists debated alternatives. Rioting and revolt were directed toward other "Americans" as much as they were aimed against England. Some states or parts of same tried to go their own way. As Rogan Kersh has shown, thirteen disparate, squabbling colonies came together. Sniffed a Tory observer, "They can never be united . . . they will be a disunited people till the end of time."[7]

The quarreling, the sniping, the clashes in interests underlined just how disparate the colonists were. A contemporary of the times observed that colonists had little in common. They varied in manners, tastes, customs, religious orientation, and traditions. They were scattered hither and yon. They enjoyed local prejudices, bigotry, jealousies, and aversions.[8] And yet, as John Adams said, "Thirteen clocks were made to strike together."[9]

Recent historians have chronicled the tendency toward exclusion by early politicians. Excluding people who differed in any way overcame local protests and yielded to the greater good of the Union. In the revolutionary period, citizens believed they were united by affective bonds, rather than by virtue or economic self-interest.[10] This set of beliefs was challenged in the Civil War. It was Lincoln who jettisoned the notion that Americans were linked affectively. He replaced this idea with a strict insistence on the rule of law as the binding element.[11] Ever since, we have had a reverence for the law because it is the institutional agent of political resolution.[12]

In addition, few people at the time really understood the realities the new nation-state would forge. Chief among them was a dramatic increase in the tax burden. In Massachusetts, for example, taxes increased from one shilling under English control to eighteen shillings in the newly established state. For some colonists, the revolution was a catastrophe. They got taxation with representation, but they paid through the nose for it.

The First Amendment ensured that the press would center on political codes of conduct that members of the press view as rules of proper conduct. Historically in the United States we have come to regard the journalist as the people's watchdog, given the task of guarding the nation, keeping an eye on the government, and protecting it from corruption of any kind through reasoned exposure. The reporter's task is nothing less than safeguarding the nation-state. Unlike law, the covenant binding the media and the public lies outside the nation-state, for it is that promise (to safeguard the nation) that gives the state its legitimacy in the first place. The law is the set of prescriptions outlining the limits of the state's power as well as the responsibilities of the citizen. The trust between elected or appointed officials and the public forms the covenant at the heart of our democracy. However, that relationship—between citizen and elected official—is brought into existence in the daily practices of the fourth estate. The state and its individual citizens are parties to one another, but only in communication.[13] Hence the importance and power of the press.

In times of armed conflict especially, the state becomes vulnerable and the basic freedoms that it promises are threatened. Witness the Patriot Act, passed on the heels of the tragedies of September 11, 2001. If nothing else, this action demonstrates the unreliability of the First Amendment, its fragility in the face of monolithic violence. War is a fault line, telling us where the fissures, the cracks, the social rifts are in our society. The importance of closely examining the evolution and development of the war correspondent is self-evident. For to understand his history is to understand our society.

The story of the press in America is interwoven with the development of nationalism. Nationalism is not a philosophical subject in the sense that Marxism or Liberalism is. It is a sociopolitical concept created in the eighteenth century and, in the ensuing years, marshaled deep psychological attachments, deep enough to sustain warfare. Since the

Second World War, as Benedict Anderson has indicated, "every successful revolution had defined itself in national terms and in doing so has
grounded itself firmly in a territorial and social space inherited from the
pre-Revolutionary past." As the title of his book, *Imagined Communities*,
shows, a nation is an imagined community. It is limited in the sense that
it is not inclusive of all humankind. It is sovereign in the sense that it is
self-governing. And it is conceived of in terms of a broad comradeship,
even in the face of deeply entrenched inequalities.[14]

Journalists act as spotlights. They ask the public to look in a certain
direction. They invite the public to examine politics and in the process
to renew the covenant of citizenship. In wartime, correspondents witness the lengths to which the state is willing to go to preserve itself.
For journalists such as Ernie Pyle, the story of war was the story of the
common man who was reduced to a name, rank, and serial number, but
who transcended that classification in death for the republic. In Vietnam,
where the tension between democracy and the realities of the Cold War
transcended territorial boundaries, journalists reinforced the value of
self-determination even as they challenged the state's agenda in that
violent, war-torn land. Women war reporters were the first to question
war as spectacle.

In some ways, the deep divisions that sprang up during the Vietnam
era (largely from the Tet offensive on) can be understood as a long period
of self-alienation. America had undergone other periods of alienation—
notably the Civil War. These periods allow a society to reinvent itself.
However, in the Civil War the journalist was not central to the process
of rebirth. In the Vietnam war journalists called into question the nation's identity—despite the fact that none of them questioned the legitimacy of the Cold War in shaping a nation's foreign policy. As the state
became less focused on its original identity, the fourth estate became
more contentious in Vietnam. No one at that time could foresee the fall
of communism that would take place within ten years of the end of the
war in Vietnam. And no one—military experts or journalists—really
understood that by this time, the U.S. Army was no longer the army of
their fathers. Rather, the army in Vietnam was occupationally professionalized. This first army of the postmodern world was one in which
each soldier was both an expert in waging war and an expert in areas
that were not necessarily tied to military matters. I mean, particularly,
soldiers had expertise in media production, specifically, television. The
military also used the latest technologies, both the computer and TV, as
a means of war-making. However, beyond that they provided radio and

television programming for enlisted men. It was during the Vietnam war that the armed forces professionalized themselves as television journalists and program directors. And, although the term "military journalist" may seem to some a contradiction in terms, these changes were regarded as matters of common sense to the armed services.[15]

It is much easier to see this in retrospect, but at the time journalists asked, Are we winning or are we losing? However, the validity of that question really died during World War II—if, indeed, it ever existed. In other words, in the period under discussion here, a truly decisive battle even during the Second World War was something of fiction. Postmodern warfare has no winners or losers—only benchmarks. This is so because between World War II and the Vietnam war the relationship between the armed forces and the American people changed from one of purely defensive purposes to one of diplomatic purposes. America need not have feared being overrun by the Vietnamese. What America was doing was furthering its socioeconomic vision.

In part, this point has already been made by Graham Green in *The Quiet American*. This book is about the idealism of an American new to Vietnam. It is an idealism that ill prepares him for the realities of that violent land.

Of equal importance in understanding the press in public affairs is the relationship between the First Amendment and other amendments. This relationship is brought to life when war breaks out. In the words of Simone Weil, "The kingdom of force renders mute all its subjects." In wartime men and women become killing machines. Hence when the gun is introduced into the equation, survival trumps the right to speak freely. War correspondents are not rendered mute by war, but a journalist by definition restrains himself from speaking or writing anything that would aid the enemy of his people. Beyond this sort of self-censoring, there usually is a state-administered censorship. The formalized procedures of censorship have been worked out over a period of about seventy-five years. In that time five wars embroiled our nation, each one having its own distinct moral environment. Censorship became the Jell-O within which war reporters and their news outlets were suspended like so many pieces of celery or carrot.

This environment of censorship operated even in Vietnam, where no formal process of submitting reporters' stories for clearance was set up because the adjutant general's office had declared very early in the twentieth century that the military had the right to censor the press only in wartime or whenever martial law was declared. Vietnam was not a declared war. Hence it is erroneous to think that the military "decided" not to censor journalistic copy. They simply had no authority to censor the press.

The inclusion of the Second Amendment in the Bill of Rights all but guaranteed that America would be a violent society. Violence in the private sector is unlawful and can be punishable, even by death. However, when violence occurs in the public sector in our country, the state protects its right to bear arms no matter what the cost. In times of war the state engages in organized violence and censors the press. Although free speech is the first in the list of rights we have, it is superseded by the Second Amendment during wartime or wherever martial law is declared. Consequently, in a land torn by the ravages of war, a viable fourth estate is usually seen as the first step in restoring peace. In real-life practices, this is why the functional democratic state's armies work to abolish the blue pencil as quickly as possible. By the same token, if the state's armies are not moving to abolish censorship, then there is no functional democracy.

Archival records show an increasing effort in systemizing the administration of censorship during wartime in the period of history studied here. However, they also indicate a range of beliefs and actions on the part of official censors, rather than a simplistic effort to ban some speech or to censor a journalist. From 1898 to the outbreak of World War II, the machinery for handling war correspondents grew ever more detailed, thorough, and comprehensive.

At the same time, government officials were always ambivalent about censoring news reports—even in World War II, when reporters had to deal with administrative roadblocks, especially in the Pacific theater. This is true because in both world wars the administrative machinery was staffed with men who were journalists in peacetime America. More than that, the military made a telling move by transferring journalists from the intelligence division in World War I to the public relations division in World War II. (It should come as no surprise, too, that a public relations agent thought up the so-called embedded journalism in the wars in the Middle East.) This view of the press as the arm of the government, rather than the watchdog of the nation-state, did little to prepare the military for the sometimes-scathing reports by the fourth estate in Vietnam.

Although the First Amendment is curtailed during war, reporters are still able to engage in an honest journalistic relationship with members of the military and the public. In fact, during war the organized office and procedures of censorship are a guarantee of press freedom insofar as they formulate and carry out agreed-upon principles of conduct on both sides. Virtually every American believes in the emancipatory properties of free speech and free press, and that includes soldiers.

This belief in personal emancipation at the hands of the First Amendment underscores the link between the state and the fourth estate. For the news reports of journalists, including modern war correspondents, are hortatory. They call members of the public to action, even if that only means turning on their televisions and watching the nightly newscasts. In reading or viewing the news about the war effort or the troops, Americans become viscerally engaged in matters of the state.

Journalism and Conscription

In the evolution of the nation-state, coercive military service of its citizens, or conscription, is worth looking into. In the context of world history, conscription is a recent development. In the context of journalism, conscription fashioned a new relationship between the journalist and the soldier. Without conscription there would be no Ernie Pyle. Conscription is also important because it pushed the boundaries of experience for all, citizen-soldier and journalist alike. Hence it became a factor influencing the interpretation of war. It is of great significance because reporting on wars constructed and shaped the felt ethical obligation on the part of those whom the public authorizes as witnesses to the slaughter of its young men and women: war correspondents.

Contrary to received wisdom, perhaps, the history of coercive military service is full of hesitations and inconsistencies. In one sense it reads as a series of evasions of military obligation. Understanding this allows us to view the set of wars examined in this book differently than we would if we imagined that World War II was the template experience—with its harnessing of all the state's resources, human and otherwise—that is, the model all wars should emulate. During the Vietnam war, people referred to World War II as the "good war."

As a social practice, conscription involved a long transition occurring roughly from the end of the eighteenth century to the middle of the nineteenth century. At the beginning of this period one usually finds imperial armies in Europe; at the end, one finds armies of the state.[16]

The experience of conscription differs from state to state. Prussia, for example, established a grid of recruiting districts from which a pool of soldiers was drawn. Although all men of the district were theoretically subject to the imposition of military service, the actual practice of recruitment exempted some—notably those who had property or were craftsmen, free peasants, or the sons of noblemen and officers. It was the rural poor who provided the human resources needed for the country's defense. The political result of this kind of recruitment was a dependable pool of disposable men and, simultaneously, the increasing authority of the state over the locality. In the case of Prussia, this meant in effect that the state began to intervene between the squire and his serfs.[17]

While Prussia imposed a system of compulsory service for a certain portion of its population, France used a voluntary system of enlistment. In both cases the rhetoric of recruitment identified a universal military obligation, yet neither state actually fully implemented the principle. Thus the idea of universal compulsory service was accepted before the methods for raising conscripted armies were used.

In contrast to the European experience, Americans have used selective service rather than universal service.[18] Such an approach requires an answer to the question, Who is to serve when not everyone is to serve? There is no doubt that poor and working-class youth were selected over their middle- and upper-middle-class brothers.

In 1862 the Confederacy enacted the first draft in the United States. A Union bill soon followed. The law at the time allowed men to hire substitutes. Alternatively, they could pay a fee of three hundred dollars in lieu of service. Hence, Union forces fought with the "rich man's money and the poor man's blood."[19] This system also operated in America during the war of 1898.

In May 1917, Congress passed the Selective Service Act. It increased troop strength from 200,000 soldiers and 9,000 officers to 4 million soldiers and 200,000 officers. This law contained many full exemptions for ministers, divinity students, and other officials. Conscientious objectors could also seek a noncombatant status. There were no commutation fees, however, nor were substitutes allowed. The president had the authority to exempt men in certain occupations. By the end of World War I, more than two million men were drafted, or about half of the total force in service.

In the two decades following World War I, there was no conscription. Then in 1940, Congress passed the first peacetime compulsory military service law. During World War II, the draft moved toward nearly universal service. By 1942, a half million men were called to duty every month. And when the draft expired in 1947, President Harry S Truman moved to reinstate it because he had concerns about the Cold War and where it might eventually lead.

The 1948 act allowed for drafting men to fight in Korea and Indochina. At this time class bias was reintroduced into the equation—that is, the new law was a selective service one. Those men selected were from the working and lower classes. In the years between 1948 and the

Vietnam war, draft classifications were codified in an elaborate set of rules establishing who was eligible to serve. A lottery system was introduced in 1969, a year after the Tet offensive. Under its rules, several kinds of exemptions were allowed. Furthermore, each individual had to meet basic mental and physical standards. Many men elected to take exempt occupations and student deferrals.[20]

Hence, the history of conscription evolved over many years to cover millions of men and women who gave their lives for their nation. During the first half of the twentieth century the draft changed the nature of the relationship between soldier and reporter. Like the sand that soaks up the ocean's waves, conscription and the culture of military solution in essence renders being a journalist ethical. This is why I say that the American war correspondent is the embodiment of the ties that bind us all, both as human beings and as citizens.

When I say that a journalist is ethos I mean he is the very embodiment of the social values our nation tried to codify in the eighteenth century. Surely journalism is a vocation rather than just a job. It is a way of life, a way of "being in the world," as the hermeneutic philosopher would put it.[21] When conscription became the means to raise an army, when no one is exempt from performing his or her service to the nation, then the ties that bind the journalist to the public are greatly intensified.

In other words, a journalist doesn't *have* ethics; a journalist *is* ethos. He is ethos not because he must narrate the deaths of our sons and daughters, but rather because in every story he writes there are present certain reciprocal claims binding the reporter to the reader, the soldier, the viewer, other journalists, and, indeed, everyone about whom he writes.

Thus, the history of conscription in the United States was selective, or class based—except for World War II, where millions were called to serve. In the world wars, too, journalists were considered an important arm of the military; they wore uniforms and had the same privileges accorded to the officer ranks. Along with those privileges came the responsibility to report about those who pay the ultimate price. A journalist's mere presence on the battlefield is a promise of sorts not only to the public but also to the soldier.

Again, a journalist is ethos because all journalists, during war or peace, are the living embodiments of one of our nation's guiding beliefs found in the First Amendment. But more than that, the war correspondent is the conscience of the nation in many ways. Conscription, or the call to duty as a citizen-soldier, intensifies the ties that bind because life itself is at stake for so many. The journalist is the embodiment of what ought to be and what ought not to be.

Because the story of the modern war correspondent is the story of his integration into the military machinery of the nation-state, it is necessary to look also at the evolution of military praxis from 1898 through 1975. All matters military had consequences for the role of the press in American history. For to be integrated into the system meant that the journalist shared what passed for common sense among citizen-soldiers.

The Evolution of Military Praxis

Historians have written about the impact of war on society, including the impact of new forms of technology and consequent changes in military strategy. Much of this work concerns the industrialization of weaponry. For example, contemporary work indicates that in Europe, modern weaponry in the age of total war frustrated the quest for decisive battles.[22] This is important for the subject matter of this book because the common view of the Vietnam war held that it was a guerilla war with no fixed fronts, and as such was a departure from previous wars. This literature indicates that even in a war of overt troop movements, like the Second World War, the concept of a "decisive" battle eluded military planners.[23] Modern weaponry in the first half of the twentieth century rendered obsolete the concept of a clear and decisive victory or defeat. Hence, Vietnam became the laboratory for designing postmodern armed forces. It was not an aberration so much as it was the beginning of a new kind of military. Neither the military nor the press at that time really understood that. Once the machinery was in place, all players worked in concert. Thus, in less than a century, "changing weaponry altered the nature of military professionalism as well as the armed services' relationship to the civilian world."[24]

Other significant changes in the navy and army from the Gilded Age to the Progressive Era contributed to the maturation of military forces. A central development was pursuit of modern weaponry. After the Civil War, the U.S. Navy went into decline. Naval officials worried about the armed services keeping abreast of developments in the world. To that end, the Naval Institute, the Office of Naval Intelligence, and the Navy War College were established. Under their auspices the officer corps underwent postgraduate work in the science and art of conducting war.[25]

Accompanying these developments, the navy changed its fleet mission from a defensive to an offensive enterprise. Under the tutelage of Benjamin Tracy, the navy began to match strategy with diplomacy at a time when America was emerging as a world power. In 1894 it began planning for war with Spain. When war was declared in 1898, the navy learned some hard lessons about its weakness in navy yards and naval ordnance. Hence the war of 1898 helped lift barriers on naval building as America made a long-term commitment to establish a first-class navy.[26]

Overall, whether dealing with politicians in Washington, D.C., doing business in Bethlehem, Pennsylvania, or educating the ranks in Annapolis, Maryland, the navy was a flexible organization. The result, over a period of several decades, was an erosion of the line dividing the public and private sectors in all matters military accompanied by the circulation of personnel, both military and civilian, in a huge modern bureaucracy.[27] All of this was not lost on the press in World War II, for reporters working in the Pacific theater of operations had to deal with this bureaucracy on a daily basis.

As for the army, it too went into decline in the years following the Civil War. However, army reform differed from the naval enterprise. It took place independent of any civilian guidance and did not proceed from the revolution in weaponry, for example, changing artillery guns.

General William T. Sherman was baptized in the Civil War, where he conducted a relentless and ruthless war of attrition in the South. He believed that the army was meant to fight methodically, using all the resources of the country to destroy the enemy.[28] To Sherman, preparedness meant having effective command and administrative systems to mobilize efficiently and train mass armies. By the time of the war of 1898, however, glaring deficiencies became apparent in both command and administrative aspects. Some of the ensuing reforms (e.g., commitment to a national reserve) met with great controversy. However, the army did experience success in some areas such as establishing schools and professional organizations and their publications.[29] The Army School of the Line and the Army Staff College began to prepare outstanding officers for general staff work.

Despite these trends in modernization, by the dawn of the twentieth century, the army had become hidebound and tangled in red tape. It had no centralized control and planning.[30] Leadership was weak.[31] It was not until World War I that the army made significant progress in preparing an officer corps for command duties. Officers began to think about ways to develop and use the citizen soldier.[32] And the Quartermaster Department became more efficient in moving supplies and troops. The most significant consequence of these changes, of course, was that they led the way toward mass conscription in World War II.

All of the changes in education, research, and weaponry meant that by the end of World War II the armed forces were a well-oiled, efficient machine where everyone had his part to play on the stage of world history.

While this situation was only minimally evident in the Spanish-Cuban-American War, by the time America entered World War I, the military was going full-throttle toward this end. The flawed organizational character in 1898 spawned reforms in the new century leading the military to scrap the office of commanding general and to give first place to a general staff/chief of staff kind of organization. By this time the system itself passed for common sense in all matters military. Everything they did or planned to do had to meet the test of common sense. Its sheer size and the complexities of new technologies in armaments, as well as more streamlined and fail-safe chains of command all depended on how well the system operated.

Besides these changes involving military culture, Americans made several other cultural transitions during the period studied here that I will not explain in great depth. But these developments, too, left their marks on future generations and so they must be mentioned.

At the end of the nineteenth century, Americans were concerned about the closing of the frontier. This concern precipitated a fear that the country might be going into a state of decline because there no longer was an environment for the pioneer, who took off his immigrant clothing and donned his American garb in the wilderness.[33]

In the first two decades of the twentieth century America took on a new form of capitalism, regulatory capitalism.[34] The country also underwent a series of transitions, changing from a group of isolated communities to a nation connected by a national rail system and telegraphic communication. And the growth of the press accompanied this as part of an integral sense of the nation's life.

At the same time, the orthodox beliefs of the genteel class—the class to which Henry and William James and Richard Harding Davis (the most famous war correspondent until his death in 1915) belonged—were being challenged. The genteel view of America rested on familiar distinctions between higher and lower classes, advanced and backward viewpoints, and "civilized" and "lawless" mentalities.[35] The group of journalists covering the war in Cuba reflected these distinctions. However, while Davis engaged the genteel life, and Stephen Crane the life of letters, men like Sylvester Scovel (who worked for New York dailies in 1898) became the prototype of the working stiffs of modern journalism to be found in the world wars.

Moreover, as a new intellectual class emerged,[36] men like Lincoln Steffens and his feature writer Abraham Cahan introduced the reader of the *Commercial Advertiser* to the "impassioned secular radicals liberated from religious orthodoxy." Among this group of radicals were a significant number of German Jews, including many editors of the new national magazines, such as the *New Republic*. Later, H. L. Mencken's *American Mercury* gave space to writers of the Harlem Renaissance, so much so that some traditional black spokesmen became suspicious of them.[37]

These myriad voices all came together and redefined America away from the previously entertained ideal and toward cultural pluralism. In this view every ethnic group, no matter the time of its arrival, becomes a cofounder of America.[38]

This chapter provides a summary of historic events affecting war correspondence in the United States. The press cannot be understood in absence of understanding nationalism. The nation-state carved out for itself certain rights, among them the right to raise standing armies through conscription. Despite the inclusion of a free press in the nation's founding documents, the military established through its Judge Adjutant General's office the right to censor the press in specific circumstances (as chapter 2 will show).

Conscription and censorship both left indelible marks on journalists. Censorship was thought to be a "necessary evil"—but only to a point. The recognition of legitimate rules regarding censorship allowed both the soldier and the journalist the freedom to do their jobs. Conscription made being a war correspondent an embodied ethos. As such both trends left the journalist more clear-eyed than he had ever been before.

War correspondents are a special breed of journalist. As chapters 2 and 3 will show, they became fully integrated into the military system by the end of World War I. They had to stay well informed about war strategy, tactics, ordnance, and command. They accompanied soldiers on the first, second, and third waves of assault, and so risked their lives. This fact alone testifies to their belief in the value of the democratic nation and commitment to its public.

2 Early Encoding of State-Administered Censorship During Wartime, 1898–1916

Nothing more clearly discloses all the thorny issues and problems surrounding the First Amendment than the history of government administrative bureaucracies overseeing what became public knowledge during wartime. The state began to concern itself with the publication of information in wartime at least as early as the U.S. Civil War. The speed of the telegraph ensured governmental oversight. President Abraham Lincoln authorized the military to seize telegraph lines in the North. Many military units in both the North and South refused to allow journalists to accompany them. Some editors were arrested, and publication of some newspapers was suspended.[1] Nevertheless, no centralized administrative guidance regarding press protocol or what could and could not be published was given to the press. Nor was the relationship between the military and the press or the press and the presidency a matter of published policy.

Before the United States declared war on Spain, reporters covered the conflict from both the Spanish and the Cuban sides. All correspondents departed from Tampa Bay and landed on Cuban soil several hours later. Once there they had to declare themselves to Spanish officials. General Valeriano Weyler issued passes allowing reporters to go where they wished as long as they did not breach the Spanish line of defense. When traveling alone, reporters stayed in hotels. When traveling with General Weyler, they messed with him and shared his accommodations—usually at a nearby sugar plantation.

When war was declared against Spain in 1898, the Signal Corps took over crucial telegraph and submarine cable lines. A newsman was appointed chief censor in the New York office of Western Union. However, those who administered censorship were more concerned with commercial (banking) transactions than with press dispatches.[2] The Adjutant General's office issued a set of press guidelines. One page in length, these guidelines were of a very general nature, stating that journalists needed a pass issued by the secretary of war. Once in the field, this pass would have to be countersigned by a designated officer. The military reserved the right to limit access to its units when such access would be injurious to military operations.

Although the guidelines, drawn up and signed by General Nelson Miles, noted that the "passes issued will be limited to the smallest number," a great number of passes were in fact handed out.[3] After giving out as many as he could, Secretary of War Lindley Garrison sent journalists directly to General William Shafter, commander of the invading armies. Instead of simply denying access to these journalists, the secretary shifted decision-making responsibility to the commanding officer in the field. "Feeling that as many passes had been granted from this office as could well accompany the troops," Garrison proposed "to leave it to [Shafter's] judgment and discretion as heretofore."[4]

One of the most interesting aspects of this early formulation of press guidelines is the military's identification of the reporter with the civilian: correspondents and all civilians inside the lines of the army were subject to the rules and articles of war.[5] Thinking of reporters as civilians ended during World War I. By then the military regarded reporters as part of the machinery of modern war—as soldiers with pens rather than swords.

In this chapter I argue that the story of administrative censorship in the United States is the story of the integration of the reporter into the military machinery of the nation-state. Over a period of fifty years, and in the face of worldwide destruction, the reporter became identified with and self-constituted by the military culture of the nation-state. In other words, in the world wars, news reporters and soldiers both construed the journalist as an important weapon in the arsenal of war. Moreover, the critical period in the evolution of this movement from civilian to military status occurred during the second decade of the twentieth century, when General John J. Pershing led punitive expeditions into Mexico. It was when the country was technically not at war that censorship practices became organized and codified.

The development of the state's overview of the press in wartime has its roots in the wars in Cuba and the Philippines at the end of the nineteenth century. In the world wars, the military recognized the importance of press cooperation and thus created "voluntary censorship." During this period, too, censorship was seen as a management concern. Finally, during the Vietnam war, censorship operations became largely a set of limited challenges to the reporters' presence in that country.

The End of the Nineteenth Century

In 1898, reporters complained bitterly about press censorship. In retrospect, however, censorship in the war against Spain was mild. Nevertheless, it was the first official, public step taken in the United States to codify press conduct during wartime. Yet, while the seed was certainly sowed in Cuba, the plant really took root during the Filipino uprising the following year (1899) and then later grew into a sturdy young sprout between 1914 and 1916 during the U.S. expeditions against Mexico. It was then that the United States institutionalized its censorship codes in response to the confusion and inconsistency of both journalistic and military experiences in Cuba. This codification was drawn up and set into practice during peacetime when neither war nor marshal law (legally the basis of censorship) was declared. Fifty years later, in Vietnam—again when no formal war had been declared—these codes were tacitly exercised. Journalists in that costly war remade the relationship between the press and the nation-state. To understand how and why we reached that point, it is necessary to track the development of censorship codes and practices.

In 1899, after the U.S. military occupied the Philippines, Filipinos disappointed with the failure of America's liberation of their homeland rebelled. As conditions of censorship steadily grew, American correspondents in Manila became increasingly restive. The Associated Press (AP), particularly, complained that censors were, one way or another, determining what sort of information was getting back to the United States.[6] General Elwell Stephen Otis, who commanded the U.S. occupation forces, responded to this criticism by saying that reporters themselves were sending their dispatches from Hong Kong and that he took great care to treat them all alike.

The dissatisfaction of the press in Manila came to a head when reporters there drafted a telegram for publication in their respective newspapers. Otis summoned them to his office and threatened "court Martial [sic]," a threat disclosing an assumption he was making about the role of the press in wartime.[7] The general was angry that correspondents had accused him of lying. Quickly denying this, the journalists amended their telegram and sent it on to Hong Kong for transmission to the United States.

While Otis reacted in the heat of anger, he did offer to make changes to the system. However, those changes were nominal in nature. In ways that are eerily similar to journalistic experience in Vietnam, correspondents charged that the people of the United States had received overly optimistic reports about the Philippines containing views that officers in the field did not share. Arguing that, contrary to published reports, the situation in the field was not well in hand, journalists said that the insurrection would not be squelched without increased force, that the tenacity of the Filipinos was greatly underestimated, and that volunteers in the military were not willing to serve any further. Reporters charged Otis with altering their stories and quoted him as saying that what reporters had written would only "alarm the people at home" and "have them by the ears."[8]

When the secretary of war asked for an accounting, General Otis wrote that he was not conscious of sending misrepresentations and that, in fact, he had been rather conservative in his curbing of the press. Otis informed the adjutant general that when he asked for documentation of instances misleading or misrepresenting reporters' views, journalists offered nothing "tangible except [to say that] my conclusions [were] unwarranted."[9] To reporters' charges, General Otis countered that they had defied military authority and were subject to punishable actions. They "courted martyrdom," he wrote. However, he also indicated that he was willing to remove censorship and let them transmit whatever they wanted.[10]

The next day, Otis reiterated that the journalists' charges were untrue. He insisted that the future would vindicate him.[11] Several days later, General Nelson Appleton Miles reissued his general orders governing the transmission of dispatches over military lines or other lines under military control. Press messages were fifth in order of priority, after military and government messages, state and civil dispatches relating to public business, and those of diplomatic agents from neutral countries.[12]

As long as they did not interfere with military business, press messages were transmitted free of charge over military lines closed to the general public. The press was allowed to use codes for reason of economy, as long as the codes were filed with the central office. Signal officers were enjoined to give journalists the fullest possible telegraphic facilities consistent with the public interest and in the spirit of impartiality and "unvarying courtesy."[13] At the same time, Secretary of War Garrison advised General Otis to treat the press liberally, "even to the point of practically meeting your expressed willingness . . . that the censorship be entirely removed."[14] But, he also cautioned that all dispatches about the military should be submitted to the censor in advance of publication. The secretary of war only wanted to curtail reports that would affect military operations in the field or offend military discipline. Although this suggests that he was fence-sitting, Garrison nevertheless acted in good faith and urged the general to effect his suggestions without advertising it: "Do it without announcing that you are going to do it."[15] While Garrison was applying pressure on Otis behind the scenes, publicly he referred to the "misstatements in the public press regarding the conduct of affairs in the Philippines."[16] It probably wasn't the first time—and certainly wasn't the last time—the military sent mixed messages to the press about which rules to follow.

Nevertheless, the AP continued to levy charges that censorship was unreasonably stringent. They insisted that the military had forced them to rewrite dispatches to suit the censor, rather than the facts of the case. The word "ambush," for example, was entirely prohibited and any news of a political nature was suppressed.[17]

Thus, by the end of the war of 1898, the administrative machinery for censorship of the press was tested and found wanting. In general, Secretary of War Garrison preferred to shift responsibility for giving out press credentials from Washington to the commanding officer in the field. Behind the scenes, Garrison went back and forth about what to do. In the same memo he directed the commanding general both to impose censorship and remove it. This milieu explains why the fourth estate was so unsatisfied with the situation, and why they responded by filing their dispatches from a neutral territory. Nevertheless, a seed had been planted that would grow into a sturdy sprout during the punitive expeditions into Mexico a decade and a half later.

The Punitive Expeditions into Mexico

It was in the period 1914–16 that the military began to explicitly address in published material the role of the press in a democracy seized by war. The appeal was to reason and caution concerning distortion of facts or disclosure of information about military movements or plans: "All right minded men agree that the greatest care should be observed in this matter. It is a fact that the press occupies a dual and delicate position, being under the necessity of truthful[ly] disclosing to the people the facts concerning the operations of the Army, and at the same time, of refraining from disclosing those things which, though true, would be disastrous to us if known to the enemy."[18]

These rhetorical strategies and appeals to reason and reflection were rooted in the powerful mythos of the Enlightenment. War was such serious business, the army observed, that only responsible men could be entrusted to it. And these responsible men would have no objection to submitting themselves to reasonable rules and regulations.[19]

The state and the fourth estate both saw reason as an indisputable arbiter in matters regarding national security. The experience of the Spanish-Cuban-American War and the Filipino Rebellion left an indelible mark on officers who were determined to avoid the confusion about press matters engendered in the wars at the end of the century and those affairs immediately subsequent to U.S. military action in the Philippines.[20]

At the onset of military maneuvers in Mexico, Secretary of War Garrison acknowledged the difficulty of creating an equitable policy for the press in such conditions. He wrote, "I realize that the whole field is a new one and that experience is probably the only guide that will lead us to a satisfactory conclusion."[21] Willing to make changes to meet exigencies that might arise, he outlined some amendments to the published field regulations. Since it was physically impossible to allow every reporter who applied for permission to accompany troops, he decided to choose a pool by lot.[22] In an effort to limit their number, the secretary allotted three spaces to each major press association and two spaces to minor associations. However, to get around *its own policy*, the War Department simply modified a reporter's bond to designate that he represented not the news service, but one of its subscriber newspapers.[23] Every rule is made to be broken—but more important, the rule breaking in the war with Mexico tells us that the War Department recognized the legitimate interests of the press and that the department had no interest in antagonizing the press.

Covering the punitive expeditions against Mexico (including maneuvers in Vera Cruz, Texas, and New Mexico) cost newspapers three thousand dollars per correspondent simply to accompany the armies. Two-thirds of this sum would be forfeited if the journalist committed any infraction against regulations. The rest would be drawn against to satisfy expenses in transportation, food, and supplies. (The army made its argument for such a high price based on the seriousness of its purpose. It feared that men seeking adventure rather than serious work would try to accompany the military forces.) In addition, journalists working for foreign papers had to have already "served" in other campaigns.[24] This requirement suggests that foreign correspondents whose nations were sympathetic, if not allied with the United States, were thought of as parties in service also to the ends of a democratic state. The mythic language surrounding the democratic nation-state used in all of these practices shows the crucial role that the concept of a free and self-determined democracy as a transcendent value played in guiding the day-to-day decision-making routines of journalists and soldiers alike.

It was also in these early twentieth century campaigns that the habit took root of appointing as censors men who had journalistic experience. Correspondents were required to wear uniforms at this time, and they had the privileges of commissioned officers.[25] If they hired messengers, as they often did, the courier would have the privileges of an army private.[26]

The story of the situation with Mexico bears repeating. On April 9, 1914, America's conflict with Mexico began to unfold when unarmed U.S. sailors were arrested in Tampico. In response, the U.S. Navy shelled Vera Cruz and the American Expeditionary Force landed and occupied the city. Mexico then severed relations with Washington. U.S. troops continued their occupation until November 25, after which they withdrew.

When U.S. forces landed in Mexico, reporters descended on Vera Cruz like flies to a spoonful of honey. Hearst's International News Service alone wanted accreditation for ten men, including photographers as well as writers. One writer could operate a wireless transmitter, foreshadowing a new problem the military would have to contend with: a medium of communication that could bypass telegraphic channels controlled by the military.[27]

General Frederick Funston, commanding officer in the field, sent an urgent message to the adjutant general's office asking for guidance on what privileges should be given the press. Many reporters were arriving in Vera Cruz by transport from Galveston. The deluge of reporters and the military's lack of preparation for it embarrassed Funston.[28] The War Department, in the meantime, was handling requests from newspaper editors for permission to send their reporters along with the troops.[29] U.S. newspapers received copies of the rules and regulations for press conduct before General Funston did. In addition, the president of the Mexican Telegraph company demanded to know what the status of reporters was. In exasperation, he informed Adjutant General George Andrews that "in view of the sensational press messages that are being received from Vera

Cruz, we respectfully suggest that it is important that the substance at least of these rules should be telegraphed to General Funston."[30]

The accreditation procedures in the first few days of the incidents in Vera Cruz were confusing. Records indicate that most military officers in the field preferred to wage war—what their training had prepared them for—rather than deal with the press. However, once the regulations were drawn up, little deviation from them was tolerated, as is the custom of a military culture. Consequently, the records of these administrative bodies tend to show incidents of *mis*conduct rather than those of good conduct, as well as the steps of decision and indecision. This pattern would reach its apogee in Vietnam.

In Vera Cruz only three skirmishes of record took place between the fourth estate and the military. Two are worth recounting here.[31] In May 1914, the military accused the *World*'s correspondent in the field of breaking regulations. Confidential cablegrams between General Funston and Secretary of War Garrison flew over the wires describing the altercations and the charges leveled at the reporter, who mailed a dispatch the censor at the cable station vetoed on the grounds that it was "farfetched" and a "mass of lies."[32]

Garrison talked with the editor at the *World*'s Washington bureau. He shared Funston's cables with the paper's managers and resolved to settle the matter by asking the *World* to replace its correspondent in Vera Cruz. While Garrison backed the general, he was also loath to make the incident public. The *World* took exception to this request, as might be expected given the occupational guidelines of a free press. The paper's position on the matter can only be inferred from Garrison's cables, because he returned the *World*'s wires to them at the conclusion of the affair.[33] The paper's principal objection, one which is representative of press reactions to military threats of disaccreditation after 1900, was that the journalist himself had not been allowed to make his own statement of fact.[34] In other words, the appeal made here and hereafter was to due process.

In the end, Murray was allowed to remain in Vera Cruz on the condition that his paper "order" him to "govern himself entirely and cheerfully in accordance with the regulations."[35] Evidently it was not enough for a reporter to obey the regulations; he was also required to be happy about it. This enjoinder to be cheerful is a cultural marker indicating the contemporary expectations (but not necessarily outcomes) for conduct becoming a gentleman or a soldier.

The secretary of war recognized in this incident what everyone concerned already implicitly understood: if a journalist wanted to circumvent censorship, he could. Censorship rules only worked with the permission of the newspapers that sent correspondents into the field.[36] General Funston himself knew the limits to which he could go. "I realize," he wrote to the adjutant general of the War Department, "I have the power to deal with Murray by withdrawing privileges or deportation as disturbing element comma but a WORLD [sic] is one of the strongest supporters of Administration [and I] fear such action might cause embarrassment."[37]

Contrary to public statements of both the military and the press, Funston's remarks indicate the degree to which the military had been aware of the hazards of political fallout consequent to its decisions. In declaring and indeed believing itself to be independent of the military, the press had supported our cultural mythos that there is a clear demarcation between military and civil interests, as well as one between military and press goals. These are fictions that function to reassure the culture that all is operating according to its founding ancestors' dreams.[38]

A second skirmish with the press concerned *Collier's* magazine, which wanted to send Jack London to Vera Cruz. The magazine's managing editor, Edgar Sisson, characterized London as "a distinguished American man of letters as well as a citizen of high character."[39] Given contemporary mores of middle- and upper-class public conduct, this was something of an exaggeration. Between the time that *Collier's* requested accreditation for London and the time the Fifth Brigade sailed to Vera Cruz, London himself had presented a telegram to officers from his editor indicating that the secretary of war had given him positive assurance that London could accompany the troops.[40] When Garrison queried him, the magazine's chief editor Mark Sullivan wrote a cryptic and curt note in reply: "I am compelled to assume that the spirit and wording of your letter was dictated by some urgency of public affairs; otherwise I should feel obliged to limit my acknowledgment of it to an expression of failure to understand its spirit."[41]

Garrison read this as a veiled reprimand for questioning the magazine about its representative in Mexico. His response was a summary of the known facts about Jack London's conduct. Garrison informed the editor that he had never given anyone an assurance that he would be able to accompany the troops in Mexico. The secretary closed his letter by telling Sullivan that if London used deception to accompany the troops he would be deported. Garrison asked for a copy of the reputed telegram, but it was never produced. At one point, General Leonard Wood was called into the matter because the magazine had argued that Wood had given London authority to accompany troops. However, Wood had done no such thing.[42]

Meanwhile, internecine wars continued in Mexico throughout 1914, 1915, and into 1916. In March 1916, Pancho Villa conducted a night attack on Columbus, New Mexico. Villa caught the town and the garrison there by surprise. He killed fourteen American soldiers and ten civilians before withdrawing back into Mexico.

President Wilson sent U.S. troops to the border, eventually reaching over 150,000 men. A week after Villa's attack, Brigadier General John J. Pershing conducted a punitive expedition mostly with U.S. Cavalry. What followed were several skirmishes with Villistas, as well as with regular Mexican troops. But Pershing was never able to catch Villa, and withdrew his forces in February 1917.

One of the most perspicacious statements to be formulated by the War Department in this period came at the hands of Woodrow Wilson's secretary of war, Newton D. Baker. It is the earliest formulated policy on the general principles of military-press relations that I found. Significantly, it indicates an understanding of *the press as an arm of war making*. Baker wrote the following to General Frederick Funston, who had charge of press matters in both the Philippines and Mexico.

> The matter is . . . very vexatious, as it is difficult to balance accurately the conflicting interests of everyone concerned. It is, of course the government's permanent duty to protect properly its military movements, and anything, which would tend to interfere therewith, must be subordinated. On the other hand, it is of national importance that a proper dissemination of military news be promptly furnished the public. . . . [The] psychological effect of a thorough diffusion of such items cannot be over-estimated. It should therefore be the policy of the Government to aid this distribution to as great an extent as is compatible with the military needs of the general situation.[43]

Baker, who was writing this letter four months into the punitive expedition, had come to recognize how crucial good military-press relations were to the interests of the nation, and the degree to which a healthy public sphere and, presumably, continuing public support rested on the work of war correspondents.

Thus, by the end of 1916, through trial and error the military had moved away from its plan to restrict the number of correspondents accompanying Pershing's troops. Baker sought Funston's "experienced advice," but with the admonition to keep in mind that several military columns would be in operation simultaneously—a comment prioritizing military needs and the growing complexity of war ordnance and industrial strategy.

The correspondence of newspaper editors with the secretaries of war during the years from 1914 to 1916 shows an unqualified desire to cooperate with military authorities. The only complaints to surface from the press about military handling of reporters concerned due process, inconsistency, and favoritism. For instance, the editor of the Chicago *Herald* wrote to Newton D. Baker that he had killed AP reports at the request of the military only to find out that the New York papers had gone ahead and published the information. "Might I ask the War Department to define the limits of censorship so that newspapers that live up honorably to not only the letter but the spirit of the law be not made to suffer through the action of other newspapers that whip the devil around the stump?"[44] This editor, like many others, argued that all patriotic newspaper publishers would respect the "wishes and orders of the War Department but they should not suffer from competition on the part of publishers who place and [sic] ephemeral piece of news ahead of their duty to the country." And he called for punishment of the parties who ignored military requests.

The Philadelphia *Ledger* and its syndicate were similar in their unmodified support of the military expeditions into Mexico. However, the *Ledger* went a step further and declared that an absence of members of the press from army troops would have negative consequences for the preparations for war. Reporters, it argued, were "the literary exponents of the nations [sic] life."[45]

The recognition of a transcendent order guiding the day-to-day decisions of responsible journalists is an important factor to consider in the history of the press in America. The press was not alone in being guided by this transcendent order, for the military and the civil government likewise assumed that patriotism was a greater value than, say, printing the latest news. But only to a point; some would print a story the military judged not in the interests of the expeditionary forces. That they did so suggests that along with this transcendent order was an interacting immanent one, the one that tells the story of newspapers' successful integration into a market economy by the second decade of the twentieth century. The significance of this, I think, is that an economic order is part of the fabric of the nation-state and at times assumes the upper hand over both patriotism and military affairs. A market economy, in other words, is not one among a number of alternative economies—for example, regulatory capitalism or socialism—for this nation-state. It is part of the fabric of the whole. Consequently nation-states whose economic spheres are not free market will host a different kind of press with different sorts of procedures and different values. Another explanation is to understand a market economy less as "the bottom line" (which a good editor was expected to protect) and more as an abstraction that clings to a perfect equilibrium in public affairs.[46]

The nod toward profitability in the press's understanding of itself goes beyond the notion that the press must concern itself with "filthy lucre." It entails seeing itself as a source legitimizing or delegitimizing the government's officers and procedures in the quotidian world. In other words, concern for the bottom line should be read—in this context, at least—as proof of the press's independence from the government.

In the case of Mexico, the secretary of war referred the question of press control to the judge advocate general, who decided that military necessity justified control over newspaper correspondents exercised at points along the Mexican border. However, this necessity did not extend to locations where U.S. troops were not on duty, in effect allowing correspondents to send (with impunity) dispatches about the American Expeditionary Force from telegraph points near the border. The legal situation made the judge advocate general reluctant to formulate rules of censorship called for by the editor of the Chicago *Herald*. In the present circumstances, he counseled, "the patriotism of newspaper editors and their cooperation for the success of the expedition in Mexico . . . must be relied upon in respect to matters of censorship."[47]

The judge advocate general's suggestion—that the attention of editors be "invited" to see the injustice resulting in some media outlets failing to comply with requests of the War Department—was naive, even for the times. In fact, the U.S. Army War College pointed out as much:

> It is not believed that an appeal to the editors of all papers suggested by the Judge Advocate General, would effect any better result than has already been achieved. Some publishers would still fail to comply with such requests, and injustice would thus continue to those complying. Since the law does not permit an absolute censorship, in the absence of a declaration of martial law, nor the punishment of offenders as recommended by this editor, editors generally cannot be logically informed of any penalty, and it is not deemed good policy to inform them of a rule of the War Department which could not be enforced by some penalty.[48]

Here is the recognition of the limits of authority and its exercise that would guide the imposition of censorship as "voluntary" in the two world wars.

In addition, as has often been the case in the history of administrative censorship, the War Department followed a practice of inconclusion. The records of the adjutant general's office are replete with memos and cables counseling no action on its own part. The view was that the best strategy in handling affairs of censorship is one of evasion. What emerges from this body of correspondence is the rhetorical strategy of evasion. These communications have a fairly predictable form. They begin by stating the "facts," usually an account of someone's complaint or infraction. Second, they refer to known practices in recent history, in part due to the practice of citing precedent in the law. However, it goes beyond legal practice because history—with all of its inconsistencies and paradoxes—is collapsed in these memos into a legitimation of present practices or lack thereof. The third movement of administrative communication is the admission that the military's legal authority or the government's civil authority is limited.

Finally, there is a resolution, one which often is no real resolution for either the military or the press, and which must have caused consternation and frustration among military officers, newspaper editors, and war correspondents alike. A clear example of this sort of administrative maneuver can be found in a letter from the War Department to a film company in New York: "I am directed by the Secretary of War to inform you that the letter from the Private Secretary to the Secretary of War dated March 28, 1916 . . . and its inclosure [sic] . . . are hereby rescinded, in view of the fact that authority for the granting of permits to the individuals and corporations to take motion pictures of Army life is vested in the Commanding Generals of the several territorial departments."[49] The office of the adjutant general then directed Mr. Rogerman to apply to the commanding officers of the territories in which he wished to film.

The military had a great many reservations about allowing motion pictures or even photos of their camps or maneuvers.[50] The fact that I came across no mention of, much less objection to, sketch artists in the military records of the Spanish-Cuban-American War (when their work was still regularly published) would indicate that the military did not question their presence on the battlefield. However, it did not regard moving pictures or photographs as a form of news gathering. In the case of photography, the army wanted to allow only one photographer who would then make his work available to all who wished it. The army chose Underwood and Underwood, a commercial firm. In part the desire for only one photographer simply underlines the assumptions being made about photographs as capturing unreconstructed events. In other words, the military understood the process of photographing an event as one free of interpretive strategies. The photo simply captured what was there.

Yet, the press, too, was operating under the assumption that events free of interpretation can be captured on film. Their objection to having Underwood and Underwood supply photographs was that the firm was a commercial concern rather than a news-gathering one. The press believed that the photo captured an untampered-with reality, but that only news photographers knew which reality was newsworthy.[51] This signals, I think, that news images had reached a saturation point in which photos were thought to prove a truth unhampered by any faulty human misunderstandings. It indicates that by the second decade of the twentieth century, news photos had established a new mythos supporting the nation-state: the mythos of transparency, referring to the deeply rooted belief that all things national could be captured in the news that was so transparent the press's legitimacy could not be called into question.

When the incidents in Vera Cruz took place, the secretary of war intimated that photographers as well as those working for motion picture companies who wished to go to Vera Cruz could do so. His permission, however, was to conduct business there, not to be accredited to the American forces. At the same time, he cautioned them that they were expected to abide by the regulations the commanding general might establish. In an effort to be noncommittal on the question of visual media accompanying troops, Secretary Baker simply observed that he had "no objection to their going."[52]

During the events of 1916, William Fox, an agent from Underwood and Underwood, was appointed photographer to accompany the expeditionary force.[53] Early in the operation, the secretary sent directives to General Pershing and his staff in New Mexico stating that he did not approve any visual media other than Underwood and Underwood.[54] Despite having a monopoly on photographing the events in Mexico, the punitive expedition proved to be an unprofitable venture for the company. The expense of the enterprise amounted to more than the proceeds from the sale of pictures.[55] Plus, the war in Europe was of more interest to magazine and newspaper editors than the were troops in Mexico.[56]

As I have suggested, a central question facing the secretary of war during the punitive expeditions was the legality of censoring press publications. As Brigadier General W. W. Macomb pointed out, censorship could only be extended to newspapers or journalists in a specific theater of operations or in an area where martial law was in force. The Field Service Regulations did not indicate the press could be otherwise censored. Since martial law had not been declared in some areas, for example, El Paso, there was no way the military or the War Department could justify absolute censorship. Macomb noted that voluntary submission to censorship had had the fortunate result of suppressing information that Mexican leaders could have used to their advantage.[57]

After the occupation of Vera Cruz, the War College Division met and drafted a memorandum regarding control of the press in wartime. It submitted several recommendations to the Army Chief of Staff, among them that the president of the United States direct censorship in the absence of any legislation. The War College urged legislative action before the occasion arose for its application. It pointed to the confusion and dissatisfaction experienced by the British in their efforts to establish censorship in the aftermath of August 1914. However, War College Division records do not indicate whether the recommendation of its chief of staff resulted in any action.[58]

While members of the press registered their displeasure with the limited number of correspondents allowed to accompany Pershing's army, their appeals to the secretary of war or the adjutant general clearly indicate that they viewed their role as ancillary to the armed forces. Clair Kenamore, who worked for the *St. Louis Post Dispatch*, pleaded for accreditation on the grounds that he had been reporting on border matters for four months. He wrote that he'd done "all in [his] power and the paper [had] given widest publicity to stories which have tended fairly to justify action of the department and army." He further noted that he "had given the army the publicity it greatly needed."[59]

Many appeals were made on the basis of a paper's connections abroad or of the number of newspapers in a bureau's association.[60] The *New York Herald* argued that the federal government had always recognized it as an important news-distributing agent.[61] Sam Hughes, editor of the Newspaper Enterprise Association (NEA), argued experience for the NEA's representative. He had covered the German Army during the summer campaign of 1915, and had done so without incurring the wrath of the German staff officers. In fact, Hughes argued, the reporter's copy had been submitted to the censor and left untouched. The reporter in question was D. H. Durborough, who was in his midthirties and who had worked for papers in Philadelphia and Chicago. Hughes closed his appeal for accreditation with these words: "If I may be allowed to say so, I think that Correspondent Durborough would be a valuable man for the army in Mexico during this campaign. He made two long trips into that country for the Newspaper Enterprise Association in 1914. One of these visits was spent entirely in the camp of General Villa himself. Villa made Mr. Durborough the recipient of very many attentions. The result is that Durborough knows Villa and his methods like a book. . . . I am very sure that this knowledge could be made of service to the army."[62]

This blurring of the line between soldier and reporter began in the punitive expedition into Mexico and became the rule of thumb for military affairs long afterward in the modern period. The identification was made, moreover, by the press rather than the military. However, the identification of the reporter with the aims of the military was either tacit or private. It was not publicly formulated until World War II when, at a press conference, General Dwight D. Eisenhower told the reporters who were to cover the D-Day invasion that they were part of his staff.[63]

This chapter traced the development of explicit censorship practices in the early twentieth century. Historical documents reveal a deep faith in reason as the source for such practices. (As the reader will see, this faith in reason reaches its apogee during World War II when an appeal to common sense became the hallmark of those overseeing censorship.) The documents indicate that despite the appeal to reason, various officials in Washington often resorted to the rhetorical strategy of evasion due to implicit questions about the legality of press censorship. However, it would be a mistake to see these situations in terms of a struggle between the military and the press because the censor more often than not was an editor or reporter during peacetime. Likewise, journalists, soldiers, and government officials all were guided by the values made transcendent by the Constitution and the Bill of Rights.

3 Censorship During the World Wars

The legal roots of state-administered censorship predate the world wars of the twentieth century. However it is in the world wars that administration of censorship becomes entrenched in bureaucracy. By World War II it is comprehensive and thoroughgoing. This chapter examines the growth of censorship during these epochal wars.

World War I

American war correspondents tried to cover the war in Europe from the beginning in August 1914 until the end in 1918. During this time they experienced four kinds of communications environments (the first three before the United States joined the Allies to defeat the Central Powers): (1) freelancing and happenstance consisting of roaming the countryside in search of military action; (2) total exclusion from the zone of the armies; (3) limited access to the front under the supervision of allied military authorities who gave guided "tours"; and (4) accompanying American troops once the United States entered the conflict.

This is, of course, a roughly chronological ordering of the situations with which American journalists had to contend. However, in all periods except that of total exclusion from the front, American journalists were aware of the propaganda dimension of what they were witnessing firsthand.

U.S. journalists covered both sides of the war in Europe beginning in 1914. Almost from the very beginning, reporters with the armies of the Central Powers were given limited access to the front. Those covering the Allied forces had a more difficult time beginning with the freelance period in August and early September 1914. During these few weeks, a reporter could successfully cover the advance of the German army from behind Allied lines, but only if he steered clear of the military command on both sides.[1]

When the armies mobilized on the continent in early August 1914, Richard Harding Davis agreed to go to Europe for the Wheeler Syndicate. He boarded the *Lusitania* for England on August 4, the day Germany invaded Belgium. When he and other correspondents finally reached Brussels, they were issued *laissez-passers*, permits entitling them to go anywhere within the stated environs. Each morning, Davis rented a yellow, Gatsby-like roadster, bedecked with the flags of several countries, and followed his leads.[2] "In those weeks," he wrote, "during which events moved so swiftly that now they seem months in the past, we were as free as in our own home town to go where we chose."[3]

In these early days, the chief problem journalists faced was not the blue pencil, nor was it ducking bullets. Their problems included having to bribe various minor officials to get through the lines, getting arrested for not being where they were supposed to be, and getting released once it was determined they were reporters from a neutral country.[4] At night they returned to their hotels where they had a meal washed down with good wine or champagne.[5] Until the German army swallowed Brussels, correspondents followed this routine.

Such heady adventures came to an end on the night of August 18 when refugees began to trickle into Brussels with news that the Germans had taken Louvain. With Brussels facing occupation by the German army, the seat of the Belgian government moved to Antwerp—in effect leaving any reporter who stayed behind without credentials. General Von Jarotsky, the newly appointed German military governor of Brussels, issued *laissez-passers* to Davis and others.

On August 23, several reporters commandeered a taxi and set out to find the Allied forces. Some turned back for fear of arrest. Davis continued on, but took a wrong turn at Enghein and came upon a column of General Alexander Von Kluck's army executing a surprise attack on one of the English flanks.[6] The Germans interrogated him as a spy. He was under suspicion for a number of reasons, the most important being that his passport was issued in London, not Washington, and his photo showed him wearing a British officer's uniform. The matter was serious enough for the Germans to have imprisoned or even executed him. Eventually he was released and returned to the United States. To his wife, Davis wrote he had a "falling out with the mad dogs."[7]

The experience of being taken for a spy was not an unusual one for journalists early in the European war. Nor was the German army the only one suspicious of reporters. Robert Dunn, for instance, accompanied the British during their retreat from Mons, the first English-German encounter in the war. Dunn was sitting in a rundown café in Busigny drinking a glass of home-brewed beer when he heard heavy fire outside. Twice he headed up the road to Le Cateau and twice he was sent back by the British. Dunn's papers only allowed him to go to Paris and the British were beginning to suspect him of spying. Thinking the risk of arrest was too high, Dunn turned back south on the road to Bohain. Once there he tried to get train passage to Paris, but failed. Because of a glut of refugees, no transportation was available. He was walking toward a hotel when a shout went up behind him and someone put a hand on his shoulder. Crowds scurrying along the cobblestones shouted, "Espion! Espion!"[8] The fingers that gripped his shoulder belonged to a British officer who asked Dunn in German where he was going. Dunn answered the officer's questions in French. The crowd became angry and derisive, but Dunn was permitted to go, feeling shaken over the ordeal.[9]

The Battle of the Marne on September 5 marked the end of the freelance period of war coverage for American correspondents and the beginning of the second phase: total banishment from the front. From autumn 1914 until spring 1915, correspondents were kept entirely out of the war zones. The front stabilized as the armies dug in and trench warfare began. Introduced at the Battle of the Aisne in September 1914, trench warfare was carried on until the second Somme offensive in March 1918. Few gains were made on either side during the whole of 1915 and 1916, whereas millions of lives were lost.

In late March 1915, the British began to allow a few American reporters to make short tours behind the lines, and thus the third phase of censorship began: limited access to the front. Reporters were always accompanied by officers and their movements were severely restricted. Later the French War Ministry began to allow journalists to accompany French troops in the fighting zone. By July a press headquarters was set up near the Allied Powers' general headquarters. The military provided mess and automobiles detailed for press use. Reporters were given maps, daily communiqués, and guided tours of the front. In the morning hours, reporters divided up the front into sections with each car assigned to a specific area. In the afternoon, they returned to their headquarters and wrote their stories.[10]

Unlike the Allied Powers, the Central Powers had been using the tour system for some time. German tours were tightly programmed, each one usually lasting about a week. The correspondent's schedule included morning inspection of behind-the-lines sites, such as hospitals, ammunition dumps, and supply stations. At noon the guard was turned out in his honor. At four in the afternoon, he watched distant shelling from behind the lines. At eleven in the evening he would crawl into bed in a French hotel, where the prices for food and lodging were controlled by the Germans. The next morning he was awakened by his guide and escorted on a similar round. After a week the military guide returned him to his hotel in Berlin, where he was often filled with the "curious feeling of never having been away at all."[11] The Austrians, too, allowed correspondents limited access to the fighting zones. Here journalists were required to wear yellow-and-black armbands to identify themselves as reporters. They were accompanied by guides and allowed to visit the eastern front to see the Russian "steamroller" in action. (The eastern front stretched from the Baltic Sea to Romania.) The Austrians provided correspondents with food and toiletry subsistence needs.[12]

Many reporters gave up trying to get to the front until April 1915. Richard Harding Davis, John McCutcheon, and Irvin Cobb all returned to the United States. Some, such as Wythe Williams, joined the Red Cross as ambulance drivers or stretcher bearers to get as close as possible to military operations.[13] However, even in these cases, there were other barriers to reporting back to their newspapers. For example, the American ambassador to France prohibited Williams from using the cable until he left the Red Cross Service.[14]

Occasionally, reporters were allowed to go to the front line. For example in January 1915, several visited the trenches south of Ypres. At noon they lunched with the German officers, some of whom were educated at Oxford and spoke English well. The conversation ranged over many topics, including the social and economic dangers of a military hierarchy. After lunch they observed the artillery exchange fire. It was only at night that they entered the trenches, where they were allowed to remain for a two-hour stretch.[15]

During the "tour" period of the war, journalists experienced several aggravations: strict regulation of their movements, censorship of all copy, and tedious evasions by the military. On some occasions reporters were required to give up their places in press cars for someone considered "more important." Such people included diplomats, prominent society figures, and actors and actresses. The latter two were thought to be molders of public opinion by tour directors who could not resist giving them tours of the front.[16]

These restrictions, over which journalists had little control, created an environment permeated by a sense of futility and demoralization.[17] Under such conditions, a reporter alternated between feeling "helpless as a package in a pneumatic tube" and as if he were "a boy scout being instructed in the bugaboos before his first night in the woods."[18]

Herbert Corey was especially fond of writing long protests. His correspondence is filled with letters to press bureau officials. Included is an interesting letter to Sir Stanley Buckmaster, the British government press bureau director. Corey publicly charged the British with forging American correspondents' reports. Newspaper headlines caused a furor at the British Press Bureau, and Buckmaster sent a note to Corey asking him to come for tea and to bring proof of his charges. Part of Corey's lengthy reply follows. I have quoted it at length because it illustrates the emotional commitment of the journalist to the truth and to his public. It also lets us glimpse the tenor of the times and the restrained, courteous, and—to our ears—somewhat archaic language of the day.

> I wish to express my thanks for this [opportunity] as it permits me to review the work of the censorship from its inception. My charges were, in brief, that legitimate news was withheld from the American and English [?] public, and that in consequence a distorted view of the war situation was presented to it; and that while free publicity was accorded to stories of German atrocities, which were in great measure improbable, or obviously untrue (please see Canon Horsley in this morning's chronicle [sic] and Mr. Irvin Cobb in the Saturday Evening Post of October 17), matter which cast a more favorable light upon the German character and conduct was deleted.
>
> In short, to quote from your letter of Monday, that an effort was made "to win the aid of public opinion in America for the Allies."
>
> I believe that I will be able to convince you of the truth of these charges.
>
> As to the forgery, which I will take up at length, I made that in one specified instance only. I so stated emphatically, I said that I had heard rumors of others, but had not investigated them and had no knowledge of their truth. I believe—I am not sure—that I said I did not credit them. I made that charge upon the best possible information. It was not then possible to get proof. It is now only possible to get proof through your office. You will have no difficulty in securing a knowledge of the truth. I shall depend upon your furnishing me with the result of your investigation, with the name of the censor, the disposition of the case, and a photograph of the additions to the letter, if such are found.
>
> You will appreciate that from my point of view the jury in this matter is the American public.[19]

We glimpse here how frustrated Corey was with what he saw as British manipulation of the American press corps. The memo also exemplifies a tactic adopted in cases where the military holds the winning hand. First, Corey indicates alternate interpretations of events (atrocity reports, which were suspiciously similar in rhetorical form), and then puts the office on the defensive by noting that the proof is in the hands of the military. The fleeting scent of military propaganda has made him stand en garde. This memo provides the backdrop against which we are able to understand the ironic stance journalists eventually took during this war (see chapter 4). But it also gives good examples of the resistant, introspective self that is at the center of journalistic practice.

The heavy censorship the military exercised at this stage of World War I threw a veil of secrecy around the war.[20] Even after journalists were given limited access to battlefields, the nature of trench warfare worked to undermine the assumptions and presuppositions about war and its coverage that reporters had entertained. They no longer were able to report the war in the tradition with which their editors and the general public had become familiar. Because they were closely regulated, journalists began to view events as spectators, sitting at a distance, removed from the action—very unlike their experience in Cuba and Mexico. Furthermore, the carnage they saw—on a scale they had never experienced—made them feel this was not the world they belonged to. The quality of detachment from the scene of action, a remote point of view, became the foundation of the irony with which reporters began to view their circumstances. Over time, irony became a habit of thinking.

In February 1917 the United States had severed relations with Germany, protesting the German policy of unrestricted submarine warfare. Following disclosure of a proposed alliance between Mexico and Germany, as well as the sinking of American ships, the United States declared war on Germany, and Pershing was selected to command the American Expeditionary Force (AEF).

When American troops landed in France, a brief spurt of romanticism erupted, much like in reporting on the Spanish-Cuban-American War. Soon the machinery of General Pershing's expeditionary force took shape and reporters were placed under the control of the Press Censorship Division, Intelligence Section of the Army (G-2-d). The story of the American war correspondent during this part of the Great War is one of a bureaucratic solution to the question of how to adequately protect military interests and at the same time keep the American public informed of the developing situation.

It is according to the spirit of these times that a committee was established to administer war information. In this arena as well as elsewhere, people sought a systematic, organized solution to the problem. Accord-

ingly, experts in the field made up the committee. President Woodrow
Wilson created the Committee on Public Information (CPI) and appointed
newsman George Creel as its head; other members were the secretaries
of state, war, and the navy. Creel's agency was to be responsible for re-
leasing war news from various governmental agencies and departments
and supervising voluntary censorship of newspapers in America.[21]

Within the context of the history of the press, the Creel Committee
was something unusual: a singular, uncustomary answer to customary
problems and procedures. Within the context of U.S. history, however,
the Creel Committee was one of many examples of the prevailing progressive politics and the tendency to solve problems by means of committee.
In *The Search for Order*, Robert Wiebe sees the drive for reform prior
to World War I as a purposeful, scientific effort made by a new middle
class of professional and scientific experts to bring organization out of
chaos. Whether solving problems of tariffs, conservation, or education,
the new middle class did so through bureaucratic means and large-scale
management.[22]

At first few, if any, newspapers viewed the Creel Committee with
animosity. Later on, however, journalists came to resent the committee's role in controlling news, beginning with an incident that came to
be known as "The Fourth of July Fake."[23] Both the Associated Press (AP)
and the *New York Times* charged the committee with giving out falsified
descriptions of a submarine attack on the first fleet of American trans-
ports to France and deliberately publishing the story on July 4, 1917, in an
attempt to manipulate public opinion.[24] The day after the Creel version
of the affair appeared in papers, the AP published a cable saying that no
submarine attack had occurred. Evidently the AP cable was the assessment of its correspondent, Frank America, whose sources were officials
at the submarine's European destination point. In the days following, the
press charged Creel with fabrication. He admitted to elaborating on the
original cable he had received. Creel's personal suspicion was that military jealousy may have prompted Frank America's source to minimize
the story of the fleet's skirmish in the Atlantic.[25] The tacit application of
the occupational culture Creel brought to his job from civilian life may
have been at work here as well. Suspicion and skepticism are a good new
reporter's tools.

Whatever the case, the Fourth of July story was the beginning of the
disenchantment felt in newspaper circles at home toward the Committee
on Public Information. From July 1917 on, the press saw the committee
as a government agency designed to "disseminate high-minded views
and policy statements about the war."[26]

As soon as the Creel Committee was set up media companies began applying for accreditation to accompany Pershing to Europe. The commanding general, however, opposed having journalists accompany him. Rather, he said, authorized war correspondents should wait until the troops crossed over the Atlantic. He was also firm in asking for the smallest possible number of reporters to be accredited.[27] His notes on this subject were always terse, but polite. For example, when the managing editor of the *Chicago Daily News* wrote asking permission to send Junius B. Wood with him, Pershing replied, "With reference to your application to send one J. B. Wood with my expedition, the matter has been referred to the War Department, which will handle the matter later. It is not intended that any newspaper correspondents shall accompany me. I remember Mr. Wood very pleasantly. Yours very truly."[28]

The secretary of war instructed Pershing to confer with authorities in Europe to determine what their wishes might be as far as news representatives were concerned.[29] Pershing reported that both the English and the French wanted the United States to handle its own correspondents independently.[30]

Having consulted with the Allies, Pershing asked that only representatives of the press associations be accredited until the first wave of expeditionary troops landed. He wanted to limit the total number of correspondents to eight. He recommended allowing magazine writers only infrequent visits with the troops and he wanted Frederick Palmer, whom he appointed major with the Signal Corps, to be the press officer in charge of war correspondents.[31]

Pershing defended his request for a small number of reporters by arguing that the French accredited only twelve reporters and the British six reporters to their armies. Further, he reported that these men were always restricted to the guidance of a commissioned officer. Pershing estimated the total expense of a correspondent, to be borne by his employer, at four hundred dollars to six hundred dollars per month.[32] George Creel, however, objected to restricting the number of the press people. He believed that "any reputable American Newspaper" should be allowed representation. These men would be under bond and required to comply with Pershing's orders. Creel noted, and others concurred, that the expense of covering the war in subsistence terms alone was so high as to self-restrict those who elected to do so.[33]

As editors applied for permission to send reporters with troops, the military began to organize press headquarters in Europe.[34] They remained reluctant to accredit photographers and motion picture operators. Because of earlier complaints about restricting photography to the concern only of Underwood and Underwood, however, the army worked to avoid any charges of favoritism. General Douglas MacArthur recommended that all companies engaged in photography or movie-making select representatives themselves and share their expenses equitably.[35]

The regulations issued by the American military for World War I were similar to those devised for the expeditions into Mexico, including the admonition against adventure seeking. There were, however, some significant changes. The military now required certification of a reporter's physical fitness ensuring that he could endure the hardships of army life. The prohibitions against photography were spelled out. Regulations covered what the reporter should wear, what he could expect from the censor, and his rights as a commissioned officer.

Thus press censorship came under one of the four divisions of the Intelligence Section of the U.S. Army. The other three divisions were Information, which collated and disseminated army and enemy information; the Secret Service, which dealt with espionage and counterespionage; and Topography and Maps, which dealt with geographic information and included schools of instruction.[36] In addition to supervising the censorship of the press, the Press Division coordinated the work of similar divisions in Allied camps, as well as with the U.S. Navy.[37] This same division was also responsible for visitors ranging from members of the U.S. Congress to actors and actresses. G-2-d handled their accommodations and travel arrangements, and provided for their entertainment too.[38] When reporters gave up their seats for a visitor (whom journalists saw as frivolous), they were forced to swallow a bitter pill.

Almost immediately, the Press Division began to systematically store and record clippings from newspapers and magazines, indexed by subject and author. Confidential accounts classified reporters according to their strength so they could be utilized according to military need. And who better to do that than men who were journalists and editors in peacetime? "Grasty and Eyre are able seasoned writers, good for constructive criticism; Wood, Broun and Bagin are admirable 'picture' writers; Johnson, Gibbons and Carroll are hard workers, particularly good on work needing patient study. The Associated Press is, as always, from the nature of this syndicate's work, probably the best for work of a 'neutral' character."[39]

The policy of the Press Division was to permit criticism "wherever criticism is constructive and not actually dangerous at the time."[40] In some cases criticism was forestalled by calling on the "loyalty of the best men in the newspaper colony," a term suggesting military annexation of the press and revealing much more than the writer probably intended.[41]

Frederick Palmer, as chief press officer, took up the task of organizing and running the censorship office and the correspondents who were accredited to follow the AEF in Europe. As with the Creel objectives, the plans for running G-2-d looked good on paper, but when it came to implementing them, all kinds of problems arose. Ideally, no newspaper correspondent was to be required to write anything contrary to his inclinations. The problems facing G-2-d (too little space, too few cars, and Pershing's belief that only a few reporters were needed in France) were dealt with one by one.[42] Finally, on July 19, 1917, the bulletin board at Castallane House, Pershing's temporary headquarters, held the message for reporters that signaled the beginning of the final phase of the reporting during World War I:

> All accredited correspondents will please come to this office at 11 o'clock on Saturday morning, July 21st, and they will go to their headquarters near the American training camp at 7:30 Monday morning from the Gare de l'Est.
> All correspondents:
> Are advised to have telegraph credit cards.
> Can carry small cameras.
> Are advised to buy a no. 6 Tarride map, which is that of the region where he [sic] will live.
> Should have a typewriter, large or portable, plenty of copy paper, carbon writing paper, etc.
> Should take plenty of tobacco, cigars, cigarettes.
> Should have a rubber bath tub.[43]

The following September, correspondents received the list of general regulations governing their behavior. Divided into two groups, accredited reporters were to live with the army in quarters provided them near the General Headquarters (GHQ). Visiting correspondents lived elsewhere, usually in Paris, at their own expense, and were allowed to come along periodically for tours of the training area and the front.[44]

The rules that applied to accredited correspondents were stringent, complicated, detailed, and as restrictive as any they had been subjected to by the Allied or Central Powers. Although reporters were genuinely thought of as the eyes and ears of the American public, the rules and regulations imposed on them by the military precluded the successful execution of their task.

In April 1918, about a month before American troops were to take part in combat, Colonel W. C. Sweeney, who was then the general staff chief of G-2-d, issued an order clarifying the basic principle underlying censorship: all information not helpful to the enemy may be given the American public. Following this general directive was a list of rules covering what could not be printed. Forced to follow all the regulations imposed by these and other directives, reporters had to be content with writing stories providing the American public with little real news. As time passed and the Press Division issued more and more memos, the journalists' situation became clearer and more discouraging.

From June 1917 to May 1918, reporters were lodged at Neufchateau—a few miles from Gondrecourt where the troops were being trained and from Chaumont where Pershing's headquarters were located.[45] After initially reporting on what the troops were doing, little happened, time dragged, and the "depressed little group" of American correspondents was starving for news.[46] The break came on May 28, when the U.S. Army First Division captured Cantigny in their first independent operation. After the Battle of Cantigny, rules loosened up and reporters were free to cover events as they saw fit. The changing situation is reflected in the official order issued on June 15, 1918:

> The newspaper correspondents who are duly accredited by the War Department and attached to the American Expeditionary Force are charged with the duty of keeping the American public informed of the activities of our forces. They are under military control, and all matter written by them is submitted to censorship. The work of these correspondents is considered to be of the greatest importance as it is essential that our activities be truly and promptly represented to the American public. All members of the American Expeditionary Forces should understand that these accredited correspondents are held worthy of confidence, and it is expected that every reasonable facility be extended to them to enable them to obtain all proper information for the efficient performance of their duties.[47]

The army defended its practice of censorship by pointing out that the censor's office dealt daily with fake stories. In all wars there are fake journalists who file fake stories and real journalists who file stories implying they were eyewitnesses when in fact they were not. No war covered in the scope of this study offered an exception to this kind of thing. The Press Division believed part of its job was to prevent fake stories from appearing in the press, as well as to correct inaccuracies or to block certain kinds of information from reaching enemy hands.[48] Besides keeping clippings of press reporters, the censor's office also began to keep files on "troublemakers," "pacifists," "socialists," and others whom they regarded with "a certain distrust."[49]

One such case involved Norman Hapgood, one-time editor of *Harper's Weekly*. He was "friendly," the officer wrote, but "known to have decided pacifist tendencies, believing that a speedy end of the war, no matter how, would be to the greatest benefit of all parties concerned."[50] Eventually a list of all American correspondents was compiled, along with brief descriptions of their work in many cases.

The significance of this development for the First Amendment is self-evident, since it flies in the face of constitutional freedoms. Beyond that, however, it demonstrates how the military combined a sense of local needs—battlefield conditions—and a deep faith in the system of general rules. For example, in late 1917, Lieutenant Colonel Nolan asked for reviews of the various censorship offices. One report noted that its rules were clear and in line with general policy. The reporting officer goes on to note that "if the rules have not operated to the satisfaction of the correspondents, I feel that it is principally the fault of the correspondents and not of the system."[51] The review conceded there were cases in which the censor failed to understand the spirit of the rules. Yet it emphasized the importance of going by the book. This faith in procedure over substance was held up as virtual insurance that both military and press goals would be attained.

Propaganda and War Correspondence

Besides greatly systematizing the censorship office, the U.S. Army Press Division also began consciously to appreciate the press as a propaganda tool during World War I. This awareness worked in such a way that by World War II, the Press Division identified itself as "Public Relations," which implies the use of propaganda.[52]

Clearly the environment spawning propaganda is one in which values are not shared. That is, no one needs to use propaganda unless he is certain that the other party does not share a particular belief and will not further its ends. Propaganda seeks to serve the interests of one party to the disadvantage of others. Thus it is important to distinguish propaganda from persuasion or rhetoric, which seek voluntary compliance and involve mutual and interactive dependencies. Courtship is not propaganda; neither is advertising. Both of these are forms of persuasion. Here we can define propaganda as *Merriam-Webster's* does: as ideas, facts, or allegations spread deliberately to damage an opposing cause and to further one's own.

Massive amounts of resources were devoted to propaganda in both world wars. World War I was the initial laboratory of propaganda use. Yet, while it is true that the military consciously engaged in press propaganda during this war, one should not leap to the conclusion that false stories were printed by journalists who were hoodwinked by the army. On many occasions the press volunteered to further the aims of the army in bringing the war to a successful end. Moreover, the military's Press Division carefully vetoed any story or part of a story it believed was not an eyewitness account.

One such case was a report by Caspar Whitney of the *New York Tribune*. The censor at Neufchateau deleted the following statements from Whitney's story: "Not many days ago an American soldier, who had been captured in a night trench raid, was shortly afterwards found by a search partly lying castrated and dead in No Man's Land. Revolting statement to cable but the naked truth which you in America need in order to understand the Bosche."[53] Clearly, the propaganda value of this account is self-evident, but the censor deleted it. Colonel Sweeney justified the censor's actions on the basis that the facts recited about atrocities must be true and must be verified as true. He noted: "Nothing would please us more than to have the evidence of the truth of such a statement of the atrocity by the enemy and I again tell you that our officers and soldiers are constantly on the lookout for such things. Anonymous, hearsay information as to an atrocity of this nature committed by the enemy, much as we hate him and capable as we believe him to be of committing such an act, cannot be published to the world unless it is true."[54]

Sweeney invited the reporter to submit proof of the atrocities. Whitney declined, saying that he had gotten the information from an officer recently returned from battle, whose name he did not know. Whitney also revealed that the soldier had been found alive, but that he, Whitney, wrote that the soldier was dead because he believed "it was wise to do so."[55]

This event is illuminating for a number of reasons. It supports the argument that in all wars there are reporters who make up facts. It demonstrates how willing the press has been to aid the military in painting a stereotypical picture of the enemy. And it indicates that the military system of censorship, ever growing in complexity, is never a simple operation for fooling the people (as Phillip Knightley states in his book, *The First Casualty*). The bureaucratic structure of organized censorship contributed its part to the ironic stance of the war correspondent in the First World War: organization down to the last detail and the reporter's task of keeping the public informed worked at cross-purposes. If, like Herbert Corey and Irvin Cobb, a reporter learned to cooperate with the military, he tried to fly below the radar and continued to report the war. If he did not cooperate, like Wythe Williams and Heywood Broun, he was sent back to the United States.

At first, reporters responded to organized censorship in World War I by organizing themselves into the War Publicity League. The aim of the group was to fight against the censor until they were permitted to tell the truth about conditions—especially supply conditions. No member of the league wanted to print critical attacks about the U.S. Army. Reporters felt, however, that censorship operated to shield from criticism officers who were responsible for mistakes.[56]

Some Congressional members shared the opinion that censorship was a means to conceal military blunders. Heywood Broun, disgusted with the restrictions placed on him and his friends, returned to New York in December 1917 and published a series of articles on the supply blunders hampering the AEF. Following Broun's disclosures, a few senators talked about a conducting an investigation, but little came of it.[57]

When trying to fight censorship restrictions, reporters adopted bureaucratic means of protest, most frequently by means of the memo. More often than not, these written protests were lengthy, serious, and styled along the lines of a legal brief. Philadelphia newsman Reginald W. Kauffman fought continuously with the military and evaded many censorship restrictions until Secretary of State Robert Lansing cabled G-2-d: "Reginald W. Kauffman sending to Philadelphia *North American* vicious attacks on Expeditionary Forces. Find out if his articles are submitted to censorship with view of expelling Kauffman."[58] On receiving the cable, G-2-d demanded that Kauffman surrender his credentials. Kauffman replied that he had already done so in a note mailed three weeks previously to Secretary of War Newton D. Baker. Kauffman explained he was giving up his accreditation because the military censorship violated the rules and obligations detailed in Article VII of the Field Service Regulations and those implied in the credentials issued to war correspondents. "These violations . . . render it impossible for a conscientious correspondent to perform those duties to the public which his profession imposed."[59]

The creation of the War Publicity League and the long, tedious written protests of reporters (of which Kauffman's is just one example) suggest that increasingly journalists' requests and protests fell on deaf ears; they soon introduced a note of mockery into their formal requests and defenses.[60] By September 1917, reporters had become very restless. To keep them busy, G-2-d organized a tour of the recently installed bake ovens near Dijon, which were used to provide food for the AEF. A three-car caravan left press headquarters for Dijon, with orders to stay close together. On arrival at Dijon, the car carrying Lincoln Eyre, Junius Wood, and Dan Dillon was missing. Eventually the three overdue newsmen arrived at the hotel, where the others were already eating dinner. They went into the dining room, sat down, and ordered their meals. They were boisterous and impolite, and threw bread at friends sitting at the next table. Obviously, they had stopped off somewhere along the way for drinks. When the reporters returned to headquarters, the military officer in charge filed charges against Eyre and Wood and recommended they be sent home. Dan Dillon, who had thrown the bread, stepped forward to shoulder the blame for the whole incident. According to his account, the three of them had stopped at a liquor store so that Wood, the current mess officer for reporters, could add to the supplies of whiskey and rum at more reasonable prices than those at Neufchateau. Dillon's statement exonerated Eyre of any wrongdoing. His statement is an example of the mockery that permeated reporters' responses to military officiousness:

> While standing about, I had the brilliant idea that a drink of rum would do some good after an all-day ride. Unselfishly, I communicated my inspiration and it was hailed by cries of "Hear! Hear!" Showing the deference due to a press officer, I handed the bottle first to Mr. Griffith, who, after taking a copious draught, passed it along to the others. I can only say from the depth of my sack cloth and ashes that it was I, Daniel Dillon, who committed this personal and professional conduct which might have injured the morale or discipline of our soldiers. As I happened to toss a few crumbs at my roommate, Lyon, seated at an adjoining table, you, Mr. Eyre, of course, had no interest in my playful antics and at no time used your powerful right arm to hurl these dread grenades.[61]

On the strength of Dillon's official statement, the case against Wood and Eyre was dropped.

Relations between the military and the press during World War I varied according to the practices of each national military unit. Reporters adopted a range of strategies to deal with each situation. Censorship had consequences, not only for what was made public, but also—and more importantly given the nature of this book—on what and how reporters experienced the war. Chapter 4 will elaborate on the experiential aspect of war correspondence.

Censorship During World War II

In the Second World War, a massive bureaucracy was created to manage public intelligence. Byron Price, manager of the Associated Press, was tapped to be the director of censorship operations in the United States. In keeping with the War Powers Act, Executive Order 8985 created the Office of Censorship (OOC). It set out the limits of a censorship program.[62] As comprehensive as it was, the OOC was only one of several government agencies detailed to censorship operations. The military censored communications from their soldiers, as well as press dispatches sent from the zones of combat. Planning for censorship in case of war began long before the Japanese attacked Pearl Harbor. The Bureau of Customs censored mail and other written material sent by freight or carried by travelers. The Board of Economics censored technical data sent over international communications lines. The Federal Communications Commission censored radio bands, for example, short wave radio, and shut down ham operators. And the Federal Bureau of Investigation (FBI) had a hand in many censorship matters.[63]

Byron Price, the man chosen to head domestic censorship, had seen battle during the Meuse-Argonne operations in World War I.[64] In 1927 he was appointed Executive News Editor for the Associated Press. In his capacity there, he streamlined the workings of the bureaus under his care. His objective was to cut down on bureaucracy and to return initiative to the individual reporters and editors. For example, he abolished all formulas for writing and directed his reporters to write according to their own intelligence.[65]

With his experience at the AP, Price seemed the ideal man to organize and direct domestic censorship once war was declared. His credo led and followed the temper of the times: "Both experience and common sense testify convincingly to the dangers which might result to a nation struggling for its life if the public prints were left untrammeled and unguided by considerations of security."[66] Over time, the call for common sense as a justification for violating the First Amendment of the Constitution of the United States would become routine.

Price was a no-nonsense kind of guy. He was also very shrewd. He understood the value of strategic communications. In trying to walk the thin line separating just and unjust restriction of the press, he remarked, "The best I could hope for would be to keep quiet and hope nobody notices. I followed this advice and said as little as possible for publication."[67]

In the difficult job of pulling together a massive bureaucracy, Price found himself going head to head with other branches of the government. It took him eight months, for instance, to get a statement in writing from the War Department saying that censorship was his job and not theirs.[68] In all matters he remained a reasonable man. He applied the same abilities for streamlining organizations and reducing bureaucracy to the censorship setup as he had to the Associated Press.[69] Unlike reporters in the war, Price found the army a tougher nut to crack than the navy. He thought that nobody paid any attention to army restrictions, whereas they did to the navy's.[70] This really does not signal another point of view so much as it signals the vantage point for evaluating the situation in censorship. Of course, if no one paid any attention to the army's restrictions, it would be easier for reporters to navigate their world and more difficult to navigate the world of the navy. As far as relating to the military was concerned, the character trait that worked most in Price's favor was an ability to stand up to a lot of gold braid and win.[71] This, I believe, was because he was a man of discretion—when he ran at loggerheads with the military, he kept it confidential. This practice was much appreciated by soldiers and goes a long way toward explaining why Price was so successful in working with a great range of people in the course of the war.

As director of censorship, Price was often called on to address problems that censorship posed for freedom. He appealed to common sense as a guide for making hard decisions, decisions that countered the person-forming creed of Americans and the belief system structuring the formation of the citizen: freedom of speech and of the press.

The citizen belief system was incorporated into the occupational practices of journalism. That is to say, the everyday practices that are routine to journalists embody the citizen belief system as it is articulated in the documents written in the founding of the nation-state. Consequently, being sensible was something Price practiced long before he became the director of censorship. For example, Price had gone to Europe to review the AP's operations in 1940. Even as he sailed to Amsterdam, where he hoped to set up a communications center for the wire service, two of the AP's European bureaus disappeared. Price's Swiss visa became invalid when the country closed its border. Travel in some areas was reduced to one operating train daily. Censors did not permit disclosures by telephone of the real situation between Paris and Rome. In some areas telephone service was entirely suspended. Several reporters were stranded, waiting in railway stations for a long shot at getting space on a train. Germany was trying to isolate England from France, and British embassy officials believed there was a 90 percent chance they would succeed.[72] Troops were massing at border areas. It was taking three or more weeks to get visas to Spain and Portugal at a time when borders could close with no warning overnight.

When Price decided to go to Berlin, and then to Budapest, the American Embassy advised him not to, unless he wanted to remain in Berlin for the duration of the war. As he explained to his boss, Kent Cooper, Price decided "to put [his] pride in his pocket, concede failure, and come home." "I certainly had the strongest reasons for believing that a continuation of the plan would have meant isolation for the period of the war in one country or group of countries. I certainly did not assume you intended this, nor is it sound management for an executive to permit himself to become bottled up in one sector of a large operation. The spectacular thrill would have been to go on. The sensible thing was to withdraw."[73]

In a nutshell, that is an account of Price's values: sound management, executive accountability for the whole operation under his guidance, an aversion to grandstanding, and the exercise of sensible, critical faculties. He would also need patience, for there were individuals and agencies in the government who, in effort to self-publicize, gave Price additional headaches to contend with. The FBI, he argued, never passed up a chance for front page news.[74]

The Government Printing Office (GPO) also caused problems. In a speech, the public printer, Augustus E. Giegengack, disclosed information about secret inks and certain paper to detect them that were given to German prisoners of war to use when sending letters to Germany. His remarks were introduced into the Congressional Record by Senator Willis and subsequently were published in a newspaper column.[75]

> Under the Geneva Convention, prisoners are privileged to write letters home once a month, I believe. We are not allowed to subject their letters to tests which would deface the messages, and therefore our first prisoners felt safe in transmitting secret reports in invisible fluid ink. Milk, lemon juice, saliva, and other easily available fluids would do the trick on ordinary paper—and some information did get out which [sic] might have been damaging. The war department asked us to do something about it. The director of our laboratories first developed a coated paper, on which invisible acid ink immediately showed up in a bright green. Invisible nonacid ink turned a fine glowing red. . . .
> About a year ago the censorship people got a new headache. The Germans had discovered a substance which could not be detected on our paper. When censorship officials caught up with it, they worked on the problem and finally came over to the Office for help. Within a few weeks we had a new paper, which is sensitive to nearly every known substance, dry or fluid. . . . We have an order for 20,000,000 pieces of this stationery. I should like to print enough for 10,000,000 prisoners.[76]

When Price learned of this indiscretion, he called the public printer into his office. Giegengack responded, saying that he had done no harm. And, although he expressed his regret, Price believed Giegengack still failed to understand that he had publicly disclosed information regarded as secret. Price saw in the incident an example of bureaucratic self-aggrandizement and petty jealousy. His solution: "We are compelled in the future to regard the staff of the Government Printing Office as an unsafe repository for confidential information, and I hope we will tell them as little as possible."[77]

During World War II, all reporters unconsciously tried to be cameras—that is, they endeavored to send home the "true picture" of what was transpiring at the fronts. This point demonstrates the degree to which realist conventions had so thoroughly permeated the institutions of the nation-state, including the institution of the free press.

In this latest worldwide conflict, the federal government imposed two main types of censorship: voluntary domestic censorship and censorship at the source. The Office of Censorship issued a code of wartime practices as a guideline for the stateside press, requesting that they keep confidential such subjects as the location, strength, and destination of the armed forces; information about weather conditions; and letters and interviews from the combat zone. The principles upon which voluntary self-censorship rested were true to the American tradition; that is, the censor could only deal with questions of war security and had no authority over editorial opinion.[78] Only questionable material had to be submitted to the censor. This simple rule, which by this time had become accepted practice, had major consequences. As a result the workload of the Press Division was manageable, with voluntary censorship accounting for only 0.5 percent of its budget. Despite this insignificant amount, voluntary censorship was considered at the heart of the whole censorship operation because once information was printed or broadcast, it was next to impossible to keep it from the enemy.[79] The minimal expenditure on voluntary censorship demonstrates that once the press agrees to a set of rules regarding publication, it begins a dance with the state that is performed with relative ease.

The second type of censorship, at the source, was conducted entirely by the military in the theaters of war. The Press Division, which was part of military intelligence during World War I, was transferred to public relations in World War II. Public relations officers (PROs) now oversaw the welfare of correspondents, ensuring they had food, lodging, transportation, and communications facilities. One of the most thoroughly organized operations was the landing on Omaha Beach, June 6, 1944 (D-Day). In London, location of the Supreme Headquarters, Allied Expeditionary Force (SHAEF), arrangements were made for briefing reporters.

During the Vietnam war, this sort of briefing would be called "the five o'clock follies." In World War II, however, journalists treated briefings—and officers—with respect as well as occupational skepticism. Reporters spent their afternoons studying photographs, intelligence reports, and operational orders. The photos of the French coast from Le Havre to Cherbourg had every pillbox and minefield marked, with corrections up to the previous twenty-four hours. The orders for one landing ship alone comprised about a thousand pages and covered almost everything a journalist might want to know: mail service to and from the beachhead, war correspondents' uniforms, the corrections of firing angles, and so forth.[80] In addition to being briefed, reporters were given a course on how to move about while keeping under cover, how to dig foxholes, how to read maps and pitch tents, and other instructions for survival on the battlefield.[81]

After June 1, 1945, correspondents detailed to specific units were called up, a few each day, and ordered to their embarkation centers. SHAEF's Joint Censorship Group had arranged for a few censors and twenty-three correspondents to accompany the troops on D-Day. Field press censors examined reporters' copy and, if approved, reporters radioed their reports to London. Radio facilities were limited, so what could not be handled was sent via air or speedboat to London for censorship there. As the Allies advanced into France and communications facilities improved, more censors and reporters went to France and less material went to London.[82]

The routine reporters followed varied from campaign to campaign, but generally before a landing or a bombing mission they were briefed as to the target of the operation, were taken to their embarkation points, and went in with the troops on the first, second, and third waves of assault. During the invasion of Okinawa, PROs opened a branch office aboard Admiral Richmond K. Turner's flagship. Spot dispatches were censored there and radioed to Guam, where they were relayed to San Francisco. If the radio was in use, the copy was sometimes sent by teletype to another radio transmission ship, which in turn sent it on to Guam. Newsreels and feature copy, both considered less urgent, were sent via landing craft to Guam, where they were censored and then mailed to the United States.[83]

There were complaints about the censorship during World War II, especially in its early stages. The British censor recalled 1942 as the most difficult year of the war.[84] Allied morale had been badly battered by the capitulation of France and the hell-bent-for-leather evacuation at Dunkirk, where vessels of all shapes and sizes took British and French soldiers (who summarily discarded their weapons) across the English Channel to safety. Statesmen and military leaders were coming and going. Their movements always incited speculation about where a second front would open up—all information considered lethal if the enemy got its hands on it.

In terms of strategy, the British and the Americans differed in their plans of battle. The Americans wanted to invade Western Europe immediately to free the French. The British, who remembered painfully the ruthlessly efficient German army at Dunkirk, wanted to attack the Germans through the "soft underbelly" of the Mediterranean. Americans, almost to the very end, considered the African operations a sideshow. However, the victory of Montgomery's Eighth Army at El Alamein was important strategically and psychologically. It was important strategically because, for once, Allied Forces had been victorious. Morale soared and the curtain was raised on the North African invasion, which took place four days later (November 8, 1942) at Algiers, Oran, and several ports near Casablanca. Most correspondents were lodged at Algiers, where General Dwight D. Eisenhower set up his headquarters.

From the point of view of the censors, the main problem in the early days of the African campaign was opposition of the Free French to Allied policies concerning the Vichy regime.[85] The Allies believed any success they might enjoy depended on the cooperation of the Vichy regime. Meanwhile the Free French believed they should have been in on the operation. Chapter 4 examines the interplay between correspondents and the censors over this situation and reveals the military consequences of rear area problems. Censors refused to pass any copy suggesting the extent of the Allied cooperation with the Vichy French. The lone exception was Ernie Pyle's column on the "small fry" the Allies allowed to retain their offices, even after the invasion was completed.[86]

Thus, in the European theater, censorship of the American forces was cautious and strict, but only in the first year of the war. The first year of any war is always the most difficult for censor and reporter alike, because everyone is trying out his legs at something new. Also, it is difficult because war experience seldom allows anyone to engage in summarizing tactics. Like someone reaching for a light switch in a dark room, reporters have to feel their way along.

The Pacific theater was an entirely different story. There censorship hassles dogged the reporter during the entire war.

The war in the Pacific was a naval affair, and since the 1880s, the navy had exercised more stringent censorship practices than any other branch of the military. It is common to have stricter censorship in the early phases of any war and is due more to the inexperience of censors than it is to military defeat, because it occurs even when the military is victorious. As censors get experience, the restrictions ease up. Not so with the U.S. Navy. Not so in the Pacific. As late as 1944, correspondents stationed in the Pacific could not write as much in their private letters as those stationed in Europe could.[87] When Ernie Pyle sent his columns out from Guam, the censor cut out the names of the men he mentioned. Since individual GIs were warp and woof of his columns, navy censorship emasculated his copy. Pyle threatened to leave the navy and go back to the army unless the navy relented and allowed names to be printed. Anxious to have Pyle in particular writing about its men, the navy conceded to his request.[88]

Many would explain the difference in censorship practices between the navy and the army in terms of security. Hundreds of men occupying one ship at sea make an easy target. As it was commonly said, "Loose lips sink ships."

However, the security of the armed fleet only partially accounts for the difference in censorship stringency between the navy and other armed forces. An explanation for the navy's heightened and inflexible censorship lies in its history. Specifically it can be traced back to 1882 to the creation of the Office of Naval Intelligence (ONI). The ONI guaranteed that henceforth naval operations would depend on banks of information. And they did.

In the war with Spain, for example, the ONI routinely gathered official diplomatic and consular reports sent to the State Department from around the world. It also routinely posted naval attachés to embassies and legations abroad. The ONI was the first intelligence gathering agency in the United States. Its reports as well as the contingency plans it drew up provided the naval fleet with a sound basis for war with Spain as early as 1894.[89]

By World War II, naval operations had a long history of data gathering. It should, then, be no surprise that the bureaucratic machinery would be as widespread, haphazard, and convoluted as it was. The navy of World War II inherited its unusually complicated bureaucratic approach to censorship, and reporters complained about it through the entire war.

For example, *Newsweek* reported that correspondents working for the morning papers nursed a grudge against the navy. Fred Pasley, of the *New York Daily News*, accused the navy of favoring the papers owned by Colonel Knox, then secretary of the navy. He charged that the navy granted the Knox papers "virtual monopoly of hot navy news." Pasley argued that the release time for the stories of the invasions of the Gilbert and Marshall islands was set for noon, February 13, 1942, a time that clearly favored the evening papers. Further, rumor had it that only Robert Casey of the *Chicago Daily News* and Keith Wheeler of the *Chicago Times* witnessed the attacks.[90]

Robert Casey, however, held a different point of view. Colonel Knox wrote to Admiral Heburn requesting that no special privileges be extended to reporters for his papers that were not also given to correspondents representing other news units. This letter was posted on the wall of the PRO office. "Nobody will quarrel about the idea of the letter," wrote Casey, "except perhaps there should also be some assurance that *Daily News* correspondents get the same privileges and restrictions as the other."[91]

One of the ironies of this series of incidents is that as bitterly as journalists complained about favoritism being extended to Knox's reporters, they also took advantage of it. The correspondents in the Pacific elected Robert Casey as their spokesperson on the idea that his connection to Knox made him the man most able to influence the censor.[92]

On the whole, Casey was miserable in Hawaii. He was fed up with the "alleged war coverage in the Pacific."[93] Believing there was no hope of straightening out the muddle, he asked his editors to relieve him of his Pacific assignment.[94] The problems of the naval operations of censorship were twofold: the organizational complexity and indecisive character of procedures and decision making, and the actual physical limitations of covering the armed fleet.

All news from the Southeast Pacific had to pass through General Douglas MacArthur's headquarters. All news from Central Pacific Operations had to have the navy's stamp of approval on it.[95] In Hawaii, the press was required to submit all copy to the fleet officers first and then to the "downtown" censors. Some of the downtown crew evidently rewrote parts of various reports, which incensed reporters. Casey wrote to Colonel Knox, asking him to intervene. Knox in turn asked Admiral Chester Nimitz to reform the censorship operation. Nimitz reorganized procedures so that reports pertaining to the fleet were filed only with the fleet public relations office. Copy pertaining to the army or to local issues went through the central office. In both cases, reporters received a copy of the censored version of their reports. That way, the correspondents knew how their reports read back home and how long it would be before they appeared in print.

This procedure continued for a number of weeks. Then the navy put into operation national censorship, theoretically to coordinate all other censorships, save time, end duplication of work, and make the whole censorship operation more efficient. Efficiency, however, never materialized. Reporters were still required to submit their copy to either the fleet censor or to downtown operations (depending on subject matter) and then, have it passed by the national censor. Thus, the navy's censorship operation fed on itself and multiplied.[96]

In April 1942 procedures were again revised. Correspondents submitted fleet copy first to the captain of the ship, then to fleet intelligence—rather than fleet public relations—and finally to national censorship.[97] The inefficient, indecisive, impermanent censorship operating in the Pacific theater was at best irritating, and at worst, impossible to deal with.

The problem was complicated further by the physical limitations of covering war at sea. In land warfare, a reporter could get to the scene of the battle even if he had to use his own legs. In modern sea warfare, even if he could round up a skiff, no reporter could follow a destroyer, much less a submarine. Nor could journalists get to the disembarkation points, as they had in the Spanish-Cuban-American War. They had to be aboard the ship engaging in battle. There was no way of telling ahead of time which section of the fleet would encounter the enemy. Chances were fairly good that a reporter could be assigned to a ship for a month-long expedition and never see any fighting.

Despite these problems with censorship during World War II, most reporters thought the war was accurately and fully reported.[98] Periodically there were storms of protest, but even in the Pacific, reporters like Robert Casey based their hopes for reform on an appeal to the admiral's common sense—what reporters felt ought to be the rule for what passed the censor's test. Consequently, the highest praise a censor or PRO could muster was that he was a reasonable man.[99] Unlike any other war under consideration, the rhetorical strategy adopted to appeal a censor's decision was common sense.

This chapter detailed the history of censorship in the world wars. As noted earlier, the turning point for establishing documented procedures for war reporters was the American expedition into Mexico. In this chapter we have seen the emergence of modern war correspondence during the world wars. The link between the nation-state and journalists went from being assumed to being explicitly stated through military practices, such as the practice of simulating rank. In both world wars journalists became officers with pens rather than swords. They were fully integrated into the military system. And they became walking advertisements for the nation-state.

It is also clear from this chapter that as the threat to national security increased, that is, under conditions of worldwide war, control and management of information became more thorough. This growth reflected the move in society toward bureaucratization as a means of management. In wartime, the use of propaganda accompanied the appearance of highly structured bureaucracies. All wars covered here had some form of news control, however minimal. The world wars, though, both exposed enemy propaganda as well as utilized their own forms to a greater degree than any of the smaller wars in Cuba, Mexico, and Vietnam.

The practice of seeing World War II as the "good" war has limited our understanding of that war in bringing about reliance on system as the orthodox way to wage war. In World War II a tremendous shift occurred in understanding the role of the journalist from one having to do with intelligence to one having to do with public relations. This change alone should make all citizens pause. While General Eisenhower was right to say that a journalist belongs to a story, not a military unit, it was a mistake to treat them as quasi-staff officers.

4 Censorship in Vietnam

The Vietnam War is thought of as "the uncensored war." However, this is misleading in many ways. It is a mistaken belief because censorship had long been the culture of war and its reporting. (This aspect of censorship—its culture—will be investigated in chapter 5.) Reporters in Vietnam had been given a legacy of expectations: everyone knew the legitimacy of censorship rested on a set of ground rules necessary to protect the lives of soldiers or to ensure military success, and no one questioned the Cold War logic that had been instilled in soldiers and reporters alike in learning about civic matters in elementary and secondary schools.

Hence it is more correct to understand war journalism as one culture being integrated into a second culture, one involving the military and its sense of system. By the Vietnam era, journalists adapted well to military life without anyone prompting them. This was especially true of journalists who had previously reported in World War II. Dickey Chapelle and Richard Tregaskis come immediately to mind.

In Vietnam military requests that safeguarded the lives of soldiers seemed reasonable, and reporters respected ground rules that did so. As in other wars, if military practices were inconsistent from camp to camp, or if another newspaper or broadcast station published "embargoed" material, reporters became angry.

To be sure, the ability of the Saigon press corps to keep the public adequately informed was compromised from the earliest days of the war by the military command all the way up to the commander-in-chief. There was a policy of dissembling, playing down bad news, and withholding it altogether, accompanied by a public stance of continued optimism for the progress being made in the war. Together these poorly prepared the American public for bad news when it did come.

The body count is a good example. The kill ratio for attacks when the Viet Cong stood and fought the Americans was five VC for every American. However, if the kill ratio included attacks by stealth, ambush, or land mines, it dropped to 1.5 to 1. In the face of such facts, the optimism General William Westmoreland exhibited about progress came under criticism. Even reporters who sympathized with the military realized the command had overplayed its hand.[1]

However, the press corps also made mistakes. Sometimes they distorted the significance of a news item. For example, television correspondents exaggerated the loss of cargo planes during the fighting at Khe Sanh. Actually, these losses were "well within expectations for a battle of that size, but when television reporters used them over and over again to build dramatic tension they took on a symbolism far larger than their actual importance."[2]

The military in Vietnam accredited and disaccredited American journalists. The most significant difference between Vietnam and the other wars studied here was the number of journalists disaccredited. In every war one or two journalists were disaccredited. In Vietnam that number increased dramatically.[3]

To understand the situation, remember that war was never legally declared in Vietnam. Nor was martial law. While the military can and did request voluntary censorship, it did not have jurisdiction over reporters, except when engaging the enemy. Hence a reporter could go up country and live for a few weeks with the GIs, then fly to Bangkok and file a report detailing troop maneuvers. That they did not do so speaks volumes about the ethics of the majority of accredited journalists reporting the Vietnam War.

The process of accrediting reports went something like this. News outlets sending journalists to Vietnam were required to send a letter to the Military Assistance Command, Vietnam (MACV), confirming their employment and vouching for their identity and professional status. News outlets were also required to assume financial responsibility for their reporters, and they agreed to inform MACV if employment was terminated.[4] It was MACV's policy to afford full cooperation and assistance to news media representatives within the "limits of security considerations."[5]

Upon arrival in Vietnam, journalists filled out and signed an application for a MACV privilege/ration card. In effect, reporters had to comply with military regulations governing the use of exchange merchandise. This list of regulations forbade the accumulation of merchandise in excess of "normal consumption levels."[6] Further, no item could be sold for profit. The records of disaccretitation in Vietnam indicate that several reporters sold merchandise for profit or engaged in money-making and illegal currency manipulation.

The full picture of accreditation and disaccreditation is very complex and detailed. For example, some men and women were bogus journalists. Others were legitimate reporters, usually freelancers, but claimed to work for bogus news outlets. If we disregard those who behaved deceitfully or illegally, it is clear that legitimate journalists did a good job trying to inform the public about this most difficult war.

In Vietnam, accredited journalists carried a MACV accreditation card that accorded the bearers "full cooperation and assistance, within the bounds of operational requirements and military security."[7] Bearers were also entitled to rations and living quarters but only on a reimbursable basis. Reporters also signed combat and flight releases. Finally, all were given a summary list of rules and restrictions governing the use of military payment certificates (MPC), U.S. dollars, and Government of Vietnam piasters (currency). Journalists were required to sign this list, so no one could claim to be ignorant of the ground rules for exchange.[8]

MACV recognized three kinds of correspondents. The first included journalists working full time for the commercial press, as well as bona fide freelancers employed by agencies other than the U.S. government or the Vietnamese press. The second group of recognized journalists were those working for the U.S. government, which included information specialists and photo technicians as well as those employed by the Joint United States Public Affairs Office (JUSPAO), *Stars and Stripes,* the U.S. Information Agency, the Voice of America, and the U.S. Agency for International Development. This second category is new to the historical mix. It demonstrates that while reporters were being integrated into the military system, the military system was itself adapting to what used to be called "mass culture." The third category of accreditation covered nonjournalist employees, such as secretaries or drivers. Members of all three categories carried a MACV press card, but people in the third category had limited press privileges.

MACV accreditation cards each carried an expiration date. A card stamped "Returnee" indicated a previously accredited reporter whose pass had expired. All returnees who were in-country for the first time after 1968 were required to reapply for accreditation as a new arrival.[9] Standard operating procedures allowed MACV to accept letters of validation from a bureau chief in Saigon, but those correspondents were accredited for 30 days only, giving them time to have their home offices write the necessary letter for a longer junket.

Some people representing themselves as journalists manufactured false letterheads for news outlets that existed only on paper. Once the military realized that, they began to check standard media reference works such as the *Ayers Directory, Willings Press Guide,* and *Editor and Publisher,* to verify the legitimacy of the organization.[10]

There were several reasons for disaccreditation. The most common was engaging in illegal money transactions. For example, James Bryant, a freelance journalist for Group W (Westinghouse stations), cashed some bad checks. In November 1971 he received a letter from Captain Paul Ceria warning him that his checks had bounced and asking him to make good on them ASAP: "You are reminded that writing checks without sufficient funds is punishable by law."[11] Because it was a serious matter, Bryant was denied check-cashing privileges indefinitely on the U.S. Army Headquarters Area Command (USAHAC), Open Mess Division. Bryant replied to the letter by leaving a note indicating he was trying to get information from his employers about why the checks had bounced. On March 25, 1972, he left Vietnam without making good on the bad checks.

Elaine Shepard, who later wrote a book following her months in Vietnam, was disaccredited because she abused the rules for postal money orders. In a period of about six weeks, she cashed money orders for $40,000, which violated military code.[12] The U.S. Embassy was asked to invalidate her passport and visa.

Stuart W. Reichstein offers another egregious example of accredited correspondents engaging in money manipulation. Reichstein initially worked for the *Lockhart Post-Register* in Texas from mid-December 1968 to mid-June 1969. In December 1969, he worked for the American Legion, ostensibly writing war news for their newsletter. In January he signed on as correspondent to MACV for *Naval Affairs* magazine.[13]

The secretary of defense received a letter indicating Reichstein had appropriated a half-million dollars in U.S. government property—generators, fans, freezers, slot machines, and so forth. Further, the letter alleged Reichstein was using unauthorized MPCs and cashing checks at government facilities. He had converted MPCs for $5,500 at the U.S. Embassy in Saigon. He had post exchange (PX) and commissary privileges under the pretext of being a reporter when, in fact, he had been an officer of the American Legion. He was also accused of buying liquor from the U.S. Embassy and using U.S. government telephones.[14]

General Creighton W. Abrams received the original complaint. Since the American Legion was "not an instrumentality of the United States Government," Abrams referred the case to the U.S. Embassy. The embassy, in turn, contacted the government of South Vietnam (GVN) and asked them to investigate the matter. On the morning of May 7, 1972, the GVN customs agents raided the American Legion Post in Saigon. They seized forty cases of liquor and 940 cases of beer, for which GVN customs duties had not been paid. They also seized $20,000 as well as MPCs used in the operation of illegal slot machines. Correspondence shows that Reichstein claimed the American Legion was entitled to duty-free import, as well as MPC privileges. He accused the GVN customs agents of being a "Gestapo-Nazi-Commie styled raiding party."[15] But the party was over.[16]

Like Reichstein, Dirk Smit passed himself off as a reporter for the *Okinawa Morning Star*. He did so to secure seats on in-country flights to visit military exchanges throughout Vietnam. His accreditation was withdrawn immediately, including his eligibility to use officers' clubs and messes, and his authorization to use MPCs.[17]

But no one compares to David Cornelius, who was accredited in 1965 and disaccredited in 1967. For two years he "reported" for the bogus "Republic Broadcasting System." Requisition slips in his file indicate that he tried to get excessive amounts of alcohol.[18] Not surprisingly, Cornelius was picked up by police for drunken behavior. When he was found out, he claimed the support of Senator Edward Kennedy and Metromedia. However, neither gave him a letter for accreditation. During the two years of his accreditation, there was no record that he flew up to or into U.S. military bases to cover the war.

As has become apparent, a complex bureaucratic machinery intervened between the journalist and military field operations, with a structure spelling out everything from the proverbial soup to nuts. For example, the military officers convening to suspend or disaccredit James P. Bennet of NBC articulated "rules of evidence" stating what could be admitted as evidence in the proceedings. The test for legitimacy was whether oral or written evidence, including hearsay, seemed relevant and material "in the minds of reasonable men."[19] (Here we find vestiges of the U.S. legal system, where all laws tacitly refer to what "reasonable people" would do or expect.)

Thus far, I have spelled out violations of rules of exchange, but other reasons were cited for suspension or disaccreditation. One of the biggest flaps concerned military charges against Ed Rabel of CBS. According to documents in the record, he consistently conducted himself in a manner violating MACV directives. On April 21, 1971, Rabel was told that Fire Support Base (FSB) Birmingham was off limits to press because it was the staging area for future tactical operations. Rabel and his photographer later arranged for "illegal transportation" there via army helicopters. Later on that same year, he violated agreements that he had made about photographing POWs or casualties in an operating room. Pictures of Lieutenant Michael L. Tournes receiving medical treatment were aired on CBS news.[20]

Toward the end of June 1971, Rabel and his photographer became combative with Lieutenant Colonel Landes. The military charged the CBS news team with taking unauthorized photographs of the confrontation. The photos were deemed unauthorized because Sam Cooke, Rabel's photographer, had filmed soldiers without their consent.[21]

Colonel Walter C. Franzen asked Rabel and Cooke to come to his office to discuss the incidents. In their conversation, Rabel denied provoking Landes into a confrontation. Rabel said he was "fed up" with the staff of the information office, whom he charged with interfering with the freedom of the press. Cooke also complained, but was even more general than Rabel in his charges, saying all army property and personnel were public property.[22]

This conversation led to a legal brief of sorts on the right to privacy, especially for soldiers. The question was whether newspaper and television reporters could record conversations of soldiers without their knowledge. Both Rabel and Cooke seemed determined to sneak up on soldiers and secretly record their conversations. In retrospect, the reporters' behavior seems juvenile. However, their actions led to the articulation of a soldier's right to privacy. As a member of the judge advocate's staff noted, the right of privacy is not protected by the U.S. Constitution, but it is protected under tort law. However, each citizen is protected from the government, not from the private sector. "The test to determine whether a newspaperman intruded is whether an ordinary man could reasonably expect that the press would be excluded [e.g., from a hospital operating room]." Even if the eavesdropping were improper, the military brief argued, it would not necessarily follow that it could not be published. "The test for publication is whether the material is of a legitimate interest to the public."[23]

All complaints and responses ultimately reached the desk of Colonel Robert L. Bryant, who conducted a further review. He concluded that Rabel and Cooke did not "sneak" onto FSB Birmingham. Bryant wrote, "Although the FSB was a staging base for future operations, *just to go there is not illegal."* He went on to minimize the photography violations and recommended that neither Rabel nor Cooke be disaccredited. At the same time, he did recommend that the army discuss their investigation and findings with Dave Miller, CBS bureau chief in Saigon, and indicated that if such conduct continued, "it may be necessary to restrict Rabel's movements on military installations."[24]

This indicates that bureau chiefs acted as liaisons between the military and reporters in the field. Given the military system of command, going to a reporter's "boss" would be logical. It indicates that the general pattern of war reporting grew from getting clearance from commanding officers in the field (in 1898) to being viewed as a part of the war effort (in WWII). In Vietnam the military was more than a fighting machine. It had become a vast network of ties and secondary relationships between the civilian population and the soldiers who provided all kinds of aid and took a leadership role in educating ("pacification" is the word they used) the populace. This was new terrain for both soldiers and reporters, and some adapted better than others.

Both the military and reporters understood that it was risky to publish sensitive information that included news of casualties, MIAs, and stories about the wounded while the military tried to notify the next of kin. But the military also knew the value of keeping the public informed as quickly and as accurately as possible.[25] Each service branch sent casualty lists to their headquarters in Washington, D.C. After notifying next of kin, the Department of Defense announced casualties on a day-to-day basis. "A full and accurate summary was published and distributed to the news media each Thursday."[26]

Lack of knowledge about the military's system of publishing information about the wounded, missing, and dead led some reporters to jump to conclusions that were not warranted by the facts. The case of Harold Ellithorpe is illustrative. Ellithorpe said that hospital personnel had led him to believe that a soldier was wounded when, in fact, he was dead. The military took umbrage with his view that a reporter could not trust the word of any officer. They laid out the guidelines for getting information in Washington, D.C. about the troops. Col. Rodger R. Bankson observed that any problem Ellithorpe had with obtaining accurate information was due to the reporter's lack of knowledge about MACV ground rules, despite the fact that those rules were distributed to all accredited correspondents.[27] And there is truth to that charge.

In Vietnam the military would routinely explain operations to news reporters with the goal of keeping the press aware of military maneuvers. Some operations were put on embargo—meaning that while they had been told about specific maneuvers, journalists could not publish that information for reasons of troop security. If a reporter wrote about such an operation, he was subject to suspension, usually for thirty days.

The *Washington Post* published a report on January 31, 1971, that in part violated an embargo on all military operations in a particular military region. The military arranged press pools to go to the region, but journalists were told they could not publish reports about it. They were note even to mention that an embargo was put on the news. Hence the *Washington Post's* violation of ground rules. Their report read in part: "Newsmen in Saigon were briefed Friday by high military authorities on details of the operation, but an embargo was stamped on the information they were given. That embargo was scheduled to be lifted yesterday at 6 P.M. (Washington time), but it was later extended for an indefinite period."[28] In other words, the military was trying to give deep background on movements to keep the press accurately informed, but the *Post* made the embargo itself the news.

Peter Jay, bureau chief in Saigon, was on his way to the airport to catch a ride to I Corps when he received notice that the paper violated the ground rules and, therefore, he was put on suspension. In arguing his case, Jay noted that all members of the *Post's* bureau had been out of town when the embargo was announced. He pointed out that no communication concerning the operation or the embargo was sent until noon on Sunday, which meant the offending story had already been released in Washington. But the story itself mentioned the embargo. Jay's wife called the paper's foreign desk. She told the *Post* that she had heard from another paper that the *Post* was carrying an incorrect story, "one that violated regulations laid down here [in Saigon] and agreed to by correspondents."[29] Later the *Post* was absolved of any part in the fiasco. The chief of information wrote, "I am happy to inform you that suspension of accreditation for members of your press bureau no longer is being considered."[30]

Sometimes journalists were not so fortunate. Such was the case of Arthur Highbee of United Press International (UPI). He was the bureau chief for the wire service in Saigon. According to statements made at a review hearing in 1972, Highbee had published sensitive information on August 13, 1971, about a downed U.S. aircraft. The story appeared before the search and rescue operation had been completed as well as before the MACV and Military Assistance Command, Office of Information (MACOI) officially released the information.[31] Highbee defended himself first by saying the ground rules had been unclear. He stated that one of his field men heard on a field radio that the pilot had been captured by the enemy and that he, Highbee, had killed the story as soon as he was advised of the ground rules violation. Finally, he said he had no intention of risking someone's life for a story.[32]

More troublesome is the record of a phone conversation between Colonel Robert L. Bryant and Highbee. Highbee told Bryant that he would appear at the hearing, but Alan Dawson, the reporter who "wrote" the story, would not appear because although the offending story carried Dawson's byline, another reporter, Bert Okuley, had actually written the story. Bryant reminded Highbee that Okuley had been disaccredited previously in 1971.[33] Hence the defenses offered by UPI only further muddied the waters. Upon review, the board suspended Highbee's accreditation for thirty days. The vote was unanimous. No minor report was issued.

Thus, we see that individuals masquerading as journalists practiced deceit in their relations with the military. Some real journalists were deceitful too. Some practiced deceit with the organizations employing them.[34] Some were thought to be unstable or mentally ill.[35] Others were legitimate freelancers. Hence the picture of journalists in Vietnam is as complicated and as muddled as the picture of the war itself.

Bogus journalists and news outlets included Robert Sheu for "Photon West" and R. H. Mitman for "Technical News Service," both firms existing only on paper. In contrast, an example of a legitimate news outlet getting shafted by its employee was Photo Service, a small concern supplying several publications in the eastern and mid-Atlantic states with photos of soldiers. They hired William Shipley in 1968 to supply photos and news captions.[36] The military accused Shipley, and an Australian entertainment group he was managing, of committing fraudulent acts. Since Photo Service refused to pay Shipley's debts, it was barred from receiving accreditation for any military or Department of Defense affair.[37] Shipley was also suspected of illegally obtaining passports and tickets.[38]

The military also disaccredited a few legitimate reporters because of the content of their reports. For example, Helen Musgrove was a correspondent for the *Florida Times-Union* and the *Jacksonville Journal*. Her managing editor, Elvin Henson, asked why she had been disaccredited. He wrote, "Mrs. Musgrove was doing what we thought to be a good job and a good service, and the dispute came as quite a surprise here."[39]

According to records in her file, Musgrove's disaccreditation resulted from an article she wrote about the improprieties in the military exchanges and commissaries. Among other charges, she maintained that concessions were obtained through under-the-table kickbacks. The military indicated that for a contract to be granted, it had to be signed by three different organizational heads: the Republic of Vietnam, the Pacific

Exchange (PACEX) procurement representative, and the commander of the installation at which the concession was to be located.[40]

The military characterized Musgrove as a reporter who had no "concern for facts when they detract from her sensational charges."[41] In a report that appeared in the Jacksonville paper, she was critical of the United Services Organization (USO) in Vietnam. The military faulted her for saying things that were simply not true, for example, that soldiers had to pay for USO shows. They also noted that Musgrove had been frustrated in her attempts to secure concession venues for popcorn and for a dress concession.

The military admitted there were abuses in the exchange system in Vietnam. But they turned the tables on Musgrove by claiming that her failure to secure concession venues was an indication that their attempts to plug the loopholes were succeeding. They wrote, "Mrs. Musgrove has been frustrated in her attempts to place herself in a position to profit at the expense of the U.S. servicemen she espouses to champion."[42]

Again, there were many reasons for disaccrediting American journalists covering Vietnam. Several lost press credentials because they engaged in illegal money-making ventures. Some accredited and disaccredited reporters were bogus—some were journalists only on paper; some news outlets existed only on paper. Several real reporters also engaged in deceitful practices in gathering the news, such as eavesdropping on soldiers who were unaware that they were being recorded. Some, like Musgrove, were real journalists who tried to profit from the war.

Over and above these instances of a "free press" profiting one way or another from the war was another group of journalists who engaged in obstreperous behavior. This too was a complex faction. Sometimes reporters were simply emotionally immature and hence "acted out" when they ran into trouble. Other reporters became unruly, feeling they were treated as errant children. However, many journalists who engaged in such behavior felt that the public's right to know was being eclipsed. Acting out sometimes signaled an overt indication that the ideals of the free press in America were being abrogated.

The UPI's Saigon bureau was cited for several "unpleasant incidents" in spring 1967. For example, Richard Growald was suspended for publishing the exact number of casualties in several battles, while Leon Daniel was accused of stealing a statue from a Saigon bar. The military police (MPs) referred him to the Vietnamese civilian police. Many other correspondents were cited for using foul language, being uncooperative with the MPs, and refusing to identify themselves.[43]

Chief of Information Colonel Rodger R. Bankson asked the Saigon bureau chief Eugene V. Risher to inform correspondents that the privilege of holding press accreditation was based on their agreement to cooperate with the military when asked to do so. He told Risher that a second incident of this type (lack of cooperation) involving UPI reporters would result in permanent revocation of their accreditation.[44]

The military kept a running diary on journalists whom they considered miscreants. UPI reporters were also involved in fighting unidentified Vietnamese males. Most of these infractions resulted from drunken behavior rather than any desire to be uncooperative. However, some reporters were emotionally immature even when sober. Growald's accreditation was suspended for thirty days because he revealed the number of casualties suffered by a "friendly unit."[45]

James Bennet was suspended for thirty days because he engaged in loud, boisterous, abusive, vulgar, and threatening behavior at the Da Nang press center. He and Jack Klein, the Saigon bureau chief for NBC, were notified that a hearing would be held. Neither attended, nor did they submit any written matters for consideration by the board.

Klein agreed with the military that Bennet had acted intemperately. Bennet sent a letter of apology to the offended party. However, Klein argued that MACV should have put Bennet's behavior in the context of the difficulties that the entire press corps encountered in Da Nang. He wrote: "To translate a bar room argument into suspension of a man's right to work is . . . to blow things all out of proportion."[46]

Another NBC reporter, Henry Colgate, was disaccredited for threatening a noncommissioned officer (NCO) and for using loud, abusive, suggestive, and provocative words and gestures. Several sworn statements were taken describing Colgate's behavior. Colgate had come to the enlisted soldier's mess, dirty and wearing only an undershirt because his shirt was too dirty to wear in the mess. MPs stopped him and told him to go get properly dressed. Hence his response to their order.[47]

This was not his only infraction. According to Sergeant Keith M. Chambers, Colgate had requested transportation to the 196th Infantry. When asked about his work, Colgate replied, "Yes, I am a freelancer. I sell my work to the major networks. See, I can go out and dig up dirt and sell it to the networks, where they can't go out and look for it. Even on occasions, I tell the GIs what to say into my cassette recorder and then sell it to someone."[48]

Both Colgate and Jack Klein attended the MACV ad hoc board meeting. They defended Colgate's behavior on the grounds that Chambers, the sergeant major questioning Colgate, was impolite and disrespectful. Colgate had shown his accreditation card, identifying him as "Free Lance

Correspondent." Then Chambers addressed Colgate as "Mr. Lance." Colgate lost his temper. He had just returned from a day in the field. He was hot, dirty, and tired. All he had wanted was to get something to eat. What should have been resolved easily with a little wisdom and a lot of patience became an incident elevated to an official board meeting.[49]

A different case was that of Terry Reynolds, an employee of the Vietnam Military Publishing Company. He was sitting in a small bar in Saigon when he noticed an MP grabbing the lapels of an enlisted man. Wanting to find out what was going on, Reynolds showed his press card and tried to question the soldiers involved in the incident. Eventually, everyone involved moved to the MP station. When an MP grabbed the soldier and pushed him along an aisle, Reynolds intervened, saying that he didn't think it was necessary to lock up the young GI. "I had seen the whole thing and I was prepared to make a statement." For this effort the desk sergeant told him to sit down and shut up or he would be locked up. Again, Reynolds showed his press card and demanded to be treated as the civilian he was, whereupon he was locked up along with the hapless grunt. He was released fifteen minutes later.[50]

Captain Richard Morrison was tapped to investigate and write a report about the Reynolds case. He concluded that the MPs were "a bit aggressive," but they were completely within their province as MPs. He also argued that the entire incident could, in some ways, be a matter of bad chemistry between the MPs and the reporter. Eventually, MACVOI sent Reynolds a letter saying a board of inquiry had issued a report on Reynold's "alleged interference" with the MPs and had recommended that his accreditation be revoked.[51]

In this and several other cases, reporters seemed to be unaware of the ramifications of the agreement that they had signed in order to cover the war in Vietnam. The basis for each reporter's accreditation was his agreement to abide by ground rules, all of which had been spelled out for him. In Reynold's case, the chief of information decided not to revoke his accreditation. He advised all parties that "even though we are going to treat this incident as closed, unjudicious [sic] activity of any nature which exceeds under questionable circumstances the pure news-gathering responsibilities of correspondents in the Republic of Vietnam, reflects unfavorably on the entire Saigon press corps."[52] From the military's point of view, any journalist who engaged in activities that exceeded his (the journalist's) authority contributed to the poor image and the dysfunction of the press corps.

The last case I want to discuss is that of the Schell brothers. Jonathon and Orville Schell indicated they wanted to see military operations in the

Duc Pho area of Vietnam. Colonel George E. Wear spent the better part of two hours explaining why and how air and artillery were used against fortified villages that the enemy defended in the south. In the course of being briefed about the military activities going on there, "it became apparent that these two young men were pacifists and were looking only for material to discredit the U.S. effort in Vietnam."[53]

Both brothers were overtly hostile during their visit to Vietnam. Orville Schell interviewed refugees in Duc Pho by asking leading questions. For example, he asked, "The Americans burned your houses, didn't they?" and "You weren't allowed to collect and bring your personal belongings, were you?" When Colonel Wear was apprised of this situation, he ordered his men to bring the brothers back to brigade headquarters. There they were furnished transportation to Quang Ngai.[54]

Other soldiers in the Duc Pho area had similar complaints about the Schells. All agreed that they were hostile. Some said the Schells were using their accreditation cards to "further their political and personal beliefs rather than objectively reporting the war."[55] Others thought that a paper record of their comments should be kept in case the brothers engaged in the same kind of behavior in the future. What was at stake, as far as the military was concerned, was the credibility of the Free World effort in Vietnam.[56] At the same time, they also tried to caution both men about their overt hostility, saying that they would be accorded the same support as any other accredited journalists, but that their manner was off-putting. The military made it clear that the absence of objectivity "might decrease [their] opportunity for obtaining the facts."[57]

One might argue that the press in general and the Schell brothers in particular were simply onto the mistakes being made in Vietnam. If that were the case, all reporters in Vietnam would have sent out similar appraisals. Military records indicate that Schell brothers even put off other correspondents. On at least two occasions, other news media correspondents who shared guest quarters with them complained to the information officer. And, finally, one of the *Boston Globe*'s editors, who agreed to pay them on a story-by-story case, tried to impress upon Orville Schell the necessity for objective reporting. "Don't write editorials. Illustrate what you have to say and prove your editorial point, not so much by flat statements as by example of one person or more who are typical cases in point."[58]

Thus, it seems that in Vietnam some correspondents were hobbled by the overconfidence and inexperience of youth—and they certainly would not have been the first war correspondents in history to be so circumscribed.

During the years between the Second World War and Vietnam, the army and the navy underwent a series of innovations that further professionalized their ranks. This included education and training that exceeded strictly military necessity. As military practices and professional specializations expanded, a more legal approach to solving censorship problems ensued. Vietnam was the crucible for shaping a post-Cold War military, one where education was as important as ordnance and television, the computer and satellites—all electronic media—were adapted to the needs of military command. In many ways the press did not really understand this bigger military picture in Vietnam. In this chapter, the records clearly indicate the range of problems and misadventures many reporters, authentic or bogus, had. In chapter 5, I want to refocus the readers' attention concerning censorship during wartime by identifying several patterns of behavior that emerged from the sources I consulted.

5 The Culture of Press Censorship During Wartime

In chapters 2, 3, and 4, I indicated that over a period of many years censorship practices evolved along with the social practices of journalism. The turning point for the establishment of behavioral codes during wartime for censor and reporter alike was the second decade of the twentieth century. From then on the story of press freedom during war is the story of the integration of the journalist into the military system.

This chapter will argue that the press—and this is an observation rather than a criticism—dances with the state at every turn. In other words, by redefining censorship as a cultural experience rather than as a set of restrictions externally imposed on the press, it is possible to reconfigure the relationship between the press and the state in the latter's civil and military operations. This reconfiguration manifests seven general patterns in a complex tango where the state and the press engage in a highly structured set of steps that are at once formalized and intense. While dancers may be moving in different directions, forward and backward, they do so in concert, because both the government, especially in its military manifestation, and the press have the same goal: preservation of the rule of the people, by the people, and for the people. For this reason, all journalistic practice—but especially practice in wartime—raises larger questions than those about truth in warfare. Ultimately, it poses questions about the relationship between the public and state authority, and the role of the press in this relationship.

The reigning assumption—at least in the United States, where the relationship between the state and the press is codified in the Bill of Rights—is that the journalist has the right, even the duty, to wade into dangerous waters and be critical of current military or political views. The whole practice of censorship asserts and strengthens the principle of a free press. Without its possibility, a free press does not exist. In fact, the ever-present possibility of censorship plays a crucial role in elevating the First Amendment to sacramental status among journalists, lawyers, judges, and scholars.

Rules of censorship are often tacit. They structure the ethics of a censor's behavior and outline the qualities of judgment he legitimately exercises. At the same time, the rules assume a set of behaviors and attitudes on the part of reporters. Codes of behavior for both parties, which have a history predating the wars this study covers, have been slowly put into place. The intransigence of such codes—either through imprudent judgment or rhetorical recklessness—evokes negative responses from the other party.

The codes of censorship comprise a set of conventions that all parties understand in a practical way. When called upon, they can articulate them—if only partially. The codes entail how far reporters can go in explicitly addressing the subject of their stories. At the same time, reporters can encode their reports in such a way that no one could make an example of them. Even when no formal office of censorship is set up, even when journalists do not have to submit their stories to the blue pencil (as was the case in Vietnam), the conventions of censorship behavior are implicit in every act engaged in by reporters, editors, or military officers. If journalists are fish, censorship is the sea. Without water, fish die. Without the possibility of censorship, journalists cease to exist.

The story of press censorship during wartime, then, is the story of the interweaving of several related but distinct factors: the occupational practices and conventions of the military and the press, the organized bureaucracy (both journalistic and military) administering judgment on the publication of a story, the strategies of interpretation invoked by journalists to adjust to any restrictions they might face, and the technologies of warfare affecting what could and could not be seen and understood about daily events in the theaters of war.[1]

Before the United States declared war on Spain in 1898, reporters tried to cover the Cuban insurrection from both the Spanish and the Cuban sides. Spanish censorship was set up shortly after the second Cuban insurrection took place in 1896. The Spanish immediately tightened the reins on news leaving the island. Press reports were checked to ensure that the importance given the uprising reflected the Spanish viewpoint, that is, that Spain kept all matters well in hand. Reporters were required to have a military pass to travel over Cuban terrain via the rails, which were under Spanish control. The first Spanish leader, Arsenio Martinez Campos, was easygoing and made few demands on journalists. His replacement, General Valeriano Weyler, was not. When Weyler assumed his duties as commander-in-chief of the Spanish forces, he confined journalists to Havana and strictly forbade any newspaper reporter from accompanying either the Spanish or Cuban armies. Newspapers raised noisy objections. Reporters began to accuse Weyler of trying to cover up war crimes, even though for over a year prior to the restriction, no newspaper had sent a representative to cover the rebellion from the Spanish side of the lines.[2]

This is the first pattern I found in the culture of censorship: when the military forbids coverage of a battle or a maneuver, news outlets judge the events as newsworthy. In other words, a military prohibition of coverage is treated as a transparent movement; it signals to the press that an infraction of constitutional rights may underpin this strategy or that some significant action that is part of the people's business has taken place. Despite the wide range of historical circumstances covered in this study, this general observation holds true in all wars. Even in World War II, the war that our culture generally views as legitimate and justified, reporters were sensitive to any military evasions. For example, prior to the Allied invasion of North Africa, reporters were furious about the censorship of stories describing the military's cooperation with the Nazi French. Only Ernie Pyle's copy cleared without the censor's amendments and deletions.

The same sort of pattern played out in military zones. Here the journalist's skepticism prevailed. Inactivity in the waiting areas, especially, was seen as a cover-up. The armed forces were alert to journalistic concerns and responded to reporters in a variety of ways. Early in 1944, for example, the adjutant general's office (AGWAR) sent a memo to all theater commanders notifying them that the press was accusing the military of concealing mistakes under the guise of military security. In this instance, friendly fire had destroyed allied transport planes off the coast of Sicily in 1943. AGWAR admonished commanders in the field to publish losses and damage due to accident or misfortune unless security reasons were obvious.[3]

Reporters often judge their own inactivity as an indication of military evasion. However, in the European theater of operations (ETO), the U.S. Army was quick to point out conditions beyond their control. In the aftermath of the D-Day invasion, a statement from ETO headquarters noted that the limited number of reporters "is by no means any effort by SHAEF [Supreme Headquarters, Allied Expeditionary Force] to prevent further coverage but that the military conditions and plans do not permit further assimilation of correspondents beyond" those already placed in the area.[4] The public relations officer (PRO) noted the limits that field conditions imposed on armies, and implored the adjutant general to stop sending more reporters.[5]

At the same time, the military was often aware of the advantage of a policy of vagueness about its own and enemy dispositions. In the Second World War, especially, a public relations policy of carefully discharging information was carried out, in particular to broadcast journalists. "Almost without exception," one memo counseled, "German division commanders captured to date have expressed their appreciation of Allied broadcasts as being their most reliable sources of information on the general military situation during periods of combat."[6]

Furthermore, the military's appreciation for press conventions worked to its advantage. Almost always, censors were peacetime reporters and editors. By World War II, the military knew enough to appoint newspaper people who had experience in war reporting and, more importantly, who were respected by other news people.[7] For their part, reporters respected military conventions, if for no other reason than to avoid censorship. As Tom Tiede observed in Vietnam, when the military asked photo bureaus not to print recognizable combat photos of casualties, the press complied because following the rules was a way of avoiding censorship.[8] In preparation for invading the continent in June 1944, communiqués transmitted by teleprinters in the public relations office distinguished between on-record and off-record background material and were sensitive to morning and afternoon newspaper deadlines. The on-record communiqués were not distributed to the public for thirty minutes after reporters received them. This small detail indicates the degree to which the military had learned to use the press to its advantage, rather than seeing it as an interference in the operations of war.

On the home front, the Office of Censorship operations, headed by an Associated Press (AP) man, illustrates a second pattern in the culture of censorship. When the Japanese bombed Pearl Harbor, many editors, managers, and reporters took leaves of absence from their companies to enlist in the armed services or to work in some other capacity for the government. Many corporations gave their management personnel allowances during the course of the war, making it possible for men to serve the nation without economic deprivation. Both the AP and Scripps-Howard

Newspapers, for example, committed themselves to remunerating Byron Price and John Sorrells, both of whom had living costs they could not meet solely on their government salaries.[9]

With the upper echelon press managers directing both the military and civic censorship operations, the scene was fully set for experiencing censorship practices in terms of peacetime rivalries between news outlets. Hence, Price appointed Sorrells as the head of press operations to remove "any lingering resentment which the United Press might have had [and there was some] that an Associated Press man had been selected as Director of Censorship."[10]

After discussion with the National Association of Broadcasters and the independents, Price appointed Harold Ryan from Toledo, Ohio, to head broadcasting. Ryan was general manager of the Fort Industry Company, which had a chain of six small radio stations from Georgia to Ohio. Both NBC and CBS were apprehensive about Ryan because they feared he would favor small stations at the expense of large ones. Describing the big corporations as "considerably agitated," Price noted he had little choice, since appointing anyone from NBC or CBS would cause resentment in other quarters.[11]

Thus, press management of press censorship ensured that the practices of competition that structure the marketplace of news would surface in the daily interrelations between the press and the state, and that censorship operations would be inclined to perceive the motives, ideas, and beliefs of journalists in those terms. Thus the second pattern in the culture of censorship: wartime censorship, when managed by news editors and reporters, reinforces and intensifies the mythos of a free marketplace of ideas that underpins all journalistic practices and signifies excellence in its practices.

As a cultural experience, this meant that Byron Price's actions, whatever they were, would be judged as favoritism. Even the AP viewed Price in these terms. When reporter Ed Angly's story about American troops in Australia appeared in the *Chicago Sun*, many papers around the country picked it up. Coincidentally, the *Sun* was engaged in an effort to become a member of the AP. Since it was not yet a member, the Associated Press could not pick up the story, but United Press International (UPI) could. Some of Price's former colleagues at AP felt he had "unnecessarily handed a good story to the Opposition." Price countered that if the *Sun* had been a member of the AP, "as it should have been," there would have been no problem.[12]

In some cases, reporters accepted pooling as a necessary evil, so long as the requirement was lifted as soon as feasible. ("Pooling" is the practice of selecting some news reporters to accompany troops. These few then share their information with all reporters.) Given a choice, editors preferred no pooling at all. This was as true of black-owned papers as it was of white-owned ones. For example, the publisher of the *Baltimore Afro-American* asked that his reporter, Ollie Stewart, represent only his newspaper, rather than the "Negro pool."[13] In all matters, however, the military favored consistency in applying policy to avoid charges of evasion or bias, to keep the media happy, and to "insure that the best interests of the press organizations are served."[14]

One of the most frequently used steps in the dance called censorship was the backstep. In 1898, journalists were able to use their Spanish passes to elude Spanish forces and travel inland to meet up with the insurrectionists. After passing through the trocha (the rail lines that acted as the backbone of the Spanish defense), they hired and rendezvoused with dispatch boats owned or rented by their employers at various secret points on the Cuban coast and sent news reports to Key West to be telegraphed to their home office. When not using Key West facilities, reporters used cable lines at Jamaica or Môle Saint-Nicolas, Haiti, to evade the Spanish blue pencil. As time passed and public opinion became more critical of Spain, General Weyler became more and more censorious. Eventually he arrested and deported errant journalists.

Equipped with the necessary military pass, Richard Harding Davis— who along with Ernie Pyle is among those people most frequently identified as representatives of the best in the tradition of war correspondence— got what he called a "car window view of things."[15] Private accounts of his experience indicate Davis thought the Spanish treated him fairly, with kindness and courtesy. They sent his cables and delivered his mail. He did not suspect them of reading his letters.[16] However, being confined to a railway car increased the difficulty of getting at the truth. "You would think," he wrote his mother, "the picturesque and dramatic and exciting thing would be the one I would rather believe because I want to believe it, but I find that this is not so. I see a great deal on both sides and I do not believe half of what I am told."[17] Davis's account suggests a third pattern in the culture of censorship: the degree of restriction of movement is in inverse proportion to the credibility a journalist invests in his sources.

In 1898, reporters had difficulties reaching the Cuban camps. Part of the difficulty rested on the military strategy of the insurgents formulated by the commander-in-chief, Maximo Gomez. Gomez designed his forces to be highly flexible, ready for quick dispersal and reunion. The success of the guerillas was tied to two elements. The insurgency had to be island-wide, thus forcing Spanish troops to disperse into smaller groups. Additionally, the war could be won only if it became economically devastating to Spain. To achieve this goal, Gomez and his troops burned out the island's sugar crops. Both of these strategies made it harder for reporters to find insurgent camps in order to accompany the armies on their campaigns.[18]

Davis and George Bronson Rea were able to establish a relationship with General Weyler that was based on shared expectations regarding conventions. Because the journalists conducted themselves in ways that suggested a gentleman's code of honor, they were allowed greater freedoms than those reporters whose middle-class or lower-middle-class upbringing did not prepare them for the world of the drawing room. This suggests a fourth pattern in the culture of censorship: to the degree that members of the military and the press shared a common code of behavioral conventions (mostly determined by class of origin, if not current socioeconomic standing) boundaries of what it is permissible to print became elastic and permeable.

The most common way to get news in Cuba was to make friends with officers. Early in 1898, Sylvester Scovel's wife (who referred to herself as the "new woman" and may have reported about Cuba for some news outlet) wrote to her mother that she and "Harry" had had dinner with the officers on the battleship Maine. "All the American officers like Harry," she later wrote. They liked his work and his method of working.[19] In Vietnam college-educated reporters nurtured ties to the unit public information officers "who will leak information."[20] The context of these friendships was always respect shot through with disdain. This disdain governs the relationship's integrity, for it allows both parties to sustain the fiction that they are at bottom on opposite sides of an invisible demarcation line.

H. L. Mencken knew as much in 1914. His diary records these liaisons with the cynicism for which he is well known. The price of propinquity, he thought, was independent judgment. Referring to news wire reporters, he noted, "They stand closest to [Ambassador James W.] Gerard, and I daresay they reflect his views."[21] The German military did not allow reporters to leave Germany for eight weeks after visiting the front. Mencken was stuck in Berlin where he made his rounds. He observed: "Plattenberg invites me to call on him daily and sample his excellent Scotch. But man cannot live on Scotch alone. . . . Plattenberg has a stiff neck, but he is nevertheless able to laugh. I told him I was reminded of the darkey [sic] about to be hanged. Asked if he had anything to say, he replied, 'This surely will be a lesson to me.' The gentlemen of the Military Bureau have a hearty appetite for such anecdotes."[22]

Cynicism is the reporter's approach to life. It underpins skepticism and is not so much a character trait as it is a way of knowing. A war correspondent always has one eyebrow raised. He knows that his proximity to the military is an essential ingredient of the job. Such was the case with Richard Tregaskis while covering the Vietnam war, which he understood as a miniature World War II. Writing somewhat apologetically to Admiral John S. McCain, Tregaskis said, "I also felt you were very tolerant of my criticism of the administration for failing to use our bombing strength to hurt the enemy more deeply. I really was echoing the opinion voiced to me many times by both land- and carrier-based pilots that interdiction targets are unsatisfactory as far as winning the war is concerned."[23]

In Vietnam, Tom Tiede referred to this method of getting news as "the cold war." Despite the gulf between them, most PIOs were willing to help journalists. Few openly disclosed sensitive information. Instead, they would say something like, "We're having a party Wednesday morning and you're invited." One PIO explained it thus: "How can I do my job and not let the press know when something is up? Newsmen aren't delinquents."[24]

George Bronson Rea had been in Cuba five years when the second insurrection against Spain broke out. He complained about correspondents who accepted information uncritically from sources. Rea was reluctant to fault General Weyler, nicknamed "The Butcher" by the press, because Rea was reluctant to accept any notion that the Cubans were oppressed at all.[25]

As previously noted, in Cuba, reporters managed to circumvent Spanish censorship by using dispatch boats that rendezvoused at secret points along the coast. However, once the United States declared war on Spain, a new sort of censorship was inaugurated. The U.S. military took over cable offices: the navy occupied the office at Key West; the Signal Corps occupied six cable offices in New York and oversaw the landlines of Florida, the French cable on the south coast of Cuba, the British cables in Puerto Rico and Santiago de Cuba and, in time, the Cuban submarine cables at Santiago. Censorship was entrusted to the respective superintendents of each office who all worked under the direction of an officer from the Signal Corps. This arrangement had long been planned. Both reporters and editors complained that censorship by American forces was worse than that of Spain.

Any mention of troop movements was automatically removed from news accounts. Censors also checked the paper daily to determine whether anything of benefit to the enemy had gotten through their hands. Any reporter who violated the censorship efforts of the military stood the chance of losing his press credentials.[26]

Other elements also worked to censor news. For example, reporters were restricted to one hundred words per story—due in part to the cost of transmitting daily reports via the telegraph, but also due to the large number of people accredited to cover the war. Virtually anyone who asked for press credentials received them. This situation was repeated several decades later in Vietnam, until the military there realized that some applicants for press accreditation were lying to them.

During World War II, reaction to press censorship was predictable. At first journalists were openly irritated and angry at the military. Eventually they resorted to dupery. Although the censorship of the Spanish-Cuban-American War did not reach the proportions of World War I, after the explosion of the USS *Maine* Jimmy Hare walked into the offices of *Collier's Weekly* and proposed photographing both the wreckage and Cuban life. He had considerable experience as a photographer, so he was hired.[27] Later he covered World War I, and noted this about the War of 1898: "Oh, we had some censors in those days too! But they had not attained their colossal proportions so a fellow could sometimes put it over on them."[28]

Hence the fifth pattern in the culture of censorship: when the military imposes extreme measures, reporters resort to evasion tactics to report the war. The more extreme the measure, the more evasionary the journalist.

Denial was a useful part of these skirmishes. Paul Manning of Mutual Broadcasting, when reprimanded for an unauthorized broadcast during World War II, simply argued that he was not bound by the security agreement he signed once he left the battle site. He and five other journalists had gone to Paris and broadcast news from there without submitting to the censor. One of his colleagues, Laurence Leseur of CBS, took another approach. He told Supreme Headquarters, Allied Expeditionary Force (SHAEF) that he had gone to the Hotel Scribe at 6 p.m. and waited until 9:30 p.m. for the arrival of censorship personnel. Then, "I undertook the responsibility of acting as my own censor at the radio station involved, in accordance with General Eisenhower's personal statement prior to D-Day that he regarded accredited war correspondents as quasi-staff officers." The army responded to any such unauthorized broadcasts by suspending those concerned for thirty days. In effect, this barred the journalists from the combat and communications zones.[29]

The character and intelligence of the censor determined the lengths to which a journalist had to go to outwit him. Reporters often thought the censor a stupid person who had "royal airs" suggesting "kingly lineage." In such cases, the reporter resorted to diplomacy.[30] If diplomacy was out of the question, reporters sent their dispatches via the mail or hired couriers who carried the reports to better points of dispatch.[31]

Historically, the military has tolerated evasion of the blue pencil by skirting the outer limits of orthodox behavior—to a point. Beyond that, disaccreditation occurred. Many examples can be found of reporters trying to get around censorship using a variety of evasionary tactics. In World War II, Dickey Chapelle (to my knowledge the first woman reporter to die while covering a combat story) had been permitted to go to Okinawa on the condition she stay aboard the hospital ship to which she had been assigned.[32] When she disembarked, she was dismissed from the Pacific theater of operations, sent back to Hawaii, and disaccredited on the grounds that she disobeyed orders. Her prints and negatives were confiscated, as well as notes she had made for a story on blood and plasma.[33] After having her war correspondent credentials revoked, to reenter the ranks she was required to sign an agreement stating "I agree to observe the same rules and ethics in regard to transmission of information as service personnel."[34] The significance of this seemingly small bureaucratic gesture is made clear when set beside the outcome of a similar incident occurring fifty-three years earlier. In Cuba, when Sylvester Scovel disobeyed orders and appeared at the flag raising in Santiago, newspapers in the United States called for his court martial.

The language used by the military and press in these and other instances, as well as the cultural expectations of the times, point to a sixth pattern in the culture of censorship: the reporter is little distinguished from the fighting soldier. The military, the public, and the press itself identified the journalist in these terms. This understanding of reporter as soldier, as a fighting arm of the military, can be found in all wars, but reached its acme during World War II. The consequences of assuming journalists are soldiers with pens are far-reaching in a society that prizes free expression. Sometimes they were used as couriers. Sylvester Scovel and others covering the war of 1898 carried letters between naval officers and the Cuban insurgents. In one case, Rear Admiral and Commander-in-Chief William T. Sampson sent a letter to the general of the rebel armies, Maximo Gomez, stating: "I have the honor to inform you of the presence of the Squadron under my command off the coast of Cuba. . . . Desiring information for my government, would be very much pleased to have you inform me as to your ideas concerning co-operation and your needs as to arms, munitions, and supplies in general. . . . The bearer, Mr. Sylvester Scovel, is empowered to treat with you in my name."[35] Gomez accepted the alliance, although he complained about the treatment of the insurgent's general delegate, Tomas E. Palma, by the American military officers. Editors as well as officers were expecting more money than the insurgents had to pay for the munitions and supplies.[36] Later Scovel's editor, Merrill (of *The World*), urged him to think and act as if he were "the personal representative of the President himself."[37]

The inclination to think of reporters as soldiers reached its high point in World War II. This pattern of behavior provides some of the strongest evidence supporting the main argument of this book: the press is a walking advertisement for the nation-state. For example, thirty-eight correspondents were authorized to wear the Asiatic-Pacific Theater Ribbon in recognition of their efforts in the war. Admiral Chester Nimitz applauded the work of these men and women, noting the "high standard of performance of their journalistic duties, contributing to the successful prosecution of the war in the Pacific Ocean area."[38] The list included journalists working for the AP, the three broadcast networks, several newspapers and magazines, and Fox Movietone News. Three women were listed; however, no black journalists were included, although black journalists covered the war, and several did it with distinction.

General Dwight D. Eisenhower melded his view of reporters as members of the military with a ready recognition of their journalistic calling:

> At my first Press Conference as Supreme Commander I told the War Correspondents that once they were accredited to my headquarters I considered them quasi staff officers. . . . As a matter of policy accredited war correspondents should be accorded the greatest possible latitude in the gathering of legitimate news. Consequently, it is desired that . . . [commanders and PROs] give accredited war correspondents all reasonable assistance. They should be allowed to talk freely with officers and enlisted personnel and to see the machinery of war in operation in order to visualize and transmit to the public the conditions under which the men from their countries are waging war against the enemy.[39]

All accredited civilian correspondents had the "simulated" rank of captain. As a memo from SHAEF makes clear, the military sometimes even decided what holidays reporters would have: "No Christmas holidays for correspondents," one memo read.[40]

In general, by World War II, the military saw the press as central to morale, "to make casualties realize the importance of their job." General Eisenhower especially recognized the value of the press, not only in terms of the national regard for the First Amendment, but also in terms of its propaganda value. A few days before the D-Day invasion, he sent a memo to his chiefs of staff observing that anything the press could do to keep the enemy in a state of nervous tension would be of the greatest possible help.[41]

By 1940, the military's understanding of the press and its value systems was quite sophisticated and was employed with a subtlety that journalists themselves often disallow. For example, reporters were thought of as "attached, not to a unit, but to a particular story."[42] Commanders were asked to apply the regulations governing war correspondence as liberally as possible to those who were working for national magazines. The recognition of the importance of magazines for a national audience and the observation that reporters belonged to stories, not to units, also suggest that officers of a certain rank regarded reporters in proprietary ways.

Even in Vietnam, where the press eventually challenged the assumptions the public was making about the state, reporters were soldiers with pens in hand instead of guns. Dickey Chapelle wrote to her editor at *Reader's Digest*, "I am writing to you from what might be considered the war room of any 20th century fighting force, the heart of their headquarters and the *pro tem* Digest's [*sic*] office."[43]

Living day and night with soldiers lends credibility to the feeling that one is, indeed, another kind of soldier. On this occasion, Chapelle was covering a Vietnamese airborne brigade. She was the first reporter, Vietnamese or American, permitted to go out on their operations. In her letters to her editor, it is clear that she identifies with the men whose maneuvers she reports on and that she is conscious of this identification. "I've so far walked almost 200 miles through head-high jungle and knee-high water with them on this kind of mission, been fired on from ambush and watched them return the fire seven times, slept seventeen nights in the field and made six jumps into drop zones reclaimed by other Vietnamese riflemen each dawn from the Viet Cong so the brigade could rehearse its jumping function."

Convinced that neither most Americans nor most Vietnamese understood that Southeast Asia was a time and place of decision, she told her editor that she is speaking "like Cassandra," with a shrill voice and an edgy desperation. Otherwise, she believed, her work could not span the great gulf between Americans sitting at home and the Vietnamese soldiers in the field.[44]

When journalists are with the soldiers in the field, they share more than just C rations. They have the same experiences as the men carrying rifles. Men were blown up before their eyes by small children wired with grenades. Tunnels had rats the size of cats in them.[45] Under these conditions, and worse, it is almost impossible to avoid psychological identification with the subject of the story.

Furthermore, journalists shared more than sleeping quarters with soldiers. They also used military communications lines. Many times in Vietnam, journalists relied on the military to process film, send out reports, and set up interviews for them. In some circumstances, the military used photos taken by reporters for their own work.[46]

In both World War II and Vietnam, reporters had an explicit sympathy for the enlisted men and a respect for the enemy accompanied by open cynicism about censors. Reporters took a dim view of anyone above the rank of second lieutenant. In Vietnam, the trade joke among journalists was that reporters were fighting two enemies: the Viet Cong (VC) and the army information officer. The VC are preferable, the joke went. They at least would not shoot you in the back. Or, as one man observed, in Vietnam, the PIO was spelled PU.[47]

Enlisted men often returned the respect the reporter had for them in letters of thanks. In one such missive, signed only "Moe," a soldier talks about Tom Tiede's stories. He writes, "We are all proud of the way you have told our story here."[48]

All war correspondents believe at an often-unconscious level that sharing in the hardships of the men fighting a war gives them—the journalists—the credentials to report on the war. This belief lives like a ghost in the attic of their "self." For a male reporter especially, there is always a nagging question deep inside, Would I have what it takes to fight like this? Military officers, too, often measured authenticity in a reporter by his experiences in the soldier's war. For example, Edward Lansdale wrote this of Dickey Chapelle: "One reporter I know who understands guerilla warfare from having seen so much of it is Dickey Chapelle. Admittedly, she is an outspoken gal who is the darling of the Marine Corps, but she does get in close and knows counterinsurgency the way Ernie Pyle knew the ground war in World War II."[49] Elsewhere, Lansdale refers to Chapelle as a "damn fine soldier in the good fight."[50]

Perhaps nothing suggests the dance the press engages in with the military more than the degree to which reporters see themselves as strategists and experts in fighting war—in effect, as opinion makers and consultants on affairs of state. Make no mistake: military strategy seduces. It can become an end in itself rather than a means to one. When that happens, whether the strategist is a soldier or a reporter, perspicacity is carried away on the winds. Kiss it goodbye.

In Vietnam, Richard Tregaskis in particular saw himself in this light. His letters refer to both Lyndon Johnson and Richard Nixon as men who would profit from a consultation with him, "to chew over some vital issues," and to make known "certain signs, very little noted in print," which give encouragement about the situation in Southeast Asia. These aspirations seem to be more hope than fact. For example, he writes that he had direct access to Nixon. However, in the next breath he says, "And I am told he would like to know what thoughts I have on these subjects."[51]

Tregaskis had made his reputation in World War II with the publication of his book *Guadalcanal Diary*. In Vietnam he was more a freelance writer than a war reporter. However, the history of war correspondence in America has many examples of journalists who saw themselves as sources of information for military officers and officers of state. Sometimes this extended to the allied governments. Dickey Chapelle wrote that she had more to do with the government of South Vietnam than she had to do with the U.S. government because the Vietnamese head of state had asked for her observations about troop morale.[52]

At the same time, the military did not appreciate what it saw as the press's influence in matters of state. Journalists, too, felt competitive with one another. Tregaskis wrote of David Halberstam, a fellow journalist in Vietnam, "the *New York Times'* correspondent (and his journalistic clique) pulled another Herb Mathews-type stunt. . . . Barry Zorthian, Ambassador Taylor's public affairs minister told me, 'It was an astounding spectacle that President Kennedy completely disregarded the advice of his embassy people and followed the *New York Times* and his (Halberstam's) satellite.'"[53]

Reporters, too, engaged in skirmishes, particularly with censors. Sometimes, the best way to get by the censor was to face him head-on. Richard Tregaskis was in the first wave of the marine assault on Guadalcanal. He left four months later because he "wanted to get the book [*Guadalcanal Diary*] out and censored and into New York before it cooled off." The biographical account among his papers tells of "helping to sink a Japanese battleship" in one of many bombing missions he flew in the Pacific.[54] As this and other accounts suggest, whether the journalist was evading or facing the censor head-on, he saw himself as a soldier without a gun, but no less a protector of the people.

However, not all movements and counter movements by the press were evasive. In World War II especially, where the system, because it was set in place, left the censor free to exercise more discriminating judgment, the dance partners drew closer to one another, as lovers might when the initial period of nervousness gives way to one of greater mutual comfort.

In this respect, a seventh pattern in the culture of censorship can be formulated: the integration of the press into the military enabled a zone of comfort to be constructed that allowed both soldiers and journalists to concentrate on their respective jobs. The army used several strategies for making the most of the press. Among them was the release of information attributed to a military correspondent or to the Official Allied Press Service whenever the true source of "authoritative information" could not be revealed. When the army thought the press was giving too much attention to one topic, it tried to attract more attention elsewhere. Such was the case when General George Patton's "colorful appeal" took attention away from other officers, such as General Courtney H. Hodges and General Omar Bradley.[55]

In World War II, journalists and soldiers worked well once both parties understood ground rules. For example, in preparation for the invasion of Africa, reporters were given a course on how to move about while keeping under cover, how to dig foxholes, and how to read maps, pitch tents, and many other things. In Britain, the censor was directed to stop all reports commenting on the violent opposition of the French National Committee and many British citizens to the political situation in North Africa. He justified the censorship on the grounds that to pass along these messages would indicate the government's approval and thus cause dissention between the United States and Great Britain.[56]

From the military's point of view, the successful invasion of North Africa depended on surprise, effective planning, and Admiral Jean François Darlan's check of French resistance. Unfortunately, however, the disharmony surrounding the political situation and complaints by the press diverted Eisenhower's attention from the military situation and indirectly contributed to the debacle at Kasserine Pass (sometimes known as Cessarine Gap) in February 1943, the worst Allied defeat on land since Battaan (1941–42). In the meantime, Rommel was retiring westward from Wadi Zem Zem and secretly accumulating armor and troops at Faid Pass. At this point the command post of the Allies' First Armored Division was located at Sbeitla. When news reached the correspondents that the Germans were advancing toward the American artillery positions near Sidi Bou Zid, they jumped into jeeps and headed for Sbeitla. Noland Norgaard (AP), Ernie Pyle, and Graham Hovey, International News Service (INS) got caught in the German blitz. The Afrika Korps overran Sidi Bou Zid and Sbeitla.

The Allies hastily devised a counterattack; reporters were stationed by the radio van and listened to the battalion commander leading the tank attack. As the battle progressed, they drove closer to the fighting, but in the midst of chaos could not assess exactly what was going on and eventually went rearward. A few hours later, with the counterattack a dismal failure, the Americans retreated. Eisenhower sent reinforcements, but the Germans moved twenty-one miles beyond Kasserine Pass and captured five thousand soldiers before they were stopped.[57]

This example demonstrates the interplay between the state and the press—the news blackout of the political situation in North Africa created a tension between reporters and the military that in turn contributed to a disastrous defeat of the Allies. Conversely, the assassination of Darlan (December 24, 1942) and the increasing activity caused by the rout at Kasserine Pass eased the strained relations between journalists and censors.[58]

As a stabilized front took shape, reporters were given jeeps and they drove from one area to another, spending a day or two with each outfit. At the front, the military did not have specific places for them to sleep, so reporters had to make do with whatever they could find. In Africa and elsewhere, this translated into sleeping in chicken houses and under wagons, in cactus patches, among fir trees or on mountainsides, and in old vacant buildings. Food at the front was supplied by army kitchen trucks, but when reporters could not get to them, they ate army C rations. In the rear areas, journalists were always welcomed at the army mess if they showed up at mealtime.[59]

The main drawback of life at the front was the toll it took on reporters' physical stamina and well-being. This is generally true of all wartime conditions and accounts in large part for the fact that war correspondents are usually young men whose youth, in turn, often leads them to romanticize battle events. On the other hand, the advantage of life at the front was freedom from bureaucratic red tape. Bureaucrats (whom Pyle called "small men of brief authority"), if antagonized, could make life very difficult for reporters.[60] Thus the importance of following codes of behavior that were mostly implicit (but which could be articulated somewhat by both the military and press), if called upon to do so. In other words, censorship—through its sheer existence—itself engendered these implicit codes, the intransigence of which would evoke penalties.

Part of every war involves the circulation of fictions created to explain the national character of the individual allied nations, the inept workings of military command, the "logic" of atrocities, and so forth. Reporters also created fictions to explain the stupidities of censorship or, at least, to vent about them. In a cable sent to George Wells of *Newsweek*, journalist Hal Boyle comments on a story circulating about Harry Zohn, a character made up by war correspondents covering the American First Army during World War II. Harry was a censor, and a real red-tape cutter. Boyle adopts the tropical strategy of irony in his observation: "If we had ten Harrys and another General Bradley, we could have cut [a] half year off the war."[61] Besides indicating the interpretive strategy privately adopted here, his comment also speaks to his assumptions about the press as companions to the fighting forces of the war.

Despite complaints, journalists got a periodic respite from the blue pencil. One such case occurred in the North African campaign. It may be that censors just missed his copy (an unlikely scenario, given the number of levels of censorship reports had to pass through). More likely, it was Ernie Pyle's recognition of the importance of the lowliest soldier and his repeated emphasis on the experience and viewpoint of the average GI in his reports that led censors to pass on the only press report about the North African political situation to be published without challenge.

Pyle wrote the column at the request of some members of the counterintelligence corps at Oran: "We have left in office most of the small-fry officials put there by the Germans before we came. We are permitting fascist societies to continue to exist. Actual sniping had been stopped, but there is still sabotage. The loyal French see this and wonder what manner of people we are. . . . Our enemies see it, laugh, and call us soft. . . . Our fundamental policy still is soft-gloving snakes in our midst."[62]

This is another example of the benefit to be had when reporters and the military share a code of value. Unlike the wars of 1898 and 1914 where men were led to stand and fight because they had cultivated a strong relationship between the soldier and his officer, in World War II, the armed forces replaced the soldier-officer bond with one between buddies. In other words, men were encouraged to stand and fight lest they let down their fellow soldiers. What I am suggesting here is that the military identified psychologically with Ernie Pyle, and so his copy sometimes became immune from the sort of restrictions faced by his fellow journalists.

This chapter began by redefining censorship, making it a culture or a medium rather than a set of prescriptive rules, that is, no prior restraint. Once the seven general patterns of behavior are detailed, it is possible to see that the relationship between the press and the military is not adversarial. Research shows that in cases where the military forbid coverage of a battle or maneuver, reporters tend to think the events are newsworthy. They are then likely to conclude that the military are covering something up. Similarly, inactivity in the waiting areas was treated as an indication of military evasion. In addition, by World War II the military had become very savvy about press conventions. They adopted a policy of appointing members of the press to manage press censorship. This strategy ensured that the practices of competition that structured the marketplace of news during peacetime would surface in the daily interrelations between censors and war reporters. But reporters tended to think censors were favoring their own news organizations. In other words, as contradictory as it may seem, the practice of appointing news editors and reporters as censors intensified the predominant mythos of the time: the news is part of a free marketplace of ideas. Favoritism, real or perceived, shown by censors for their own news outlets outraged war correspondents' sense of fairness.

Another pattern in the dance of censorship was the backstep, that is, the way war reporters treat their sources when the military restrict access to battle events. The fewer restrictions on a journalist, the more credibility he assigns his sources. Likewise, the greater the limits on a reporter's access to war zones, the less he believes his sources before, during, and after he gets there.

In addition to the consequences of restricting press movements and access, another factor played an interesting role in military and press relations: the reporter's class of origin (not necessarily his current socioeconomic class). Often when a reporter and a censor share value systems tied to each other's families, they get along well together. In fact, the boundaries of what is considered permissible behavior on the part of both censor and reporter are elastic and permeable. At the same time, a war correspondent always has one eyebrow raised when it comes to a censor. For a journalist, cynicism is more than an attitude. It is the way he sees life; it is his way of knowing the world. His gut instincts take over when the military impose extreme measures of censorship on him. The more extreme the measure (e.g., total exclusion from zones of fighting), the more extreme the evasionary tactics the journalist will use. Historically, the military tolerated unorthodox behavior by the press—but only to a point. Once lives were put in jeopardy, once the reporter exceeded the rules and ethics of the military itself, his accreditation was suspended or completely revoked.

Another pattern to emerge from this research is the identification of the reporter as a soldier. Here I mean that everyone—the public, the military, and the press itself—has historically assumed that war reporters are soldiers with pens rather than guns—even though many reporters actually carried guns into the arenas of war. It is a serious problem,

I think, when reporters forget they are not soldiers, when they begin to imagine themselves as couriers, government agents, or counselors to the sitting president. A reporter who understands the limits of his calling as well as his position in the nation-state (not to say the government) is the real McCoy.

The final pattern I found in the culture of censorship will seem contradictory to what I have written above. Life, war, and reporting are filled with contradictions. And so I want to conclude this chapter by noting that the dance the press and the military do during war also creates a zone of comfort for each partner. Once the rules for both partners are clear, each can fully commit himself to the dance. Each is able to concentrate on his job, whether that be fighting the war or reporting it. Taken altogether, these patterns suggest that it is an oversimplification to regard military-press relations as adversarial. Instead, journalists begin to dance with their partners. Reporters keep themselves aloof from military officers, but endeavor to establish honest relationships with their sources and their public.

In chapter 6, we will leave our analysis of censorship and turn to the war correspondent's experience. Here I will set forth the instances of genre I found in my research and give an account as to what they represent.

6 *Experience and Interpretation*

Modern war correspondence involves a set of judgments composed simultaneously of experience and interpretation. The report is only one part of a much larger design that governs being a journalist. The act of reporting war is a situated one with many elements involved: the kind of war being waged, the presence or absence of bureaucratic procedures for clearing stories with the military, and the occupational problems common to a particular time in history.

Conscription pushed the boundaries of experience and consequently of interpretation of war. This chapter casts the journalist's experience and interpretation of war into the larger context of genre to give some indication of the association between reporting wars and a felt ethical obligation on the part of society's authorized witnesses to the slaughter of its young men and women. I will examine the interpretive journeys taken by reporters to identify the most dominant tropes or organizing strategies for understanding experience and then speaking or writing it. To see trope as a strategy rather than a figure of speech prepares us better to understand why the journalist should be viewed as an embodied ethos, the main argument of this chapter. The tropes I found most often in the archival data include irony, tragedy, surrealism, romance in its epic sense, and common sense as a matter of realism. Each of these interpretive stances can be linked to the set of circumstances, both social and material, within which reporters worked. Each presupposes a particular political and social reality. Each speaks to the relative presence of bureaucracy in a war, as well as to the moral context within which war was fought as a solution to political problems.

When journalists depart for war zones they begin a long and arduous journey, both physically and mentally. The ever-present possibility of death will keep them hyperalert. Their task is to create reports. Historically the report has been a very capacious medium. Some reports are simply chronicles of events. Most, however, are stories. The significance of the traces of tropes, whether in a journalist's copy or in his private papers, is that when you find them you can be sure that the journalist is using his critical faculties. In fact, traces of irony or references to realism as a matter of common sense are guarantees of a critical intelligence at work.

Conscription and the culture of a military solution to political problems make being a journalist ethical in essence. Journalists don't have ethics. What a reporter is, in the marrow of his being, is ethos. He is ethos because he is a teller of tales and because all his tales present reciprocal claims binding the reporter with the listener, the viewer, or reader, with the soldier, and with other reporters. Ethics involves recursive, contingent, and interactive dramas of encounter and recognition, linking responsibility to interpretation. No matter where a report appears—in the *Detroit Free Press, Reader's Digest, Springfield Journal Register,* the *New York Times, Newsweek,* on NPR, CNN, CBS, or a local radio station—a national public is always presupposed by it and present in it. These stories are the ties that bind.

Further, each interpretive trope has corresponding, identifiable genres in the larger discursive world of fiction and literature. Unlike literature, the tropic aspect of "telling" is scattershot through a journalist's letters, diaries, and journals; the primary evidence for this book simply indicates that these kinds of experiences occur in the reporter's workaday world. It is not that reporters imitate literature, it is that literature imitates life experience—in this case journalistic experience.

The sets of interpretive strategies I encountered sometimes issued in published accounts and sometimes not. In other words, by experience and interpretation I mean to refer to an interwoven interior landscape of the modern and postmodern journalist, an individual-in-community who makes war meaningful for himself and soldiers, but most especially for his public. Most of the time the reporter situates himself in the larger community of his fellow Americans. On a few occasions, he will situate himself in the community of other journalists. When this latter case occurs, the reporter is signaling the failure of the process at some level. This happened in Vietnam where it set off noisy alarm bells indicating that something was seriously amiss.

Seldom does a reporter go beyond the national unit to situate himself in humankind—a point that supports the main argument of this book: the journalist is an advertisement for the nation-state. If a reporter goes beyond his national identity, he usually does so to support the principles that nationalism is thought to convey, those he identifies with his country such as freedom of speech or the inalienable right to self-determination. And these are values he readily consigns to others, regardless of their history or culture.

Such was the case in Vietnam, where the foundation for a new world order and for situating America in the global community was laid. The pervasive influence of American public and popular culture made it likely that the nation was moving beyond the Cold War and settling into a sense that it was not land or territory that America wanted but rather a world living by democratic values and a consumer ethic. All together, the journalists in Vietnam began to provide the American public with an extranational covenant, one that was the first sign of the failure of the Cold War logic that journalists themselves never questioned.

In the course of investigating the interior (some would say spiritual) landscapes of members of the fourth estate, certain anomalies, conundrums, and inconsistencies arise that need examination and resolution. One such problem can be framed by asking, Under what circumstances do reporters select the appropriate tropical interpretation? Another question arises when one compares what reporters write in private and what they decide to publish. In two wars, there is no discernible difference between their private and public accounts: the Spanish-Cuban-American War and the war in Vietnam. And in two other wars, there is no discernible resemblance between their private and public accounts: World War I and World War II. How can we explain these phenomena?

In this chapter I will argue that war correspondents live and work in the world of romance in its philosophical and political sense; they embody ethos. Ethos finds expression in many different ways: through irony, surrealism, romance in its sense of epic proportions (the most explicitly nationalistic trope), and so forth. With Northrop Frye, whose work greatly enriches our understanding, this chapter argues that romance is the master blueprint, subsuming all others.[1]

Even the most hard-bitten invoker of "the facts and only the facts, ma'am," the kind of no-nonsense guy carrying his press card through the halls of the Pentagon, is romantic at heart. And this romance can be traced to the three little words Americans cherish more than any others: "We, the people." These three words have the power to raise standing armies.

If the rise of the democratic nation-state was coextensive with the rise of romanticism as a worldview and the rise of a consumer ethos, it should be no surprise that journalists (whose occupation also comes out of the eighteenth century) would be the personification of those three integrated trends. What follows here is an examination of romance as it pertains to journalists. Once romanticism is examined in terms of a general orientation to politics and, indeed, all of life, this chapter will analyze the interpretive judgments war reporters have made since in 1898.

Journalists and Romance

Journalists covering wars have been called many things. Robert Capa referred to his colleagues of the fourth estate as a "worn-out bunch of unromantic scribes."[2] However, taken altogether, the records left by war correspondents indicate that romance has, indeed, been the master trope guiding their interpretive strategies and classifications, harnessing a wide range of experiences among war reporters even of the same generation. Social categories, particularly class of origin, mediate and construct all experience for the rest of one's life. Yet reporters seem to agree as a group about what is important to know about war and how we should understand it.

At the same time, the news report is a very capacious genre—more so the case with printed reports than with broadcast ones. Broadcast journalism introduces reflexivity into the mix. Hence broadcast journalists seem to form a bond of trust with the television audience. In telling the television audience about the situation in the war zone they are establishing a bond rooted in truth. They are basically saying, "Would I lie to you?"

Romanticism historically referenced a widespread popular movement that arose in the eighteenth century. As a movement, it can be theoretically divided into aesthetic, metaphysical, political, and economic (the consumer ethos) components. No sensible person would claim to define it in a comprehensive way. Indeed, the journalistic version of romance is quite different from the literary or philosophical movement bearing the same name. They are all rooted in a shift in attitudes and social behavior sometime in the 1700s. It was a general movement on a par in its significance and consequences with the Renaissance or the Enlightenment. Isaiah Berlin called it a shift in consciousness that eventually "broke the backbone of European thought."[3]

In journalistic terms, romanticism is a theory of politics (democracy) and metaphysics (the self-governing and autonomous self) integrated into an occupational ethic. The significance of the journalistic occupation lies in its tacit reference to a transcendent order—an order implied in every act a journalist engages in. This tacit relationship is inculcated in his schooling (whether educational or of the hard-knocks variety) and becomes a part of what a good journalist takes for granted as valuable. When I refer to the transcendent, I do not mean idealism or patriotism; I mean a transpersonal commitment to a particular social ethic. It includes a way of answering the existential questions we face daily, as well as a mode of feeling.[4]

Romance, as it is applied to journalism, also does not refer to a penchant for reverie or dreaming, a leaning toward the mystic, or a tendency to engage in escapism or fantasy. Nor is it what Erik Durschmid means when he says, "I never romanticize wars. Anyone who thinks wars are beautiful is mad."[5] Rather, it involves a reverence for the individual as the repository of inalienable rights to life, liberty, and the pursuit of happiness. Romance applied to journalism eschews the power of the state, even as it is its chief broker for the public. Consciously or unconsciously, journalism appeals to a transcendent order variously thought of as "a higher law," "a moral imperative," "freedom," or "truth, justice, and the American way."

Romance is used in two distinct ways in this chapter. The first usage denotes the general movement that uses this term (as explained above). The second usage is a particular tropic term indicating a journalist's interpretive strategy. In the latter sense it is found in the Spanish-Cuban-American War and in the opening days of America's entry into the First World War. After that it seems to lose weight as an appropriate way to understand war as America fought it until Vietnam. The Vietnam war was not reported as an epic battle. However, almost all of the young men who reported that war did so in the context of a very romantic view of the proper conduct of the nation-state and its military operations. Journalists would describe their reporting as realistic, no doubt—but the further America got from its ideals in Vietnam, the more vociferous reporters became.

The problem with writing about romance is that it is indeed an embattled term.[6] Among journalists, this tension arises from a certainty they have about the legitimacy of their profession to fairly and accurately report the facts of the matter. This, and this alone, is the reporter's raison d'être. The most he will likely concede in reference to an interpretive trope is that journalism is a distant cousin to realism because he is a witness to empirically observable instances. When a reporter says he is being realistic, he is really telling us he is a romantic. In this case, realism is a synonym for empirical instances felt as irreducible. The denial of romance is what makes the journalist able to engage in it so deeply. The denial is part of the reportorial stance, of the reporter's claim to being a realist. Whether he is satirical or down to earth, a journalist claims he is a "real realist." The denial of romance is necessary because a journalist cannot do his work in the shadow of "sentimental claptrap."

Romanticism, then, in its largest sense is a name for interrelated ideas, attitudes, and behaviors or actions. It includes the journalist's bearing and demeanor. Seen in this vein, romance involves an infusion of certain beliefs—including ones about the redemptive power of art and love, and the liberating power of politics. Romance celebrates skepticism as a way of knowing that leads to truth. Its ethic, which only began to be articulated in the early part of the twentieth century in journalism, is middle class, involving a perceptiveness absent of exaggeration and one, above all, that is never for purchase.

Journalistic romance equates the natural with the good and generally disdains a transcendent world, even as it is guided by it. It is this transcendent world that sacramentalizes a reporter's experience. Journalists treat the "natural" the same way older cultures treated the supernatural. That is, they give the natural world primacy over all things. The rhetoric of journalism is often anti-intellectual, even though a reporter engages ideas for a living. He just calls them "facts." And he believes in their irreducibility.

Journalistic romance has at its center the individual, whose rights include self-expression. Hence the reporter's passionate defense of the First Amendment. The individual in this view is an infinite reservoir of possibilities. The best government is one that arranges and rearranges society such that oppressive orders (like bureaucracy or, worse, despotism) are destroyed in order that these possibilities can be effected.

Journalists like everyone else have a sense of self. There have always been "selves," but the sense or experience of the self has not been a uniform or universal one. Ulysses and Penelope had a sense of self, so did Abelard and Heloise. Theirs was not, however, the modern sense of self as an interior space to which one goes for sorting and dialogue. Historically the gendered sense of self is a very recent phenomenon, arising in the same century as journalism was born. If you read the Pentateuch, you will find no psychological difference between Sarah and Abraham or Rachel and Jacob. In the New Testament, no psychological differences existed between Mary and Joseph or Elizabeth and her son John. Nor will you find these differences in later periods of history, for example, between Teresa of Avila and John of the Cross.

Rather, the sense of self the journalist experiences in the years covered by this study is a modern one, in which women and men are different creatures in psychological as well as physical makeup. The gendered self began to be inscribed with the novels of the eighteenth century. Over the course of two hundred years, the gendered self lost its aura of convention and became synonymous with what is real. This partially explains the reluctance on the part of male journalists to allow women into their ranks and especially into the ranks of war correspondents. When women insisted on covering war, they helped to break down this old mythos, but even as late as the Vietnam era, one can find it still operating. Women like Dickey Chapelle, who paid with her life for covering Vietnam, Martha Gellhorn, Frances Fitzgerald, and Gloria Emerson made it much easier for today's female war correspondents to accomplish their goals. Christiane Amanpour stands on their shoulders.

Journalism should be understood as an important component of the revolution in thinking during the eighteenth century. It developed into an occupational ethic mediated by certain generic traces in the reporter's experience. War correspondence is a major component of romanticism in the general sense, and romanticism is a major component of war correspondence. The generic traces I found were irony, surrealism, romance in its epic sense, common sense as a form of realism, and tragedy. In the following section I will examine the traits I found in the war reporters' letters, diaries, notebooks, and reports.

Journalistic Experience in Wartime

In late February 1895, Cuban belligerents inaugurated the second insurrection against Spain. The United States took little note of the rebellion's start. Newspaper accounts mentioned only that an insurrection had taken place, and because it occurred in the Pinar del Rio and Santiago de Cuba provinces, it was island-wide. It meant that this time, in contrast to an earlier rebellion, the entire island supported the Cuban insurrectionists.

Eventually major papers in the States dispatched reporters to cover the conflict. Although reporters, like everyone else, believed in the importance of character with a capital C, few if any left for Cuba with wide-eyed wonder. They had to get supplies, secure tickets, and gather clothing suitable for tropical weather. They were eager to report the conflict that most Americans thought of as a second-rate skirmish led by a group of rag-tag Cuban bandits.[7]

Joseph Pulitzer of the *New York World* and his reporter, Sylvester Scovel, were exceptions to this rule. Scovel is the prototype of the modern war correspondent. He is missing from many historical accounts, I think, because the diaries containing his notes for Cuba are written in a code that has not yet been broken. He is mentioned by many other correspondents, including Richard Harding Davis and George Kennan.[8] These sources importantly indicate that journalists were making a distinction between Scovel and the literary stars Davis and Stephen Crane.

Arthur Brisbane, William Randolph Hearst's right-hand man, said that virtually no one at the newspapers really believed that the famous fiction writers had a nose for news. For that reason the famous writers were handed over to "real" reporters (Crane to Scovel and Davis to Christopher Michaelson) whose job was to see to it that their charges got to where the news was, wrote their reports expeditiously, and sent their copy back to the newspapers as soon as possible.[9]

In this war the journalist admired reporters who managed to get the news in the face of great personal risk and to do so first. These qualities of courage and timeliness were the basis of admiration for Sylvester Scovel. Davis, too, proved he could compete with the best of them, noting that success as a war correspondent depended on intelligence and character. A good reporter was the guy who saw more of the war, both afloat and ashore, than anyone else and who was "able to make the public see what he saw."[10]

When the interpretive trope in reporting a war is epic, the reporter's sense of truth includes both truth of correspondence and truth of significance. In the war of 1898, reporters reported facts, but they also reported their significance. Because truth of significance was included in their reports, war correspondence was basically *de te fabula*—in other words, they said, "This story is about you, the reader."

The man in charge of the Fifth Army Corps was General William Shafter. His first problem was transporting twenty-five thousand men to Cuba on ships not able to hold even half that many. He ordered his men to commandeer any ship they could lay their hands on. Because Shafter knew his troops were inexperienced, he chose to invade Cuba at Daiquiri, where the fighting would not be too fierce.[11]

Once troops were mobilized on the island, reporters followed. It soon became apparent that they could not reconcile Shafter with their view of what a military officer should be. "Propinquity spoils illusions," and in the case of Shafter illusions were soon shattered.[12] The press corps began to ridicule him. Some attributed the poor press he got to his rough manners and bearing. (Shafter was obese, weighing well over three hundred pounds.)[13]

From the trenches of France in World War I a new type of journalist would emerge. Its stereotype is celebrated in the movie *Front Page*. The trench-coated journalist, cynical in outlook, suspicious of the powers that be, and usually a little drunk, is the legacy of the Great War. While they went into the conflicts of 1917 with the spirit of adventure, they came out of it changed men. A remark made by James Creelman illuminates the sort of person the reporter used to be. In a moment of anger, General Valeriano Weyler, the head of the Spanish forces in Cuba, threatened to expel Creelman for writing stories sympathetic to the Cuban insurgents. Creelman turned to Weyler and informed him that nothing would stop the presses from printing the truth, not even his own expulsion from the island. He, the reporter, was "a mere cog in a vast machine."[14] Twenty years later, the same phrase might have been uttered as an expression of despair.

In August 1914, at the outbreak of conflict in Europe, everybody was predicting that the war would be over by Christmas. With modern weaponry and the rapid depletion of vast resources, a long and costly war was thought to be out of the question. The mood that summer was one of relief, enthusiasm, and elation.[15] Journalists from all over the world flooded into France, Britain, Germany, and Russia in hopes of getting the necessary accreditation from the belligerent armies. From the United States came veterans Richard Harding Davis and Frederick Palmer, as well as rookies Westbrook Pegler and Herbert Corey. Whether veteran or rookie, it never occurred to any of these journalists that they might not be able to report this Great War at all.

As to the events of the period preceding the taking up of arms, most historians and critics are inclined to agree that all belligerents were equally responsible for the situation that developed into the first world war. When the details are assessed, however, some historians will argue that while all participants were responsible for the war, Russia and Austria were more responsible than the others. Regarding Lloyd George's view that all nations "tumbled" into war, it is true that once the machine was put into operation that only a political genius could have reversed the direction being taken to one of peaceful negotiation. However, events leading up to Sarajevo suggest that at several points along the way the political volcano in middle Europe could have been dealt with more effectively. What made a continental war inevitable, perhaps more than any other factor, was the German *weltpolitik*, aided and abetted by the development of German industry (e.g., the steel industry) beyond the needs of the German economy.[16]

The Balkan and Moroccan crises led the Germans to believe that their nation was being encircled by enemies intent on bringing them to the level of a third-rate power. The German concept of a preventive war, a local or continental war, developed from the notion that Germany in the face of encirclement could either stagnate, decline in power, or move forward to grasp the reins of world power. With a picture of Germany as a "fortress besieged by enemies," with the ring around the country growing tighter and tighter, "the idea of a sudden desperate charge out of the fortress became respectable."[17]

Whether one agrees that the outbreak of war was a tragic miscalculation or not, there is little doubt that after events in Sarajevo transpired, the crisis got out of control. Austria declared war on Serbia, the French general staff drove the Russians (willingly) down the fatal path to mobilization, and Germany delivered an ultimatum to King Albert requesting passage for the German armies in Brussels. Meanwhile, Minister of War Sir Edward Grey had informed members of the British cabinet that if they chose to remain neutral during the conflict, he was not the man to carry out their policy. By August 4, Great Britain had declared war on Germany, whose army was pressing towards Paris.[18]

Unlike the war of 1898, the First World War did not present problems of food and supplies for reporters. This war was fought in densely populated urban areas. In France and Belgium, especially, food was good and plentiful. The most difficult problem correspondents had in 1914 and early 1915 was evading officials who sought to keep them out of the war zones. After the belligerents began to conduct tours, soldiers were detailed as reporters' servants.[19] With all the fuss being made over their comfort, reporters began to feel uneasy. In a letter to his mother, Herbert Corey wrote from Berlin that "the consensus of opinion is that correspondents are almost too well cared for."[20]

The strict regulation of movements, the tedious evasions of the military, and the censorship of copy all worked together to bring on a sense of futility among reporters. Demoralized and at the mercy of a great, unseen power, the journalist felt, on the one hand, that he was "helpless as a package in a pneumatic tube," and, on the other, as if he were "a boy scout being instructed in the bugaboos before his first night in the woods."[21] Cyril Brown, who worked for the *New York Times,* took advantage of his extraordinary gall and his fluency in German to go where the Germans forbade reporters to go. Knowing the value of stage management, Brown wore a long black coat and a black derby that fitted well below his ears, carried an umbrella, and sported a cigar.[22]

At first, beating the military and the censor was great fun. Soon, however, it became all too clear that the military generally held the winning hand and could completely suppress journalistic reporting from the war zones. In the face of such odds, reporters had no choice but to become as agreeable as possible without totally surrendering their reportorial integrity.[23] Some avenues of protest were available. Journalists could complain through their editors to the government's ambassadors or other officials of military and state. Some wrote formal letters of complaint to press officers.

Some reporters became aware of Allied efforts to win the war of public opinion through suppression of news in such a way as to cast favorable light on Britain or France. These elements all provide the backdrop for the irony with which reporters tended to experience the conflict. In a war where news was sometimes integrated into propaganda, the very existence of journalism was at stake. The machinery of the modern army favored the military's version of events. It is understandable, given these odds, that journalists would begin to see the world around them in terms of irony.

At first, the veil of secrecy thrown around the war contributed to a sense of unreality. Forced to be content with getting a glimpse here or there, the correspondent began to see the war as vague, confusing, immense, and sinister. "The thing was vast beyond all human conception; and it was covered by the mists of secrecy."[24] A whole army of Englishmen vanished into the fog of war, none knew where.[25] The "wall of the disappeared" is in a churchyard in Brittany—the names of men who had gone to the front and who had never returned are inscribed there. One name, dated 1915, is followed by the epithet, "disappeared in the Battle of the Marne."[26] With secrecy went rumor, and the rumor was often more terrifying than the thing itself. Arthur Ruhl, while sitting comfortably at a café table, reading the papers with morning coffee, "saw the dawn coming up over the Oise and Aisne, heard the French 75's and the heavy German siege-guns resume their roar. . . . And these thrills repeated over and over again, without sight or sound of concrete facts, in that strange still city whose usual life had stopped, produced at last a curious unreality."[27] The journalist of World War I had to constantly nudge himself to believe that the war was a reality.[28] This experience would repeat itself in Vietnam.

From the unreal, it was a short step to the sinister. The German army, with its concentration and discipline, became to reporters an inhumanly perfect, well-organized, indomitable machine.[29] It started out as a vast, unseen power rolling through the neutral territory of Belgium. Those caught in Antwerp knew the Germans were approaching. Then, "all at once it was there, materialized, demoniacle, a flying death, swooping across the dark into [one's] very room."[30]

One of the most gripping accounts of the German army actions came from the pen of Richard Harding Davis who was in Brussels when the Germans passed through on their way to Paris. (This was Davis's last war; he died in 1916.) The German army was a machine—endless, tireless, with the delicate organization of a watch and the brute power of a steamroller—that roared and rumbled for three days and nights through Brussels, a cataract of molten lead. Davis called it a Frankenstein's monster.[31]

The German army's parade step, sometimes scornfully referred to as the "goose step," added to the uncanny quality of the march. For some it represented everything German about the army. It stood for unity, physical fitness, and determination. The German parade step sent the lethal message that nothing could stop their army.[32]

Besides the parade step, the sheer size of their forces stunned some. H. L. Mencken saw the German defenses on the eastern front. "They almost staggered me," he wrote.[33]

Knocking about between the poet's "snow-dazed" and "sun-dozed," reporters gradually cultivated a new logic, a different way of seeing events in the war zones. Indeed, this logic began to permeate all of life's experiences. This was not the world into which they had been born; it was surreal and grotesque, in the sense of being monstrous. When reporters like Davis and Scovel reported the Cuban war, they were easily able to divide their experiences into discrete categories: the normal and the abnormal, the moral and immoral, the heroic and the evil. It was not that there were no gray areas for them; there were. However, no one questioned the principles of conduct they learned in order to navigate the gray areas. In 1914 that world passed away. After the guns of August fired, journalists covering war no longer saw much difference between the real and the unreal or the living and the dead.[34]

Elements of the everyday and the normal began to take on a sinister appearance, suggesting an outside-the-skin hazard, a force neither predictable nor controllable. Eventually, when the Allies allowed American reporters to tour battlefronts, journalists found themselves facing a relentless, insurmountable wall of censorship. "Touring" war itself was an unreal experience. The journalist became a Chaplinesque figure, the lovable tramp trying to cope with problems beyond his ability to solve. Getting around the wall of censorship in the first eight months of war was so difficult, it seemed futile to try. He began by trying to scale the wall of secrecy the military had erected. Gradually, however, the wall itself took on a "dreary aspect and encompassed the whole range of human experience."[35]

In 1915, once the journalist began to tour the fronts, other aspects of the war worked together to create a sense of the grotesque and the sinister. The great stench of decaying human flesh and the sight of bodies piled on top of each other, as well as the desolation surrounding bombarded cities—all left the reporter with a feeling that the end of the world had come and he was the only survivor.[36] Soldier stragglers described ghastly scenes of bodies looking like "gray worms squirming about . . . a mess of arms and legs."[37]

From a German trench, Robert Dunn described bodies: "Bodies, bodies unburied, unrecognizable, unless we had been told. Lumps of matter like swollen sacks, in hundreds, scattered haphazard, upon one another, heaped like socks. Without visible flesh or clothing, all mud colored, drenched, gleaming terribly with the slimy pallor, like verdigris, of that awful field. It resembled a vision undersea; as if one saw through a green translucence the encrusted toll of some old disaster. . . . Life might exist for, might endure, even justify all manner of deeds, purposes, monstrous perversities—but not such as these, not this."[38] What Dunn and fellow journalists were witnessing was a nightmare from which no one ever wakens.

Surveying the rack and ruin at Gerbeviller, Wythe Williams felt he finally understood the meaning of the word "spectral." The Germans had burned the town to the ground, leaving the houses in charred, irregular shapes.[39] In nearby fields the bodies of horses were strewn. Their positions in death were ghastly. Some lay on their backs, legs stiff and sticking straight up, others with their legs horizontal to but not touching the ground.[40]

Faced with these and other horrors, Herbert Corey voiced a sentiment he held in common with his colleagues: the show no longer amused him. Despite this fact, unpleasant forms of death still held a fascination for reporters.[41] While they might be revolted by the sights of war, at the same time, journalists couldn't take their eyes away from them.

For instance, one day Corey's German chauffeur took him out to the Russian front where the German army under General Georg von der Marwitz was driving what was left of the Tenth Russian Army into retreat. The press car followed closely behind. Soon it passed a row of one-story outhouses. "Someone is watching us," Corey said to his driver, with a nervous giggle. Through the door of one of the outhouses peered a white face. It was canted slightly to one side, as if its owner were hiding his body behind the door frame. Hours later, when they returned by the same road, "the white face still peered through the open door."[42] It was the face of a woman who had been hanged.

The censorship and touring conditions did much to alter reporters' perception of their task and their relation to the military. The extensive carnage, the destruction they saw, and the circumscription of their movements removed reporters psychologically to a surrealistic space, a space experienced as unreal or hyper-real. On the eastern front the threat of cholera, on the western front the use of gas warfare—these powerful agents suggested to journalists an objective, relentless force stalked them. Examples from each front, eastern and western, illustrate my point.

On a journey from Austrian headquarters, Robert Dunn of the *New York Evening Post* spent three days and nights trying to reach Przemysl, Poland, a journey of scarcely sixty miles. Delays were caused mostly by Red Cross trains carrying the sick and wounded. Many passing cars bore the legend "cholera *verdachtig*" in white chalk.[43] The legend did not mean much until Dunn joined the press jaunt to a battle sector in the Carpathian hills. There every third word on every man's lips was "cholera." In the days he covered the sector, Dunn began to get overly concerned with the trivialities of daily existence. He became obsessed— his obsession targeted the dim existence of the peasants in the fields who accepted what happened to them with passivity, or the bleak, damp, dour, raw November days common to the Baltic plains, or the icy east wind cutting through his coat, or the bewildering futility with which he viewed the roadside madonnas in stucco niches.[44]

The threat of cholera worked its havoc, eating away at what little sense of safety a man behind the lines might feel. Dunn describes it well: "You may swear that you feel no dread of cholera, since vaccination had reduced its mortality from ninety per cent to seven per cent; but your diminishing supply of alcohol to boil water for washing hands and face grows to be almost an obsession. You spend half a morning trying to buy chloride of lime for disinfection."[45]

Dunn's colleagues on the western front feared poison gas. No journalist, not even the official eyewitness for the Allies, Major General Sir Ernest Swinton, saw the gas attack in Flanders at the second Battle of Ypres. At about 5:00 in the evening of April 2, 1915, a brown-yellow vapor drifted from the German lines into the trenches of the French colonials. As the fumes inundated the trenches, panic spread through the troops, and those who had not yet been overcome with the gas fled gasping to the rear.[46] Close to 150 tons of compressed chlorine had been released from the German cylinders.[47]

United Press International (UPI) reporter William Shephard was thirty miles away with the British forces when the gas attack was launched, so he did not see it. However, he learned of it that same night. The censor would allow only vague and obscure references to the attack, which failed to get across to Shephard's editor or the reading public what had really happened. As long as the military situation remained confusing, journalists could publish nothing of significance about the attack. Eventually reporters were allowed to talk to gassed victims, and the world learned about a new method of warfare.[48]

Actually, gas warfare was not completely new, nor were the Germans the first to use it. The French had already used small gas-diffusing projectiles called "cartouches suffocantes" in various places on the western front as early as 1914. Moreover, there is strong evidence that the French used them against the Germans in the Argonne sector from mid-March 1915 on. Yet the attack at Ypres evoked great indignation among the Allies and in the United States. The Germans were denounced for flagrantly violating a basic sense of humane principles.[49]

The historical and military significance of the German gas attack did not lay in its being first, nor did the lethality of compressed chlorine account for its importance. Rather, the significance of events at Ypres was due to the massive scale of the operation. For the first time in history a high concentration of gas over a large area of the front had been militarily successful. After Ypres, Allies and Germans alike continued to use deadly chemicals on the battlefield.[50]

As for journalists of the time and the general public, the importance of Ypres lay in its enhancement of a vague feeling that this war defied all previous notions they had understood about battle. The stories of African survivors of Ypres and the dramatic reports of the twisted, blackened limbs of its victims augmented the already overwhelming sentiment reporters felt. As time went on, journalists—like soldiers—got used to the sight of gas masks on the battlefield. No one, however, got used to the ever-present hazard of poison gas.

One of the most graphic descriptions of gas warfare came from the pen of Erich Maria Remarque. "Soldiers who had been gassed were found with blue heads and black lips. Some . . . took off their masks too soon; they did not know the gas lies longest in the hollows; when they saw others on top without masks they pulled theirs off too and swallowed enough to scorch their lungs. Their condition is hopeless, they choke to death with hemorrhages and suffocation."[51] Faced with seeing, understanding, and trying to explain gas warfare, journalists of the Great War psychologically set themselves apart from their surroundings and the distance between what they thought "civilized" war was and was not made it possible for them eventually to embrace irony as an appropriate interpretive strategy.

Battle wears many faces, as John Keegan has told us, but none so enigmatic as trench warfare. The war in Vietnam would challenge this statement, but in the context of the second decade of the twentieth century, trench warfare was cryptic. Although censorship was a common complaint, in all probability reporters would have known little more than they did had they been allowed to accompany the armies from the beginning. As far as reporters were concerned, the great irony of World War I was that while technology—responsible alike for the telegraph, cable, radio, and modern weaponry—had allowed them access to events all over the world, at the same time it restricted their vision.

If he could have gotten high enough to look down at the line of trenches, the war reporter would have seen a set of dugouts, usually arranged in three parallel lines on each side of no-man's-land, crisscrossing for four hundred miles through Belgium and France. One estimate places the total amount of trenches, both Central and Allied, at twenty-five thousand miles.[52] The front was a vast catacomb, everywhere and nowhere. One could not pick "the site of butchery."[53] Consequently, when he was finally allowed to enter the frontline trenches, the war reporter saw that there was very little to see.

Although World War I gave us the stereotype of the modern war reporter—the trench-coated, womanizing, detail man who had a whisky in his hand when he wasn't writing something—it was the Vietnam war that came to stand as the prototypical flight from reality for Americans. Nothing about the Vietnam experience was familiar. Even the context for fighting there changed rapidly, making it seem a series of unconnected events. In fact, for many soldiers as well as reporters, this unconnectedness was a defining trait of their experience.

The surreal aspects of the war in Vietnam can be found in many instances. Two important ones were the perceived discrepancy between the logic of American policy and policymakers and the logic of the Vietnamese, and the type of warfare being waged.

When Malcolm Brown and Dickey Chapelle arrived in Vietnam in the early 1960s, it was already a routinely violent country. Brown set up the Associated Press (AP) office near the Gia Long palace where Ngo Dinh Diem was in residence. Brown ran the bureau where he briefed newly arrived reporters on the do's and don'ts of Vietnam. His "Short Guide to News Coverage in Vietnam" covered both routine reporting and cautionary advice. It warned about official news sources and encouraged the development of private sources, both Vietnamese and American military. It emphasized the importance of protecting these sources. The manual also dealt with health and money matters. It focused on practical elements, for example, what a reporter needed to pack for field work: jackknife, canteen, mosquito netting, a rubber air mattress, water purification tablets, aspirin—and a gun. Brown told reporters that they would need firearms because, like the soldiers, they could find themselves in combat situations. And in such situations, he argued, reporters needed to respond as any soldier would, that is, "by doing everything you can to keep yourself alive and unwounded."[54] The importance of staying alive and healthy guided all of Brown's remarks. For example, he cautioned journalists to stay away from the radio man because he was a frequent target, as was the head of the column or point man. The safest place was next to the commander (who had the most information anyway).

All of this was in pursuance of the news. As the seasoned journalist well understood, "The whole idea of covering an operation is to get the news and pictures back, not to play soldier yourself." Nowhere did Brown mention the importance of being brave. It was all "save your ass and get the story back."[55]

American reporters were in Vietnam at the pleasure of the South Vietnamese government, who often took a dim view of members of the fourth estate. One way to handle "troublemakers" in the press corps was to refuse their visa renewals. At one point, the word went out, "[Neil] Sheehan and [David] Halberstam chances were very bad." Halberstam wrote some cablegrams and notes in code to smuggle information out of Vietnam. The South Vietnamese, he argued, tried to probe out their enemies in ways only a reporter on the spot could "judge in appropriate seriousness."[56]

Halberstam, arguably the best political reporter in Vietnam, suffered a triple indignity there. He was making waves within the Kennedy administration such that the president wanted the *New York Times* to replace him in Southeast Asia. Halberstam's editors were always trying to rein him in, even as they gave him written assurances of their support. Finally, some members of the press corps set Halberstam and "his clique" apart from the rest of the reporters. Friends in the States wrote to him, "You must have felt mighty low at times . . . I know you feel you have not been appreciated by the Powers [that be] . . . What we in New York are doing is, almost without exception, crap . . . *what you are doing is serving a nation.*"[57] Here these friends make explicit our implicit understanding of the role of the true journalist when his nation goes to war: service alongside the soldier.

This rhetoric of service to one's country was never really questioned in World War II where it was as familiar as old wallpaper. The seasoned veterans who had reported on the Second World War and who were now reporting on Vietnam remembered the earlier conflict in a way that completely elided the ambiguities that can be found in any war. Since World War I the "front" diminished because of all the modern weaponry. The notion of a "decisive battle" became extinct by World War II. Nevertheless, by Vietnam, many remembered the Second World War as a series of decisive battles and well-designated fronts. In reporting Vietnam, journalists invoked this old rhetoric. They also tended to use the strategies and tactics that worked in reporting the world war, even in the face of sure knowledge about the nature of guerilla warfare.

In June 1964, General William Westmoreland was put in charge of Military Assistance Command, Vietnam (MACV). Given his record, news reporters tended to see his appointment as an indication of military policy and effort. That is, they believed that the armed forces would step up their use of conventional troops and wind down their use of Special Forces. The "straight legs" were going to replace the "bent legs."[58]

Very few reporters in Vietnam really understood the South Vietnamese. An exception was Frances Fitzgerald. In general, reporters as a group did not treat the South Vietnamese as people with authority, people who had something authentic to say about themselves. Those who were given voice on television and in front page news were people such as Nguyen Cao Ky and Madame Ngo Dihn Nhu. The former was represented as a dandy, a "cowboy," running a corrupt organization. Madame Nhu was seen as a dragon lady, a view implying their understanding of the role of the female in affairs of the nation-state. When a report referred to the South Vietnamese, they were generally spoken for by either North Vietnamese or Americans. The South Vietnamese were seldom allowed to speak for themselves.

The South Vietnamese lived in a world in which oral conventions of communication dictated the running of contemporary institutions. They were bound by tradition and the importance of ancestors. Their community was a sacred one in which kinship connections stretched infinitely into the past as well as the future. Meanwhile, western reporters lived in a world governed by literate conventions, one in which society was thought to march as one through history in a present that was radically different from the past. This "past" was one in which the South Vietnamese appeared to be "mired."

Americans created a version of Vietnam that bore no simple relation to the country the Vietnamese live in. This version was condensed into a set of statistics: with the logic of numbers, the American military had flattened the landscape of Vietnam into points, lines, and spaces, sweeping a geography of strange and untidy names away beneath plane geometry.[59] Furthermore, the military used paper analyses to determine their "progress." Defense secretary Robert McNamara said, "Every quantitative measurement we have shows that we are winning the war." This point is significant because it indicates the degree to which failure in

traditional military terms did not have its source in being overly optimistic or arrogant.[60] Its source was a version of Vietnam that had little
to do with the reality or the social order as it was experienced by the
people of South Vietnam.

Many reporters were aware of the divergence between the official
view of the war on the part of U.S. military and political authorities
and the Vietnam they were reporting on. Even journalists who openly
supported military goals recognized problems. For example, as early as
1961, Dickey Chapelle remarked that a military victory in Vietnam was
in doubt. She came to this conclusion once she realized there was no
"doctrine for licking guerillas."[61]

Chapelle had covered the war in the Pacific during the later stages of
World War II, as had Richard Tregaskis, who made his name covering Guadalcanal. Despite his own tendencies to see the war in Vietnam in World
War II terms, Tregaskis acknowledged that many military commanders thought of the war "in archaic terms, including Westmoreland who
would like to transform [Vietnam] into a World War II type."[62] To General
Westmoreland, North Vietnam was "the Prussia of the Orient."[63]

At the same time, both Chapelle and Tregaskis assumed a kind of
proprietorship over affairs in Vietnam, sometimes with a 1950s sense
of America's "manifest destiny." Tregaskis, for example, wrote about
the Seabees in World War II language. He tried to dramatize them in a
"super-adult Western context." He also depicted the fighting in Vietnam
in words more appropriate to the open movement warfare of the Second
World War. For example, "Operation Starlight was a perfect execution
of classic incirclement [sic] at Cannae, when the Romans defeated Han-
nibal in 216 B.C."[64]

In an interview on Jack Paar's television show, Chapelle made an
effort to describe the war in Vietnam in simple terms. "The trouble is
Americans don't know whether we want to lead the free world, or what
we want in Asia. The Communists do; they want the real estate. We've
got to make up our minds about South Vietnam. It's . . . our last piece of
real estate on the Asian Continent." Paar responded, "But isn't that the
problem that it isn't our real estate—aren't these sovereign people?"[65]
Besides indicating proprietorship, Chapelle's comment also highlights the
degree to which the Cold War, which would end less than two decades
later, was guiding her analysis. She was not alone. Even reporters most
critical of the U.S. mission adhered to the Cold War rhetoric.

One of the best writers of World War II was Martha Gellhorn. She
was born on November 8, 1908, in St. Louis. Her father, an immigrant
from Poland, was stern and critical with his daughter. Her mother had

graduated from Bryn Mawr and eventually became a leading suffragette in St. Louis. She was a role model for involvement in civic affairs.

Martha Gellhorn's first newspaper job was a commission from the *St. Louis Post-Dispatch* to write fashion articles. Her first experience as a war correspondent was covering the Spanish civil war. She reached the war by hiking over the mountains separating France and Spain. Gellhorn's work chiefly appeared in *Collier's Magazine*. She saw herself as a modern war correspondent in the sense that she did not cover "women's work" or "women's issues." This was thirty years before Vietnam, where women still had to fight gender stereotypes about the proper work for a "lady." Gellhorn went on to do distinguished writing amidst the pointed remarks about women's place in society. Even other journalists were more interested in her marital status. To Gellhorn it was a complete "oddity" that her reputation was as "the very ordinary wife of an extraordinary man."[66]

Gellhorn and other women correspondents reported the war in Europe by dodging military press officers. To cover the Allied landings in France on D-Day Gellhorn snuck aboard one of the hospital ships and hid in the bathroom until the ship weighed anchor. As her biographer writes, "No one questioned her presence on Board." She had a winning combination of good looks, lots of courage, excellent writing skills, and a complete disregard for authority. These traits often opened doors for her. However, her talent as a reporter was paramount in the equation. Altogether, she gave *Collier's* "a jigsaw puzzle of fighting men, bewildered, terrified civilians, noise, smells, jokes, pain, unfinished conversations, and high explosives." Harold Acton, who worked as the censor for her dispatches, regarded her reports as some of the most acute stories that he passed during the war.[67]

Gellhorn was in her late fifties when Vietnam became the focus of military forces, which is pretty old for a war correspondent. She tried to get an assignment from several newspaper editors. They were aware of her intense hostility to the war and turned her down. She finally persuaded an English paper, *The Manchester Guardian*, to take six articles on the war from her.[68]

In the collective memory of the contemporary American public, Vietnam was its most enigmatic war. This is not to say that Vietnam was worse than any other war, because from the standpoint of soldier and journalist alike, any war is terrible and every war offers its participants the ever-present possibility of instantaneous death. As in every war, those present experience it as episodic. Phil Caputo who, along with Tim O'Brien and Michael Herr, wrote lucid and compelling accounts of his experience in Vietnam, described it as a series of incidents: "brief, terrifying dramas of death and blood separated from each other by long spells of boredom."[69] Although this description might have been written by someone in any war, in Vietnam a peculiar limbo-like atmosphere permeated day-to-day affairs. This was partly due to the long periods of inaction combined with the pervasive sense that one's actions—in skirmishes, ambushes or battles—had no real effect on succeeding events.[70]

Tom Tiede called Vietnam a land of confusion. A reader later wrote to him thanking him for writing the first true, "and I mean really true report on the soldiers of Vietnam."[71] A recurrent theme of speeches and reports coming out of Vietnam involved a commitment to tell people what was *really* going on there.[72] A dominant trope for reporting Vietnam was this discrepancy between appearances and reality.

The sense of unreality in Vietnam was partly connected to the unconventional fighting tactics used there. Guerilla warfare creates a different experience of war than the open field and mobile warfare of World War II and the war in Cuba. Dean Brelis, reporting from Phnom Penh, Cambodia, for NBC, spoke into the camera lens: "This is the front line, defending Phnom Penh against the Viet Cong who have crossed the Mekong and are supposedly headed for the capitol. For a front line, it is extraordinarily unwarlike. There were four hundred troops here. They settled in as though this were a picnic."[73]

The war in Vietnam had no identifiable course.[74] Every reporter had his own way of describing this phenomenon. Richard Tregaskis called it a "peace paralysis." In his account, soldiers tried to avoid getting hurt because the "big shots" weren't saying anything and couldn't make up their minds about what to do with the war. "I've never seen anything exactly like this," he wrote to a friend.[75]

While every war is a terrible thing, Vietnam was a tragedy largely because of the long, drawn-out irresolution toward it on the part of military and political leaders. Further, it is the only war in American history in which men were drafted to fight and then repeatedly told by their leaders that there was nothing over there worth fighting for.

The gulf between the rear area and the frontline was reminiscent of the British experience in World War I, with one exception. The British command was ignorant of real battlefield conditions; the American command, while often misguided in its prosecution of the war, was well apprised of conditions in the field. Furthermore, the American command was inconclusive about both strategy and tactics and more responsive to the political situation at home and to taking advantage of the war for officer advancement than to the plight of its own soldiers. Therein lies the story increasingly thought of as tragic by members of the fourth estate. There were, indeed, heroes in that war, but they were dead and too easily forgotten.

Just as people in decision-making capacities and ordinary soldiers were being pulled simultaneously in different directions so too were journalists. Almost to a person, reporters in Vietnam experienced a good deal of ambivalence about the war. Thus while Frances Fitzgerald paints a picture of two worlds side by side yet never meeting, she is inconsistent in her portrayal of some aspects of the war. While David Halberstam, perhaps more than any other journalist, called into question a war waged in Asia, he also was driven by a Cold War rhetoric. Ward Just and Neil Sheehan both understood that leaving Vietnam would be good for the American soldier, but disastrous to their South Vietnamese friends and colleagues. While Richard Tregaskis understood the folly of seeing Vietnam in World War II terms, he still used World War II tropes and images to convey his thoughts and experiences. This was particularly true when he was trying to sell a story to Hollywood, which stayed away from stories about Vietnam, in part because the North Vietnamese guerilla "seems too pitiful a foe." However, the desire to sell material does not explain many of his portrayals. Some comments seem almost dissociative, as when, for example, he wrote to a lecture circuit agent that South Vietnam could become a tourist industry because it has some of the best beaches in the world.[76]

Reporters as well as soldiers made an interior journey like Alice through the looking glass. This was true whether going from the rear area to the front, or going from Vietnam back to the United States. As one reader of the *Village Voice* noted, Frances Fitzgerald took this journey even though she kept "far from the slaughter and modestly faced the madness of the rear echelon."[77] While the rear echelon was highly efficient in many respects, it was also floating in jello.[78]

Many journeys through the looking glass had profound consequences. Vietnam was a divide; those who crossed it could not remember in a feeling way the days before they came of age. Phil Caputo, who believed he had failed morally in Vietnam, said, "I could not remember any existence other than that of war. . . . It seemed impossible that I had once possessed the sensibilities to enjoy Keats and Shelley." Caputo credited the transformation he underwent in Vietnam to Washington "planners" who had divided the war into phases before any American soldier had set foot in South Vietnam. Although he and his buddies did not recognize it at the same time, the briefings they received prior to going to Southeast Asia "turned out to be an experience in unreality."[79]

The most scholarly journalist in Vietnam was Frances Fitzgerald, who wrote for magazines. She relied on many documents she read for

research, as well as on interviews with U.S. military officers and Vietnamese officials and other citizens. She also used articles appearing in the
Vietnamese Courier, an English language information weekly designed
for a foreign audience and published in North Vietnam.[80] Fitzgerald was
at her best when distilling the overall picture from a massive set of col-
lected data. Her observations about the Vietnamese in particular are
measured and economical. For example, she describes the bureaucracy
of the South Vietnamese government as one run by people who had not
left their villages spiritually.[81] Fitzgerald understood the war from the
point of view of the Vietnamese peasants and her writing conveys that
point of view very well. While other reporters distinguished themselves
in political analysis (David Halberstam), spot news (Peter Arnett), or word
portraits of the U.S. soldiers (Ward Just and Tom Tiede), Fitzgerald was
able to go beyond Western stereotypes of the secretive and dissembling
Southeast Asian. She recognized the Vietnamese preference for clever-
ness and agility over brute force. She understood their disdain for the
military, their view of American soldiers as stupid "big noses."[82]

At the same time, her writing as a whole was sometimes inconsistent.
On the one hand, she said villagers were inclined to avoid the conflicts
outside their villages; on the other hand, she observed that the National
Liberation Front brought "the exciting air of the outside world."[83] While
she gave us a glimpse of village culture in Vietnam, largely an oral culture, at times she also analyzed it in terms of literacy's conventions.[84]
Fitzgerald portrayed peasants' belief in fate, for instance, as passivity that
denied them a true voice in government.[85] As good as she was in analyz-
ing the Vietnamese, she still privileged a model of government based on
a western-style democracy.

Martha Gellhorn's experiences in Spain and during World War II made
her a seasoned correspondent. In Vietnam she never traveled outside
Saigon. Although she was accredited, she avoided other correspondents.
She never attended briefings—she was not interested in military strategy
and tactics, much less ordnance. Instead, she visited the wounded and
dying in hospitals and toured refugee camps and orphanages.

One day she persuaded Ward Just to go with her to the First Cavalry Division; she had known its commander, General Jack Norton, in
Germany. She dressed well for dinner, drank liberally, and played the
coquette. When a mortar exploded nearby, all the soldiers put on their
helmets. Gellhorn openly laughed at them. Later she told a friend that
the Americans were frightened and showed the wrong spirit. In her view
an officer should exhibit cheerfulness and gaiety at all times.[86]

In Gellhorn's work and in the talks she gave on book tours for *The Face of War* there was a muted fury about Vietnam. She had a strong personality, and other reporters reacted negatively to her. She had her defenders though. Upon returning to London, she tried to turn her articles into a book, but it never materialized. She tried several times to get back to Vietnam, but was unable to secure a visa. A friend of hers tried to find out why from an official at the South Vietnamese embassy. The official's face drained of all color. It seemed that when he had told Gellhorn her application for a visa had been turned down, Martha threw a pile of books at him. "The language, Madam, the language!" he said.[87]

Gloria Emerson was an admirer of Gellhorn, and viewed her as a role model. Both women killed themselves many years later because of declining health (not because of the wars). Emerson was a generation younger than Gellhorn, born into a wealthy New York family, some of whom were alcoholics.[88] She left home at an early age and landed a job with the *New York Times*, eventually becoming one of their foreign correspondents. Besides the Vietnam war, she covered conflicts in Ireland and in Palestine.

Like Gellhorn, Emerson opposed the war by the time she arrived in Saigon. However she was a different breed of war reporter than many others in the press corps. As Ernie Pyle had done, she wrote about ordinary people, soldier and civilian alike. Emerson had already visited Vietnam in the 1950s, so she knew the people and their customs well. She felt deep empathy for the Vietnamese people and all they had been through.

Emerson felt that war was "not ennobling but debasing: a misery that inflicted suffering and psychic damage on civilians, children, and soldiers, on both sides."[89] Her book on Vietnam, *Winners and Losers*, won a National Book Award in 1978. She was also convinced of the importance of women as war correspondents because she thought men tended to see war as a grand spectacle.

Most reporters did indeed see war as a grand spectacle. This generation of journalists had been raised on the rhetoric of the Cold War. They had been given a steady diet of Iron Curtain and Bamboo Curtain.

The initial interpretive response to World War I and the war in Vietnam was surrealist, the experience of being carried away from reality. Once that distance between reality and experience is established, irony often ensues. In the Great War irony fed on the bureaucracy and censorship, both of which forced reporters to take a spectator stance. In Vietnam the irony was fed by the military culture of system juxtaposed with the eastern ethos of the Vietnamese and their bureaucracy; the experience of soldiers in the field juxtaposed with "rear area types" and the vast psychological distance between the experience of Vietnam and the American public's understanding of it.

Sometimes a reporter's words can be read as ironic only after the fact. For example, H. L. Mencken's diary during the early days of World War I quotes Paul von Hindenburg: "Our front is secure on all sides. We have the necessary reserves everywhere. The morale of our troops is sound and unshaken. The general military situation is such that we can accept safely all consequences of an unrestrained U-boat war. And inasmuch as this U-boat war offers us the means of doing the maximum of damage to our foes we must begin it forthwith." Mencken described von Hindenberg as a man who was "stingy with his parts of speech," but whose words had the effect of "divine revelation."[90]

Both politicians and Hollywood were targets of the reporter's scorn. In 1945, Dean Brines wrote that Los Angeles was not a good town for news about the Pacific war because people there were more interested "in news about Charlie Chaplin."[91] Two decades later, Richard Tregaskis would make a similar complaint. "In Vietnam any officer above the rank of Second Lieutenant was ripe for the picking. This was the case, in part, because the day-to-day conduct of the war often seemed to be in direct contrast to the officer mentality. A few months after the Tet attacks in early 1968, Col. Jack Giannini wrote about a rocket attack in Saigon. The Constituent Assembly Building took two hits and the windows at the Caravelle Hotel where reporters often lived were cracked. Giannini wrote, 'One might presume that the communists are finally getting the range!'"[92]

In some of her accounts in the *Village Voice*, Frances Fitzgerald sustains an amused distance when she tells of an officer who described the ambush and loss of twelve men the previous day. He ends his account with the observation, "It's a dirty little war." Fitzgerald's assessment: "The war in this part of the delta does not suit him."[93] A year later, this time writing for *Vogue*, she recounted an incident she apparently witnessed while out in the field—a brigade commander telling his men that the operation was outstanding: "Beaming, he turns and goes to his helicopter with strides that are longer than necessary. Though nothing, after all, has happened. There has been 'no contact'—no contact between the Vietnamese and the Americans, no contact between two closed systems."[94]

She deftly painted a portrait elsewhere of these two closed systems. On one occasion she went out in a land rover and visited various sites. Upon returning, Major Stapleton said, "Learning the war is a long slow process." Captain Ferelli said, "But we've made a good deal of progress." Fitzgerald observed, "The District Chief says nothing."[95]

Common Sense

As soldiers left the United States for Europe and the Pacific islands in 1941, sounds of "Blues in the Night" wafted up from the holds of the transport ships.[96] No one was singing "Over There." No one was predicting that the war would be over by Christmas. In the UPI offices, Earl Johnson sent out a memo to all bureau managers exhorting them to prepare for a long war.[97] Along with the soldiers went news reporters. By the time the war ended four years later, more than sixteen thousand journalists had been accredited to the army and navy.[98]

Common sense was the hallmark of the imagination and manners of the journalist reporting World War II—the predominant sentiment underlying his view of his job, the things he valued, and his aspirations. For reasons having to do with technological innovations, by 1941 the grit and resolution of the individual soldier and reporter alike counted for little on the field of battle. Gone were the flamboyant days of the nineteenth century; in its place stood the down-to-earth reporter of modern times.

According to the *Oxford English Dictionary*, "common sense" originally referred to an internal sense that functioned as a bond of the five senses. It was the center of the senses in which various impressions were united in a common consciousness. In the seventeenth century, it meant a bond uniting mankind, a feeling of community. In the eighteenth century, a philosophy of common sense developed in opposition to the works of Berkeley and Hume. According to this school of thought, the ultimate criterion of truth was the primary cognitions of humankind. In other words, the theory of perception rested on the universal belief in the existence of a material world. It was a philosophy used by all men and women to test the truth of knowledge and the morality of their actions. As such, it was remarkably well suited to the spirit of the times. Despite variations in the meaning of common sense, ever since the sixteenth century it has also referred to good, sound practical judgment, a combination of tact, and readiness in dealing with the everyday affairs of the workaday world. Like irony or romanticism, it is a way of constructing reality.

In 1726 the *Secret History of the University of Oxford* defined common sense as "the ordinary ability to keep ourselves from being imposed upon by gross contradictions, palpable inconsistencies, and unmasked impostures."[99] The definition is all the more interesting given that the correspondents of the Great War, faced daily with contradiction, cross-purposes, and inconsistencies, assumed an ironic stance to cope with their problems.[100] The next generation of war reporters modified the cynicism of their forebears. A generation haunted by the First World War and raised during the Great Depression, these reporters were trained in "the school of hard knocks." Their reports were not reflections on events but details of the events themselves, a matter-of-fact recording of the scenes before their eyes. The sartorial sloppiness of a Heywood Broun gave way to such shirt-sleeve journalists as Ben Hecht, Eric Sevareid, Ernie Pyle, Richard Tregaskis, and Don Whitehead.

Bill Mauldin's portrayal of the infantry, for example, was both realistic and ironic. His combat men did not fight the Germans using the Marquis of Queensbury's rules; they shot the enemy in the back, blew him up with mines, and killed him in the quickest and most effective way. The philosophy at the heart of this attitude was simply this: if you don't do it to them first, they'll do it to you. The GI's language was coarse; his manners rough. He might sum up the assets of a particular general by saying, "His spit don't smell like ice cream either."[101] Like Willie and Joe (everymen for the regular enlistees), he thought the insignia on the shoulders of officers "looked a hell of a lot like chips."[102] But—and this is important—at the same time, he knew that as long as you have an army, you have officers, and it was a matter of common sense to adjust.

COMMON SENSE: HOMELY WISDOM

As the hallmark of imagination and manners, common sense translated into realism, reductiveness, and homely wisdom. Homely wisdom was not so much a tendency toward the proverbial as it was a "Show me, I'm from Missouri" attitude. It was down-home horse sense, characterized by shrewd and subtle observation. Journalists writing in this vein were distant cousins and kith and kin to such fabulists as Mark Twain and Bret Harte. Some credited their matter-of-fact, levelheaded, unpretentious reportage to the "rigorous downrightness of . . . American journalistic training" and to their small-town upbringing in Indiana, South Dakota, Kansas, and other places across the nation.[103]

Besides professional training and small-town beginnings, other factors contributed to this vein of reportage. For one thing, the sheer magnitude of the war—in terms of distance and complexity—made it virtually impossible to report it in the older traditions. As late as 1939, when war broke out in Europe, military leaders in the United States still envisaged a single-front war with its nucleus at a single general headquarters (GHQ). Nobody thought about mobilizing hundreds of thousands of soldiers in many different theaters. In 1941 the army tried to activate a GHQ but realized almost at once that it would not do in a global conflict.[104] Unlike World War I, in which there was generally only one fight going on at a time, the battles of World War II were multiple, continual, and occurred in far-flung areas. Unlike World War I, this war was not one of fixed positions that correspondents could visit on an organized field trip from a centralized GHQ. The fronts changed, sometimes daily. Anyone who wished to report the war firsthand had to go with the troops. That meant reporters had to face hazardous situations, chaos, and confusion.

Moreover, the magnitude of the war and its chaotic and confusing progress were such that reporters often found themselves concentrating on a small group of soldiers or on one particular man. GI Joe became the subject of their reports. Once they chose an ordinary person as their subject, reporters had to use the language of the vernacular. Their words were concrete and plain. European towns such as Bricquebec and Isigny were rechristened "Bricabrac" and "Easy Knee." The ideas of correspondents were the ideas of the vernacular hero, the guy with the sense to come in out of the rain, who stayed away from slow horses and fast women, and who avoided putting all his eggs in the same basket.

During the war, Ernie Pyle's column centered on the GI. He loved GI Joe because Joe was honest and dirty and hungry. Pyle liked to take him apart to see what made him tick.[105] His column, written in the first-person singular, employed a central consciousness as its angle of vision. Although present in his stories, Pyle was there only as a storyteller, never as a participant. Underlying this emphasis on the individual soldier or civilian was a tacit belief that war was something that happened inside a person. Or, as a colleague put it, "It happens to one man alone . . . A thousand ghastly wounds are really only one. A million martyred lives leave an empty place at only one family table."[106]

This tendency toward homely wisdom, then, manifested itself as an attitude of disbelief. Unless a correspondent saw a shell land with his own eyes, he was disinclined to believe it had been fired. His attitude can be traced in part to his small-town upbringing and to his journalistic training. But his report also was affected, at least indirectly, by the sheer magnitude and complexity of the war itself. As soon as the ordinary individual became the subject of a report, the language of the vernacular had to be employed.

REDUCTIVENESS

A second characteristic of commonsense imagination is reductiveness. Reporters had a knack for taking a situation having all the elements necessary for high drama and bold adventure and reducing it to size. To put it another way, reporters following a commonsense tradition utilized perspective and restraint.

The Normandy landing called forth all kinds of reminders of Pershing's disembarkation on French soil. Pyle's story of a soldier on the Normandy beachhead replaced drama with down-to-earth humor:

> So far as I know, we entered France without anybody making a historic remark about it. Last time, you know, it was "Lafayette, we are here." The nearest I heard to a historic remark was made by an ack-ack gunner, sitting on a mound of earth about two weeks after D-Day, reading the *Stars and Stripes* from London. All of a sudden he said, "Say, where is this Normandy beachhead it talks about in here?" I looked at him closely and saw that he was serious, so I said, "Why, you're sitting on it." And he said, "Well, I'll be damned. I never knowed that."[107]

Similar to Pyle's putting the historic liberation of France into perspective, on another occasion Turner Catledge of the *New York Times* put the military in its place. At the point of disembarkation after traveling by air, troops would witness an officer enter the plane and announce in a loud voice, "You will now leave the aircraft in the order of your rank." Catledge had landed in New Delhi and was standing by the plane's exit, loaded down with heavy bags and other paraphernalia, when the officer made the customary speech. In an equally loud voice, Catledge replied, "I presume that means American taxpayers first," and walked off the plane.[108]

By and large, reporters restored the hard edge of proportion to the events they wrote about.[109] Convinced that "no catastrophe is so complete that it can quench out life," they exercised dignity and restraint in reporting the tragedies and victories they witnessed.[110] They exacted emotion from the scenes around them instead of infusing those scenes with passion, sentiment, or sensation.

PRACTICALITY

A third quality inherent in commonsense imagination is practicality. Gone now is the regalia of Richard Harding Davis. The army was good about providing transportation, but the amount of equipment one had to take to the front made traveling difficult.[111] The solution for reporters—as it was for GIs—was to eliminate everything but the bare necessities. Clothing, too, became eminently practical. Dress uniforms were for the rear areas. At the front reporters wore coveralls with no ties. Being practical meant, in one sense, knowing how to cope, making the best of a difficult situation. The practical reporter knew how to improvise, patch, and fix. He learned that a direct question usually got a direct answer. He was a specialist on the "advantages" of different shells. Those that were dropped gave you more warning than those that came straight at you. But, then, those that came straight at you might miss you and keep on going; those that were dropped could kill you even if they did not hit you directly.[112]

One element contributing to this practicality was the sheer physical hardship of life at the front. For veteran reporters, physical hardship was probably the number one problem they encountered as they endeavored to get the news. It was dangerous and draining work, accompanied by the possibility of dying. For war correspondents, covering the war was costly. About 50 were interned in prisoner-of-war camps; 112 were wounded, and 37 lost their lives, a casualty rate four times that of the military.[113]

Few correspondents remained unmoved when news of the death of a fellow reporter reached them. Barney Darnton of the *New York Times*, long considered the best reporter in the Pacific theater, was killed by a bomb fragment while covering advance troops moving up the northern New Guinea coast. It was with affection that his friends insisted that Darnton was the inspiration for the story of the butler who, when announcing to his mistress that seven journalists had called, said, "Madam, there are six reporters here, and a gentleman from the *Times.*"[114]

Many journalists who faced death daily either dismissed the occupational hazard of covering a war or joked about it. Most, however, assumed a matter-of-fact air when they spoke of the possibility of getting hit. "Not getting hit is just plain gambler's luck," Ernie Pyle wrote to his wife.[115] But the levelheaded approach to death, the belief that there were worse ways to die, was periodically punctuated by grief at the loss of a friend and fear of having to die. Discussion about death's possibility evoked matter-of-fact resignation; the actual death of a comrade elicited fear and anguish. Raymond Clapper was killed while covering the invasion of the Marshall Islands. The plane he was aboard collided in mid-air with another. His death devastated Ernie Pyle, with whom Clapper had played poker in the UPI Washington bureau.[116]

In one of the bloodiest fights of the war, the Tarawa landing, reporters dug in alongside the military on the beachhead. As they were shoveling out their foxholes, Robert Sherrod (*Saturday Evening Post*) turned to Bill Hipple (AP) and said, "Well, Bill, it hasn't been such a bad life." Hipple replied that he was still too damn young to die. Hipple's remark was not made in jest. It was a simple, straightforward, matter-of-fact assessment of his chances for survival. Both Sherrod and Hipple had little hope that they would survive the night.[117]

Generally, physical exhaustion and the hardships of primitive living conditions most often broke down reporters.[118] In Africa, where many correspondents were "broken in," they slept in tents with dirt floors. The wind blew the dirt into everything. They ate cold C rations (even the coffee was cold), bathed in their helmets, and slept on the ground with no blankets. Under continuous artillery fire day and night, they moved along with the infantry (including night marches) and were "part of about all the horror of war there is."[119]

In the Pacific theater, reporters argued over which island was the most uncomfortable.[120] The difficult conditions of war were further enhanced by the isolation of Pacific atolls, the cramped quarters of navy ships, and the unrelenting heat. Each theater, then, had its own special version of hardship and danger. The Pacific had its Tarawa; Africa, its Kasserine Pass; Europe, its Normandy beachhead.

The bedfellow of physical exhaustion was monotony and, consequently, emotional exhaustion. After six months or so, one became adjusted to the sights and sounds of warfare, even to the sight of the dead being buried in bloody bed sacks.[121] The emotional fatigue of a hard-hitting campaign was as difficult to deal with as survival under enemy fire: "It's the perpetual dust choking you, the hard ground wracking your muscles, the snatched food sitting ill on your stomach, the heat, the flies and dirty feet and the constant roar of engines and the perpetual moving, the never sitting down, and the go, go, go, night and day, and on through the night again. Eventually it all works itself into an emotional tapestry of one dull dead pattern—yesterday is tomorrow and Troina is Randazzo and when will we stop, and God, I'm so tired."[122] Under conditions such as this, practicality, in the sense of being able to adapt, was essential to both physical and emotional survival.

In its most narrow sense, being practical meant being pragmatic; in its wider sense, however, it meant being sensible or "wising up."[123] The prevailing sentiment about the war was that nobody wanted to go into battle, but so long as the world was fighting, America had better damn well do its best to win. This quality of being sensible lies behind Richard Tregaskis's remarks about the fighting on Tarawa: "From Hell Point, on Col. Pollock's end of the spit, volleys of firing sprang out and the Jap was killed as he swam; even the kindliest Marine could not let the swimming Jap escape, for he would be apt then to swim around our rear and throw grenades, as several Japs had done earlier in the day."[124]

Attitudes toward censorship also had a "let's be reasonable" ring to them. It was for common sense that Byron Price made his appeal to newspaper editors: "In all of these things, let's be sensible."[125] He was referring to domestic voluntary censorship, of which he was director, but reporters also used good sense as a yardstick by which to measure whether the censor in the field was playing fair.

Periodically reporters were dissatisfied with the way the news was handled. Yet, even in the Pacific, where censorship was most stringent, men like Robert Casey based their hopes for reform on the admiral's common sense. It was this everyday sentiment of common sense that reporters felt ought to rule what passed the censor. Consequently, the highest praise a censor or public relations officer (PRO) could muster was that he was a reasonable man.

REALISM

The fourth quality inherent in a commonsense approach to life is realism. Using the term "realistic" to describe a certain outlook has the same kind of drawbacks as using the term "romantic." In our everyday conversations when we say someone is romantic, we usually mean that he sees life through rose-colored glasses. In other words, he does not see life as it really is. Likewise, being realistic implies a lack of a broader vision. We have come to think of realistic people as literal-minded people who have little capacity for seeing the world poetically.[126] Applied to journalists, the term encompasses the concept of objectivity. Realism also implies a lack of imagination and a dearth of moral vision.

The truth is that the moral vision of the commonsensical, realistic reporter is solidarity. The "common" part of common sense, narrowly defined, means "average" or "everyday horse sense." But common also means "shared" or "general."[127] This moral vision is what lies behind Huck Finn's determination to go to hell with Nigger Jim rather than adhere to an unjust social code. It underlies Ernie Pyle's guilt when, upon leaving war-torn Europe for a brief respite at home, he felt as if he were a deserter.[128] This solidarity was partially derived from months and years of rubbing shoulders together during the crisis of war. It is solidarity that is at the heart of a scribbled note found on Pyle's body: "The companionship of 2½ years of death and misery is a spouse that tolerates no divorce. Such a companionship finally becomes part of one's soul and it cannot be obliterated."[129] Solidarity is also the framework for the tacit acknowledgement that, while nobody wants to go to war, "we are all in this together."

Solidarity is a moral vision connected to a time-honored belief that common sense, the domain of the rugged individual, allows one access to higher truths, truths accessible to spontaneous reason. Because common sense is a universal form of reason and the property of all men, "the people can serve as a better source of authority for truths than philosophers [so the argument goes], who can be corrupted by aristocratic notions and institutions."[130] So, common sense as a moral vision is tied closely to the philosophical underpinnings of the American form of popular democracy—a form made legitimate, moreover, by the institution of the watchdog press.

Being realistic meant being accurate too. Compared with the previous wars, there were significantly fewer unfounded atrocity stories and reports of glamorous heroics and victories without the shedding of American blood. Reporters went behind the commonplace and sought "real facts."[131] They strove for accuracy in the sense of exactness, but also in the broader sense of keeping things in proportion and perspective.[132] Realistic reportage relied heavily on the recording of a great number of details. The so-called romantic reporter also paid attention to details. The realist, however, provided an accurate recording of the event for its own sake. Common sense and objectivity took the place of brilliant showmanship.[133] If the columns of Raymond Clapper lacked the fireworks of Westbrook Pegler's, they courted fairness by reason of their factual quality and their freedom from animus.[134]

Over and above the presentation of factual details in a precise manner, accuracy meant keeping one's perspective. A consequence of the accurate, realistic viewpoint was the demise of the universally wonderful American soldier. When the actor Joe E. Brown said he thought the GIs were a wonderful group of men, Pyle retorted, "Bullshit." Neither did death in the service of one's country redeem the reputation of a blackguard. For example, one day in France, some reporters were talking about a person none of them liked who had just been killed. A. J. Liebling, the New Yorker's wayward pressman, slipped into the conventional custom and remarked that he had not really been such a bad guy. The rest of the group, however, agreed that "a son-of-a-bitch is a son-of-a-bitch even if he is dead."[135]

Reporters also courted realistic notions about their own chances for survival. Perhaps Ernie Pyle is not a fair example. He was plagued by bouts of severe depression during which he speculated on his own fate. He often felt lonely, bored, and fed up. Landings, which he dreaded, were preceded by a last-minute sense of fatalism. Others besides Pyle had similar feelings, but Pyle's depressions were not caused solely by the war or the difficulties of reporting it. His private life was in shambles. His wife was an alcoholic and frequently required hospitalization. On several occasions she tried to kill herself, the last time being a particularly gruesome attempt. They were divorced and remarried by proxy when he was in Africa. When Pyle wrote his friend Paige Cavanaugh, "If you think of anything to live for, please let me know," his words reflected his personal agony as much as it reflected anything else.[136]

At the same time, the war itself and the duress under which he had to report it took its toll. There were days when Pyle felt he would crack up if he saw combat again. The daily grind of turning out a column was emotionally draining; it was an "all-consuming everyday thing which exalts a little and destroys completely." When he said there was no sense to the struggle and no choice but to struggle, he was referring to life in general.[137] However, he felt the same about the war. War was "dead men by mass production."[138] As it was for others, the war was too huge, too complicated, and too confusing for Pyle. On especially sad days, he mused, "It is almost impossible for me to believe that anything is worth such mass slaughter." Only when he could see the end of the war did he think he could recapture an eagerness for living.[139]

Ever since the nineteenth century, reporters have tried to be a camera. In this way they are connected to the world of novel, since both they and the storytellers from the eighteenth century on have been concerned with ordinary lives. Like novelists, journalists have always wanted to send "the true picture" into our homes and offices. Reporters covering the Second World War were no exception. With the moral vision inherent in solidarity, they tried to communicate what the war was really like. The map of their inner lives reveals a realistic view of life resting on the homely wisdom of the ordinary man and the average guy. With shirt sleeves rolled up and ties askew, these men developed a habit of letting a story tell itself, of exacting emotion from the scenes around them.

In the process of covering battle, reporters used common sense as the frame of reference to organize and interpret the scenes they witnessed. Common sense as a perceptual tool is connected to the heart and meaning of American democracy, the idea that each man is his own source of authority. Reporters covering World War II personalized the common-sense tradition and incorporated its characteristics in their reports.

Despite the apparent diversity of talents making up this "worn out bunch of unromantic scribes," they all had one thing in common.[140] Whether columnist, spot reporter, photographer, or broadcaster, all believed that in carrying out their jobs they should recognize two restrictions: military security and common sense. Because they developed a habit of going to firsthand sources, they rarely indulged in wild speculation or peddled gossip. Occasionally they were wayward and capricious. But they always went about their work determined to give the public a comprehensive, realistic picture of what was happening in the war zone.

If nothing else, this chapter presented a wide range of interpretations of wartime experience. Each interpretation was a response to specific field situations, as well as the moral tenor of the times. Whether he saw the war in terms of irony or realism, his critical intelligence is the clearest indication that the reporter is an embodied ethos. Everything we know to be true about censorship and experience has prepared us to plot out in chapter 7 the basic characteristics of a reporter's occupational culture.

7 *The Occupational Culture of the American War Correspondent*

The kinds of experiences the journalist has had in reporting the wars this nation has fought were demarcated and examined in chapter 6. This chapter will present a brief sketch of his occupational culture, a kind of summary understanding that a good journalist has when he must accompany troops and write about their campaigns.

In every war, the correspondent sees the censor as an adversary. Never mind that the latter is a peacetime journalist. When the rules about what can and cannot be written are laid out for him, the savvy reporter will know them thoroughly and obey them in order to avoid the censor's blue pencil. Even in wars where there is no censor, the reporter will be careful with his copy. In Vietnam there was no censor, but there were news embargoes on certain troop maneuvers. While today many believe the Vietnam war was reported by journalists who bucked the system, it is possible to count on the fingers of one hand the number of times news embargoes were disregarded.

The true journalist wears invisible antennae that he uses to gauge when and where the military is being evasive. If he has to wait too long for a story, if his movements are restricted, or if he sees any discrepancy between what he has been told and what he experiences, he will begin to balk. "Military security" in these instances is code for "military cover-up" as far as he is concerned.

The fact that censors had been journalists before the war is both reassuring and unsettling to him. It is reassuring because a war reporter believes a newsman will understand the needs of the press in day-to-day operations. It is unsettling because when the censor exercises his authority to prevent publication of certain information, he is doing something that goes against the fundamental belief every true journalist holds dear: that the timely publication of the facts regarding the people's interests is the bedrock of democratic life.

In situations such as this, the reporter will be successful to the degree that he and the censor share common values—especially those connected to their social class of origin. Yet even when reporter and censor are very much alike, the journalist will show respect for the officer, but it is a respect riddled with disdain.

When the balance between disdain and respect starts to tilt more toward the former, the journalist will use evasionary tactics. When he does so he is signaling to the censor, the bureau chief, his editor, or the news director that he detects the imposition of extreme measures. By extreme measures I mean unreasonably harsh and restrictive measures. These sorts of measures give a real reporter justification for both the right and the duty to get around them. The key word here is "unreasonable." The bottom line in all interactions between the reporter and the military is that they must be reasonable.

No matter where or when he works the war reporter believes he is a soldier of sorts. The more he shares in the hardships of enlisted men, the more he will think he is performing a service for the nation. The degree to which he shares the life of the soldier on the frontlines often determines the extent to which he considers himself an authentic war correspondent.

The authenticity he finds is very much connected to his gut. "Gut" includes the suspicions he has as well as certain beliefs that are so fundamental that he does not experience them as beliefs, but rather as a facts. He is, above all, a no-nonsense kind of guy who can never be bought, in either a literal or a metaphorical sense.

Whenever his gut is involved in his decisions, he is surely operating according to an ethic. These are the times he will use words that imply a critical interpretation, words like "dirtbag," "chicken shit," and "scuzzball." These sorts of epithets are pervasive. A war correspondent doesn't leave them on the frontlines when he goes to rear areas or when he leaves his office for home. This is because journalism is a way of life rather than a job. Journalism permeates the answers he will give to the existential questions we all face: How shall I die? Can death be meaningful? What does a true friend do? What is love?

No true journalist is interested in theory. In fact, his disavowal of it is one of the chief characteristics of the authentic reporter. This is especially true of war correspondents because they deal with the deaths of men and women on a daily basis. In today's world there is no perceived difference between men and women journalists—although women journalists do not have the freedom to sleep wherever they happen to find themselves because to do so is to risk becoming the object of violence themselves. But in all the wars studied in this book, the war correspondent was a gendered self. In other words, he saw the job of being a reporter as part of being a man. Being a real man was part of being a true journalist. In each war studied here women reporters were present. At first they wrote about "womanly things" or what women would be interested in. But in every war there were women who wanted to be the same kind of reporters as the men were. This view of women as no different from men came to a head in World War II. In Vietnam, most of the women reporters insisted on reporting all aspects of the war. Men, however, were reluctant to let go of their beliefs about the unsuitability of women on the battlefield.

Whenever a war correspondent goes on or off "duty," he carries within himself a transcendent order that always interacts tacitly with the immanent one. This transcendent order refers to the national good and to his role in providing information to a nation's citizens so they can make informed decisions about their democracy. This transcendency is with the true war reporter 24/7. It is scattershot with structured feelings.[1] These emotional states have architecture built over the course of his life. They include affective bridges made between experiences—especially between a past experience and a present one. This is why a reporter tends to see the war he is presently covering in terms used in previous conflicts he reported, for example, why Richard Tregaskis and Dickey Chapelle saw Vietnam in World War II terms.[2]

It is generally the case that war correspondents are unable to divest themselves of their first experience of war. Hence, the seasoned veterans in Vietnam and in Washington, D.C., and New York (Scotty Reston, Marguerite Higgins, and Joseph Alsop) continued to experience the war in Vietnam as they had World War II. Consequently, news organizations run a great risk in sending journalists who have had significant wartime experience to cover a new *national* war. I emphasize "national" because it is only when the United States is one of the parties engaged in war that this phenomenon seems to occur—a fact that supports the main argument of this book: journalists are walking advertisements for the nation-state.

Should there be any lingering doubt of the truth of this argument, I refer to a story about David Halberstam, who distinguished himself in

Vietnam. He was stormy when the military were deceitful or (in his judgment) incompetent. On Thanksgiving Day 1962, General Paul D. Harkins launched the largest combat helicopter operation in history without alerting any members of the press. When Halberstam learned of it, he was furious. He told the information agency that the news blackout had changed him from "a neutral bystander to an angry man." "The reason given is security. This is, of course, stupid, naïve and indeed insulting to the patriotism and intelligence of every American newspaperman and every American newspaper represented here."[3]

Contrary to what many believe, truth is not the first casualty in war; a soldier is. And it is this fact that fuels a correspondent's fire. He knows that the statistics of war are nothing when compared to an empty place at the family's dinner table. It is because men and women die in war that the journalist justifies his desire to circumvent the censor.

Whatever the topic of his report, he sees himself as someone working for John and Joan Q. Public. He is a citizen working for his fellow citizens. In his heart the reporter knows with Thomas Jefferson that the price of democracy is eternal vigilance. In his day-to-day world, he breathes the air not of patriotism, but of democracy.

While working in a battle zone a reporter relies on rules to give him a sense of normalcy. He works well within a set of guidelines and regulations, whether they come from his editor or the PIO. He knows instinctively how much he can get away with. Sometimes he can be found trying to tweak somebody's nose. For instance, he has almost no tolerance for people who have an overdeveloped sense of entitlement, whether Hollywood star or military officer. It galls him to see his place on a military transit plane given to a movie star.

The authentic journalist will arrange and rearrange his words until a story emerges—the correct story, that is. It is part of his anti-intellectual bent that he tells everyone in both words and gestures that he is only interested in the facts. He might say that theory is what the French do. "Lafayette we are here" is a lot of bunk.

The organizing element of the war reporter's life on the front is rhythm or tempo. This rhythm is connected to how he does his work, as well as to the report he ultimately submits to his editor or news director, and the gratification he has in facing the camera or seeing his byline in print.

When he wakes up in the morning he decides his schedule in conjunction with a military representative, including what interviews he will conduct and what action he will see if he has been cleared to be with the troops. Then he writes his story, limited to seven hundred or eight hundred words. After a short time the word limits become embedded in his experience. They become invisible at times. He knows the situation he wants to write about and quickly begins melting it down to six or seven paragraphs. In this way his report is part of himself. It always walks within him. This is what he means when he talks about his "beat."

Every war correspondent has someone he looks up to. These role models are usually seasoned journalists who know the ropes and teach their younger colleagues how to work the system: who will open doors, who will waste time, who is the straight shooter. While disdaining the lazy and the false, war correspondents engage in hero worship of more experienced reporters, but never in public. Hal Boyle wanted to be another Ernie Pyle, as did Tom Tiede. David Halberstam thought the world of Homer Bigart, the man who preceded him in Vietnam. Working journalists typically have not emulated literary war correspondents such as Richard Harding Davis or Stephen Crane. This is not to say these men were not good reporters or that their fiction was not admired. It is to draw attention to the fact that working journalists—men whose vocation is to report the news—emulate other good, working journalists. These are the guys who get to the story first and report it accurately and fairly. They tend to see literary stars as poachers in the guise of gamesmen.

Reporters in wartime can show an immature cynicism that is a cover or a lid to keep fear manageable. They often act out this fear by engaging in juvenile behavior, such as throwing food at one another during mess hall or engaging in an adolescent response to authority figures. But journalists are not immature people—what happens to war correspondents is the normal process of age regression when under stress. Even the most mature adult, given enough stress, will regress to adolescent behavior. And war is very stressful.

A journalist is intelligent in both shrewd and bookish ways. During the wars considered here, there were as many high school graduates as college graduates who became correspondents. This trend started to change in Vietnam, where the majority of reporters were people with college degrees. Even then, reporters believed that if you were good you did not need a sheepskin hanging on your wall. At the same time, a good reporter is nothing if not knowledgeable.

As for his fellow journalists, the reporter does not admire literary stars who do a brief stint as journalists. Rather, he esteems the journalists who get to the story first and tell it accurately. Secretly, he ranks other reporters according to an unspoken grid of values that include timeliness and a feel for fabula (story). He despises fortune hunters and adventure seekers of any kind. They can be found in every war, but they abounded in Vietnam.

Every reporter is skilled at lying. He has tunnel vision and will say anything to get to the source of information. He does not see this as a moral lapse because he is doing it for a greater good: the well-being of the public.

As for those reporters he likes and admires, a journalist conducts constant, low-wattage surveillance. This is done chiefly in bars at the end of the working day, or after he has filed his report. He does this mainly to ensure he won't miss out on something important. If everyone is in the bar drinking, his logic goes, then he isn't missing the big story. What looks like an alcoholic culture is really a front for monitoring the current situation or conducting occupational surveillance.

Every journalist dreams of the really big story. And for that encounter he arms himself with the tools of his trade: good interviewing skills, a prescient nose, and clear writing. It is no wonder that he despises the censor whom he feels is blocking him from his goal. This is especially true if the censor is an idiot—which the true journalist defines as someone who doesn't know his ass from a hole in the ground. The war correspondent is nothing if not visceral. The younger he is, the more likely his experiences will be full of skirmishes and retorts. In these situations a war correspondent may resort to using codes—as both Sylvester Scovel and David Halberstam did.

Every once in a while a good war reporter will get into a bind. In these situations his editor or bureau chief will step in and ask for due process. This is how the Constitution of the United States permeates journalism. When a reporter is covering a war he is adamant about being an independent, objective journalist. There is no place in his heart for being "embedded" with the military—as reporters in most recent years have been described—because it smacks too much of being "in bed with" them. Hence he tends to see a clear demarcation between civil and military matters.

Part of the journalist's independence has to do with economic solvency. It is not so much a market economy that he sees as the bottom line, it is more that he sees the bottom line as proof of his independence from the military in making his livelihood. He behaves as if he were unaware of censorship as a medium. If you asked him about it, he may concede a need for censorship, but that won't diminish his view of himself as an authentic journalist because in his mind he is very much the adversary in all his relationships—except in the one with his public.

When war reporters are not high on alcohol or nicotine, they are often high on adrenaline. Adrenaline is a necessary ingredient in reporting a war and getting a good story. An adrenaline high becomes dangerous and counterproductive when it becomes an addiction, something clung to when the job of reporting a war is over.

A war correspondent has firsthand knowledge of the sheer madness of war. If he allows himself to think about it, he can make the descent into nihilism. This is especially dangerous in worldwide wars. In dealing with an incipient nihilism, he may turn to adrenaline. A journalist may feel lost without the rush danger brings. He senses, though, that his addiction is really a relief from other overwhelming emotions, ones he would just as soon not look at. Most of the time he honestly doesn't know what they are, it's all he can do just to keep them at bay. The last thing he wants to do is to examine his life, much less live the examined life, as Socrates advises us to do. This is partly why he writes about the facts—the knowable, tangible facts. In a tiny web-filled corner of his mind he knows that he, too, could become a casualty of war.

Every good journalist disdains the guys who make things up from notes they read as they rifled through other reporters' mailboxes. Rearline reporters, no matter their excuses, are failures. Although the public commonly believes that reports of the war in 1898 were often fictional, the truth is in every war some reporters make things up and some news organizations publish them. No war covered in this book was an exception to this general state of affairs.

Although journalists are often compared to historians, they seem to me to be more like secret agents. Their job during wartime is a dangerous one and it is done for their country. Sometimes it gives them access to the powerful, and they are tempted to become statesmen, to consult, to strategize, to offer advice. Military strategy is a very seductive mistress. Among those who were seduced are Richard Tregaskis, Dickey Chapelle, and Walter Cronkite. When Cronkite came back from Vietnam to report what was going on there, he made himself the news. Television is a reflexive medium, but making oneself the news turns citizens' eyes away from the truths of the social conflict and toward questions of truth reduced to the personality who uttered it. The public is short-changed by a journalist who conducts himself as if he were a statesman.

After 1915, no war reporter claimed to be a gentleman or a lady. The well-bred, mannered war correspondent who had upper-class mores passed away when Richard Harding Davis died. With every generation of reporters an older moral order fades away and a new one is born. War is so strenuous, the young are often the only people physically able to cover one. Being young does not mean being inaccurate. The old guard in the Washington press corps charged the journalists in Vietnam with inexperience. David Halberstam and Neil Sheehan were not reporting events and situations the way they were because they were young or inexperienced. They were reporting what was actually happening in Vietnam, what they were seeing and learning about. They exercised good judgment about what was newsworthy and did so even when they knew they were making waves.

A true journalist will not stand for certain things. Besides giving up his seat to actors on a junket, he cannot abide the meddling editor. The editor is the boss and for that reason the journalist tends to have a love-hate relationship with him. As the reporter sees it, he himself knows the situation better than someone chained to a desk. A good war correspondent will respect only those editors who give him the freedom of his own initiative.

This relationship to his editor is of crucial importance in the webs of significance tying a journalist to others. I have never read anything written by a reporter in praise of his editor. Neither private nor public communications are laudatory of the editor's judgment. The war correspondent navigates rough waters in this relationship for it is one of both mentorship and reprimand.

The editor is the boss, but he is hundreds, even thousands of miles away. In the field it is possible to forget about him, but the boss's arm reaches across oceans and continents. Richard Tregaskis itemizes editorial behavior thus: "As usual—after all these years it never ceases to amaze me—I was startled by the inflexibility of the editorial mind, the unwillingness to extend a little, oh so very little, beyond their [sic] rigid proscription of what is A Money-Making Property."[4] Money, in fact, is the most central concern in the cables and letters sent by editors to their reporters in the field. Neil Sheehan is an extraordinary example, if only because he went so long in eluding the requests of his home office to be more fiscally responsible as a bureau chief in Vietnam.[5]

While the AP wanted fiscal responsibility, the UPI practiced the most miserly tactics of all the wire services. During World War II, the UPI home office hired a new reporter and sent him to London. It cabled reporters in London, announcing that their living expenses would be docked a dollar each to provide the new journalist an allowance. The men in the London office mutinied. They wired back, threatening to remain idle until their allowance was restored. The home office quickly resorted to their usual strategy of claiming that a mix-up had occurred. They had never intended to cut anyone's allowance.[6]

William Dickinson illustrates the adversarial nature of a journalist's experience with almost everyone connected to his occupation. He was convinced, for instance, that Sid Williams, the London office manager for UPI, was making wrong decisions on copy. One day, Dickinson drew the line. Williams had shoved a cable over to him, a "really silly" one. In a letter to his folks back home, Dickinson told this story: "I looked at it, tossed it in the wastebasket and said, 'No such blankity-blank cable will go over the desk when I'm operating it.' [Williams] turned white, dug it out and told me to send it. 'That's an order,' he said."[7]

Of course, most of these sorts of observations by war reporters are found in their letters home, especially those to their parents, who are always assured their son is safe, if tired and broke. Such comments are seldom if ever recorded in their journals or notebooks and almost never found in letters or cables to their editors or office managers.

Many editors also decided what the story was, in effect becoming armchair war correspondents without having been eyewitnesses. Herbert Corey's dispatches about the Germans in the first year of World War I were never published because his editor thought they were propaganda. Hobart Lewis of *Reader's Digest* directed Dickey Chapelle to stop jumping with the marines and reporting her experience in an "I was there" sort of story. Her editor wanted "top, objective reporting and not first person . . . material."[8]

Yet, the personal story came to be as important as the objective account in the period under study here. Personal stories had always been the meat of letters to family and friends. By World War II they had become a respected journalistic form. The reports of Ernie Pyle, Hal Boyle, and Tom Tiede were thought to be very good. In many ways these sorts of reports brought home the stark reality of the war more effectively than did objective or analytic pieces. Tom Tiede's work was quite vivid. It was far more intense than anything the wire services could do.[9]

A generation younger than Pyle, Tiede covered a very different war than his predecessor. A reader who enjoyed Tiede's work often wrote to soldiers in Vietnam about his reports and compared him to Pyle. "Imagine how old we felt," she remarked, "when three boys wrote back asking, 'Who is Ernie Pyle?'"[10]

In some ways Tom Tiede stepped outside Pyle's long shadow because he was reporting a war that was not a war. Another of Pyle's admirers (who had actually met him) recognized how Tiede went beyond the older man's work: "Your pieces are far greater than [Pyle's]. . . . I hope you know how much they mean to all your readers. In their fierce simplicity they paint unforgettable pictures of this terrible undeclared war and it is good that we know the truth, as you write it."[11] This reader understood the difference between the moral universe Pyle lived and worked in and the one Tiede grappled with. She was also intellectually mature enough to understand

and accept the many faces of truth. As such she reminds us of the importance of not underestimating the intelligence of the American public.

Dickey Chapelle, whom columnist Bob Considine described as "one heaven of a woman," was also likened to Ernie Pyle. Here the comparison was to their mutual fates. Chapelle succumbed to the "law of averages."[12] She died after stepping on a land mine in Vietnam.

Chapelle began her career as a war reporter in the Pacific theater during World War II when the attitude was that women didn't belong in a war zone. General Douglas MacArthur banned women correspondents from his operations. Consequently, women sometimes had to rely on stories about other women. For example, Chapelle wrote, "A woman reporter captured by the Japs in Manila in 1942 brought back one of the outstanding stories of the Philippine campaign."[13]

In the 1940s if women were allowed to accompany invading forces, they were seen as an encumbrance. Their heroism in facing danger was not appreciated. After chasing stories for days at the front, some learned later that their work, if published, would be regarded as "embarrassing." Associating women with "men's work" was tantamount to calling men girls. Playground taunts of being "like a girl," instead of like a man, still clearly rang in women journalists' ears during World War II. In Vietnam this attitude was not as visible, but still worked underground where it was more difficult to deal with.

The occupational culture of the American war correspondent is a complex thing, living in the unconscious as well as the conscious. It incorporates general rules covering any situation that good journalists might find themselves in. It is always circumscribed by the mores and the sex roles of the time. And, wherever you find the war correspondent, you will find also a walking advertisement for the nation-state.

Conclusion

In America's history, the First Amendment has played a key role brokering the relationship between the nation-state and the citizen. When the First Amendment is curtailed, the freedoms it guarantees begin to withdraw into the shadows thrown up by the machinery of warfare. The constant presence of the First Amendment—its towering importance in our value system, and its centrality to our way of life—forces us to recognize that during war the work of the journalist is cast into the path of the moon's passage between the sun and the earth, that is, into eclipse. Like an eclipse, where the sun is still shining, so too the free press still exists and its members are able to function without compromising journalistic integrity.

This book has shown the military's recurring reluctance to engage in censorship—unless the stakes are high. Such was the case in World War II, when General Eisenhower "drafted" the press as part of his military forces.

Some citizens have skewed notions about wartime censorship. It is as if they believe an uber-consciousness is running the war, setting its rules and trying to muzzle the press. There is no such thing as an uncensored war. Censorship can never simply be reduced to a list of do's and don'ts or rights and wrongs about the release of information during war.

Rather, censorship is a medium we all live and work in. In war it is a culture that may be thick, like Jell-O, but not blinding. In fact, censorship has advantages under certain conditions. Once everything is spelled out, everyone is able to go about his work more freely. Both soldier and reporter understand the rules of procedure. This situation usually occurs in the second stage of a war because it takes the first stage—several days or weeks, depending on the war—to iron out the kinks in the plan.

Records in libraries and archives indicate a deep faith in reason as the hallmark of good practice for both the press and the censors. Early in the twentieth century, a major question was explicitly raised in military, political, and legal circles: Is press censorship ever really legal? The Judge Advocate General's office answered the question. The turning point came during the punitive expedition into Mexico, when America codified its stand on the nation's right to censor news copy in any form during war or the imposition of marshal law.

After this, doing good work was only a matter of trying to cultivate good working relationships between reporter and censor. As the steps to ensure passage of the news reporter's copy became more explicitly formulated, the war reporter's role in the life and internal integrity of the nation-state became more visible.

By World War I, American journalists were successfully integrated into the military system largely through the offices of censorship. Both soldiers and journalists constructed reporters as weapons in the arsenal of war. This was especially true in World War II. The strikingly easy and thorough assimilation of the press into the military was due in part to the peace-time status of most censors: they were reporters and editors.

Conscription, too, played a major role in the history and evolution of war reporting. Conscription meant that every able-bodied male citizen could be swept into battle, ultimately facing a strong possibility of loss of life. The citizen at risk might have to pay the ultimate price. Hence the ethics of reporting the war: someone must speak for the dead and in America that someone is the journalist.

It was this blood sacrifice of the nation's youngest and fittest that made the war correspondent an embodied ethos. When soldiers are drafted or choose military service, those who tell their stories become embodied ethos. The ethics of war correspondence led Ernie Pyle, Tom Tiede, and Gloria Emerson to write about enlisted men and women and the people whose lives were affected by war. Once the journalist understands he is an embodied ethic (a gut reaction rather than an intellectual exercise), he begins to realize and effect the greater calling of journalism in America: the ever-present, but usually tacit belief that a reporter is America writ small.

The First Amendment is both a right and a responsibility. Reporting war is the one side of the coin, journalistic ethos is the other—the responsibility side—of the coin. Journalists don't *have* ethics; journalists *are* ethics in motion. This is so because during war all of the highest values of their people are on the line. Life itself becomes an endangered species and the nation's storytellers must take this central truth of warfare into account as they write their reports. This is the one existential fact that any thinking person has a tendency to forget. As Tim O'Brien observed in one of his novels, "The problem with remembering is you can't forget." In other words, remembering both objective facts as well as subjective experiences of soldiers and those who cover wars is uncomfortable—to put it mildly.

Whenever the military imposes extreme measures on the press, the fourth estate responds by honing its evasionary skills. To the war reporter, extreme measures indicate the censor is being unreasonable. In the absence of common sense, the reporter feels justified in assuming the right and even the duty to get around the brass. As far as the journalist is concerned, the American public is his highest authority.

In all its varying appearances in this book censorship is a social tool used when the country is at war. At one level, censorship rules establish the zones in which both soldier and reporter are able to do their work, creating expectations and regulating the behaviors of all concerned. At a second level, censorship rules guarantee the continuance of "We, the people," insofar as they protect information of use to enemy combatants.

Soldiers are always the first casualty in wartime. To say that truth is the first casualty oversimplifies the process and progress of fighting for one's people and reporting on the fighting. It minimizes the sacrifice of the soldiers who give their life and it caricatures all wartime endeavors.

Military-press relations are symbiotic. The American public seems to believe that the press and the military have an adversarial relationship. I got a good first-hand look at this relationship when I attended a war correspondents' convention in Washington, D.C. There I realized how difficult it was to tell soldiers from correspondents. They both dressed and talked alike.

Hence it is more accurate to see them as dancers rather than adversaries. It is more accurate to see this relationship not only as a dance, but as a tango—the most strategic dance of all. There is a constant give and take. There are a few backbends and long strides across the floor—all while holding a strictly averted gaze. Inconsistencies, dissembling, prevarication, or rhetorical recklessness are missteps that lead to foul-ups.

Being an embodied ethos calls for critical intelligence. Hence reporters describe their experiences in wartime by using tropic arrangements. Each trope implies a particular politics. Irony is sympathetic to its subject, whereas sarcasm is not. The irony I found in Vietnam was directed to dissembling military officials. There was in Vietnam a certain sarcastic ring to some reporters' observations. The irony found in World War I was the identification of certain facts and predicaments beyond the soldier's control and the sense of empathy a reporter felt for the soldier's plight. (In Vietnam there was little empathy for soldiers ranking above second lieutenant.) Romance is the flavor of revolutionary politics. Common sense invariably points to the possibility of instant and massive annihilation. Under those circumstances, everyone agrees on the importance of being realistic. When half the world could go up in smoke, survival depends on being realistic.

One of the most reassuring aspects about war correspondence is this presence of the tropic dimension in a report, a journal entry, or a letter home. It indicates the reporter is fully engaged, using his critical faculties. Tropes suggest the best kind of work is being done.

Being a reporter involves taking events in the order of reality and arranging them into events in the order of a story. In other words, the journalist makes choices about meaning. He tells readers or viewers how events are related to one another. In the order of existential reality there is no ending. In the order of a story, there is. And, very often, the ending of the story is followed by predictions of what will happen, what the future will be. It is no exaggeration to conclude that the journalist is a contemporary shaman: the person whose work is to tell us about the powers that be.

Not everyone who reports a war is a true journalist. Philosophically every real reporter—and especially every real war reporter—juggles the requirements of the immanent world with those of the transcendent one. When I say a reporter is "real," I mean he simultaneously inhabits this world (the battlefield, the rear areas) and the transcendent world (his occupational ethic, the constitutional roots of his work). The immanent world may feel episodic, but the transcendent world is beyond the reach of individuals to change.

Over the years from 1898 to 1975, sex roles changed dramatically. Early on, women were thought best suited for covering women's work, for example, the Red Cross. By World War II they insisted on covering combat, although the military continued to resist. Martha Gellhorn asked to go to sea with a submarine crew, and she was allowed to do so. At least she was under water! In Vietnam something important happened. Not only did women begin reporting alongside soldiers, but they also made important contributions to the content of reports. Martha Gellhorn wrote about the effects of the war on soldiers and civilians. Likewise, Gloria Emerson thought that the story of war was not military brass or weaponry but rather what happened to the civilians bearing the brunt of the war. Thus, women (with one or two exceptions) did not treat war as "spectacle."

Besides the different configurations regarding sex roles in both fighting and reporting wars, postmodern warfare includes a central trait to this new era: undecidability, a trait central to postmodernism. Are we winning or are we losing? Does this military approach work or does it not? Did the enemy win in the Tet offensive or did we? This trait characterized the military, the press, and the politicians.

The range of the wars studied in this book differ in battlefield terrain, type of front lines, type of armor and ordnance, and in the degree of military training. But these conditions of warfare make it almost impossible to compare with the current wars in Iraq and Afghanistan. If anything this book has indicated the drawbacks of understanding present wars as if modeled on previous ones.

Besides training, terrain plays a central part in both fighting and reporting the wars. The trophy will always go to those who use the terrain to their advantage. In Vietnam the terrain really belonged to the Vietnamese. In Iraq, the desert is flat and sandy, making it a mobile war. In Afghanistan, Americans have superior firepower that in some cases allows soldiers sitting at computers in the United States to direct the Predator drones to their targets thousands of miles away. Computers were used in Vietnam, but not for point-to-point communication. (At that time, computers were in the "horse and buggy" stage of development.)

Long gone are the days of requiring journalists to bring a small set of supplies. In World War I, the list posted in press headquarters counted seven or eight items. Today's war correspondent has over 170 items to bring along, including a portable satellite phone.

Besides different terrain, supplies, and communications channels, there is always the human element in war. This is as true in today's wars as it was in the wars of the past. Both the military and the press make mistakes. But it is a serious error in judgment to dissemble to one's own people, as military officers of high rank did in Vietnam. Dissembling is good for the enemy, but not for America. For their part, reporters have a constitutional duty to report facts that do not compromise troop safety. From the early days on in Vietnam, the military played down bad news or withheld it altogether. The thing is, eventually the news is going to get out. Dissembling only makes working conditions for both the military and the press more difficult than it has to be.

However, the military were not the only ones making mistakes in Vietnam. Many reporters seemed unaware of how the interlocking parts of the military system worked. Casualties were announced by military authorities in Washington, D.C., but some correspondents attributed that to dissembling. Some of it was; but not all of it.

Reporters on the whole also failed to put casualties and loss of ordnance into a context that would help their countrymen reach a more accurate understanding of the state of affairs in Vietnam. Whether dissembling or the failure to contextualize losses is the case in the wars in Iraq and Afghanistan remains to be seen. At this writing it is difficult to get any reporting on either war, much less good reporting. The exception is Richard Engel of NBC, whose work is thorough, timely, and contextualized.

Furthermore, it helped neither the military nor the press that many adventure seekers got into Vietnam (a recurring problem with small wars). Some were bogus journalists working for nonexistent news organizations. The potential for adventure seekers was anticipated in Cuba and the Expedition into Mexico. In Vietnam, however, it was only after the fact that the military realized that con artists were passing themselves off as journalists.

Once the illegitimate claimants were weeded out and relieved of their accreditation papers, there were other problems to solve. Legitimate reporters tried to make money on the black market. Some tried to set up exclusive concessions for profit, for example, dress concessions.

Certainly, the public raised questions about the Saigon press corps, but reporters did not write about the mistakes they were making. And the military continued to play down their own errors.

I have tried to make sense of a wide range of experiences found in letters, diaries, journals, and reports. In truth the experience of war is a tangled mess. However, we can say a few things about it.

War is experienced as episodic. Hurried activity is followed by long stretches of waiting for something to happen. Once a battle begins, the reporter's horizon shrinks to the pinpoints of his senses. It is only later, during debriefing, that the pattern of the existential instances starts to emerge. The pattern is not a fixed one, nor will it ever be. It is in the nature of experience to be ambiguous. Perhaps it is better to say experience is multidimensional.

I also found several repeated patterns in the letters, diaries, and reports of journalists. I sorted them according to their tropic dimensions. Once the dominant trope is figured out, it becomes a matter of figuring out why one trope was clearly preferred over another.

In the Spanish-Cuban-American War the trope was romance whose politics is revolution. Americans in that war believed that helping Cuba would rid the island country of the Spanish occupation forces, allowing Cubans to gain control of their own destiny.

When the doughboys landed on the European continent in World War I, there was a resurgence of romance. Popular songs rang with the fervor of those who were about to be heroes. Again, it was a matter of liberating a nation from enemy occupation and assimilation.

By World War II, the stakes had become very high in terms of loss of life. The sheer scale of the war was astonishing. Both the East and the West were engaged in the fighting. And the progressing development of military weapons made annihilation a distinct possibility. Realism and common sense became the standards to use in decision making.

Vietnam was tragic. The world had by that time moved into the postmodern era. No one really understood that America's economy had made a fundamental change from one led by the manufacturing sector to one led by the information and services sector. War itself seemed to lose the "grand spectacle" trait. Although the military later used words like "shock and awe" to describe their methods in the Persian Gulf, many reporters, mostly women, had already begun in Vietnam to deconstruct that picture and put in its stead a picture of the effects of war on civilians.

Unless we return to worldwide wars, postmodern wars like those in Iraq and Afghanistan will not be reported as if they were scripted in Hollywood. Instead the focus of the camera will be on the consequences, human and financial, that all wars have.

Finally, a word about the working scribe. I tried to paint a good picture of the journalist—he is, indeed, our shaman. He tells us what is happening in the nation. In war, when the nation's existence is on the line, it is the journalist who keeps us apprised of events in the fighting arenas—or "theaters" as they are euphemistically called. He sizes up events and then writes about them so the rest of the country's citizens can know what is happening to their people. It is no exaggeration to say the American war correspondent is the walking advertisement for our nation-state.

FURTHER READING

A large body of material has been written about American war correspondence. W. Joseph Campbell's *The Year That Defined American Journalism* identifies 1897 as a defining time in American history. He gives Harry Scovel his due as the prototype of the modern journalist. Charles Brown's *The Correspondent's War* is an important source for material on the War in Cuba. *The Splendid Little War* by Frank Freidel about the same war is not a reliable piece. But it is useful for tapping into the spirit of the times in the sense that it is a celebratory text. James Landers's *The Weekly War: Newsmagazines and Vietnam* is a thorough account of its subject matter. Gary C. Tallman's and Joseph P. McKerns's monograph "Press Mess" documents the Buddhist crisis through the eyes of David Halberstam. Another book on Vietnam is William Prochnau's *Once Upon a Distant War*. Daniel Hallin's book *The Uncensored War: The Media and Vietnam* is a much cited sociological study of that war. Another excellent work is William Hammond's *Reporting Vietnam: Media and Military at War*. It corrects a lot of misinformation on the part of both the military and the press.

One of the oldest and finest works on war reporting was Joseph Mathews's *Reporting the Wars*. Nothing I subsequently found in archival records undercut his book. Probably the most popular book on war correspondents is Phillip Knightley's *The First Casualty*. However, in trying to cover so much material, this book is sketchy and given to exaggeration. Michael Sweeney wrote about the period from World War I to the wars in Afghanistan and Iraq in *The Military and the Press*. But this book collects facts rather than demonstrates his claims.

Two very well-researched books are Jeffrey Smith's *War and Press Freedom* and John Byrne Cooke's *Reporting the War*. The latter's approach examines the ways the press has satisfied its constitutional responsibility.

Many books and articles, too numerous to mention, discuss propaganda in the United States during wartime. Among those I consulted were Garth Jowett's *Propaganda and Persuasion* and J. Michael Sproule's

Propaganda and Democracy. Another source, especially for the student of the subject is Lawrence Doob's "Propaganda," found in the *International Encyclopedia of Communication*.

For readings on communications, including the history of journalism, see Gerald Baldasty, *The Commercialization of the News in the Nineteenth Century*; Michael Emery, Edwin Emery, and Nancy Roberts, *The Press in America: An Interpretive History*; Michael Schudson, *Discovering the News: A Social History of American Newspapers*; John Nerone, *The Culture of the Press in the Early Republic*; and Kevin G. Barnhurst and John Nerone, *The Form of the News*.

NOTES

Introduction

1. See "Pros and cons of embedded journalism," www.pbs.org/newshour/extra/features/jan-june03/embed_3-27html.

2. I use the term "he" for stylistic simplicity. I found women reporters in all the wars I studied. In today's world social science has reached a point where the terms "male" and "female" no longer necessarily refer to biological genders. These terms are now thought of as social categories, that is, social scientists currently see these terms on a continuum, rather than seeing them strictly as gendered. An example: Dickey Chapelle from the beginning of her career in World War II did not want to write from the "women's perspective." She saw herself as a journalist, not as a woman journalist.

3. "Bracketing" is a specialized term found in philosophy and literary studies. Here it means noticing when a journalist seems to be in a sacramental state and asking why he is experiencing this.

4. I was influenced in doing so by the work of Annabel Patterson.

5. Newton, *Narrative Ethics*, 3–69.

6. See Carey, *Communications as Culture*, 13–36. See also Munson and Warren, *James Carey*, especially "Afterward: The Culture in Question," 308–39.

7. See my account of these three approaches to communications studies in Mander, *Framing Friction*, 1–27.

8. Geertz, *Interpretation of Cultures*, 45.

Chapter 1: The Historical Context for Understanding American War Correspondents

1. Kersh, *Dreams of a More Perfect Union*, 15.

2. Ibid., 17.

3. Ibid.

4. There are several good histories of journalism: see my suggestions in Further Reading.

5. See Habermas, *The Structural Formation of the Public Sphere*.

6. Kersh, *Dreams of a More Perfect Union*, 17.

7. See ibid., 1.

8. Dr. David Ramsey, an officer in the Continental Army, *An Oration on the Advantages of American Independence*. Charleston, SC, 1778, p. 18. Quoted in Breen, *The Marketplace of Revolution*, xi–xviii, 1–29. Breen's argument is that

the colonists' shared experiences as consumers in an imperial economy gave them the resources needed to develop a radical strategy of political protest: the first consumer boycott.

9. Quoted in Breen, *The Marketplace of Revolution*, 4.

10. Kersh, *Dreams of a More Perfect Union*, 4.

11. Ibid., 17.

12. Ibid., 168. In comparison, Frederick Douglass argued from a different vantage point. He believed that the destiny of blacks was one united to America, and was based on mutual relationship and equality. See 160ff.

13. John Dewey's seminal work *Experience and Nature* argues that all things exist in communication; see 166–207.

14. Anderson, *Imagined Communities*, 7.

15. Military journalists appear as early as World War I, of course. In this context I am referring to Vietnam and television journalism.

16. Kersh, *Dreams of a More Perfect Union*, 143–45.

17. Ibid.

18. The American experience is based, at least partly, on having been a set of colonies. For insight into an anticolonial state, such as Vietnam, see the analysis of Merlin, "The Socioeconomic Background and War Mortality During Vietnam's Wars."

19. Unseem, "Conscription and Class," 28. Three hundred thousand men were called up to serve in the first draft call in 1863. Of that number 9 percent hired substitutes; 18 percent paid the three-hundred-dollar fee; and 70 percent used medical and other exemptions.

20. Ibid., 29. Cf. Segal, "How Equal Is Equity?" and Fligstein, "Who Served in the Military, 1940–1973." Thirty percent of the armed forces in Vietnam were conscripts.

21. For an explanation of "ethos," see definition 2 in the *Oxford Dictionary of the Social Sciences*. Available at http://www.oxfordreference.com/pub/views/home.html (accessed April 21, 2008).

22. See the collection of essays edited by Boemeke, Chickering, and Forster, *Anticipating Total War*.

23. Of course, the limits of warfare were an enormous part of the experience of Europeans in World War I where military leadership cut itself off from the soldiers in trenches. The American experience of World War I was not that of Europeans. Americans engaged in open-movement warfare almost immediately upon arriving in the zone of the armies.

24. Boemeke, Chickering, and Forster, *Anticipating Total War*.

25. Koistinen, *Planning War, Pursuing Peace*, 67–68.

26. Ibid., 67. This building drive went hand in hand with industrial smelting, as the Bethlehem Iron Company made good ordnance.

27. Ibid., 68–69.

28. Ibid., 71–73.

29. Examples of publications include the *Journal of the Military Service Institution of the United States*, the *Cavalry Journal*, and the *Infantry Journal*.

30. Koistinen, *Planning War, Pursuing Peace*, 72–73.

31. An exception to this state of affairs was the period when Henry Stimson served as U.S. Secretary of War and Major General Leonard Wood was Army Chief of Staff.

32. Koistinen, *Planning War, Pursuing Peace,* 74–75.

33. See F. J. Turner's classic essay on the significance of the frontier in American history in *History, Frontier, and Section.*

34. Koistinen, *Planning War, Pursuing Peace,* 58. See also my article on radio: "Utopian Elements in the Discourse on Broadcasting," *Journal of Communication Inquiry* 12:2 (Summer 1988), 71–88.

35. See Higham's essay, "The Redefinition of America in the Twentieth Century," 301–26.

36. There were intellectuals before the twentieth century, but men like Thomas Jefferson did not perceive themselves as a distinct social class.

37. Higham, "The Redefinition of America in the Twentieth Century," 312, 314.

38. Ibid., 316. Some historians have proposed seeing the early twentieth century in American history as a period of "finance capitalism," i.e., an economy dominated by banking. Another view argues it was a period of "corporate capitalism." These two labels are not interchangeable. See Koistinen, *Planning War, Pursuing Peace,* 64–65.

Chapter 2: Early Encoding of State-Administered Censorship During Wartime

1. For the Union's public communications strategies during the Civil War, see Blondheim's examination in "'Public Sentiment Is Everything.'" This article examines Abraham Lincoln's policies and practices concerning communications. For Blondheim's comments on Civil War correspondents, see paragraph 23 where he says, "Technically . . . reporters with the armies were camp followers subject to military law as exercised by the officers whose activities they were reporting."

2. Squires, "Experience of a War Censor," 425–32.

3. General Orders, Headquarters of the Army, Adjutant General's Office, Washington, DC, April 23, 1898 (printed date was April 30, 1898). Adjutant General Documents File 75898, National Archives, Washington, DC. Hereafter the Adjutant General's Document File, which is a different collection than the Adjutant General's records, will be abbreviated AGDF. The Adjutant General records' collection will be designated as AGO.

4. Letter from the Adjutant General to Major General Shafter, June 7, 1898, in AGDF 90131, Box 658. Some newspapers solved access problems by having soldiers write letters for publication. See letter to Commanding Officer, August 15, 1898, and letter from R. M. Stribbe to Russell A. Alger, Secretary of War, July 29, 1898, both in AGDF 1113583m, Box 789. During the Filipino uprising and the wars against Mexico in the early part of the twentieth century, military regulations explicitly barred soldiers from writing anything for publication in media.

5. General Orders, Headquarters of the Army, Adjutant General's Office, Washington, DC, April 23, 1898 (printed date was April 30, 1898), in AGDF 75898.

6. Unsigned cablegram from the War Department [?] to General Elwell Stephen Otis, June 29, 1899, in AGDF 245396, Box 1592.

7. Cablegram from General Otis to the Adjutant General, July 1, 1899, in AGDF 245396, Box 1592.

8. News clipping from the *Washington Times,* July 18, 1899, in AGDF 245396, Box 1592.

9. Cablegram from General Otis to the Adjutant General, July 20, 1890, in AGDF 245396, Box 1592.

10. Ibid.

11. Cablegram from General Otis to the Adjutant General, 21 July 1899, in AGDF 245396, Box 1592.

12. General Orders, Headquarters of the Army, Adjutant General's Office, August 1899, in AGDF 277240, Box 1854, p. 1.

13. Ibid.

14. Cablegram from the Secretary of War to General Otis, September 9, 1899, in AGDF 245396, Box 1592.

15. Cablegram from Secretary of War to General Otis, January 20, 1900; see also cablegram from Otis to the Adjutant General, January 21, 1900; both cables in AGDF 245396, Box 1592.

16. Letter from the Secretary of War to the Secretary of State, April 7, 1900, in AGDF 245396, Box 1592.

17. Memo from the Associated Press correspondent in Manila to the AP's main office in New York, October 19, 1900; see also the Adjutant General's cable to General MacArthur, October 19, 1900; for related material see cables from the Adjutant General to General MacArthur, November 1, 1900, and March 19, 1901; all cables are in AGDF 245396, Box 1592.

18. Regulations Concerning Correspondents with the United States Army in the Field, issued by the War Department, April 24, 1914, in AGDF 2152565 fw 2151000m, Box 7483.

19. Ibid., p. 1.

20. Ibid.

21. Confidential Memorandum for the Press, May 21, 1914, in AGDF 2152565 fw 2151000m, Box 7483.

22. Confidential Memorandum for the Press, May 21, 1914; and Memorandum for the Adjutant General and Chief of Staff, May 16, 1914; both found in AGDF 2152565 fw 2151000m, Box 7483.

23. See the letter from Henry Breckenridge, Acting Secretary of War, to the INS News Bureau, May 22, 1914, in AGDF 2152565 fw 2151000m, Box 7483.

24. Ibid., p. 2.

25. Ibid., p. 3

26. Ibid., p. 4.

27. See letter from R. T. Farrelly to Brigadier General George Andrews (the Adjutant General), April 23, 1914, in AGDF 2151752 fw 2151000, Box 7482.

28. Cable from General Frederick Funston to AGWAR, April 23, 1914, in AGDF 2151752 fw 2151000, Box 7482.

29. Not all news representatives were reporters. The *Chicago Tribune,* for example, distributed its editions daily to soldiers and sailors at Vera Cruz free of charge. The paper asked for and received permission to send a circulation manager to Mexico. See letter from J. C. O'Laughlin to Captain Frank McCoy, April 28, 1914, and letter from Adjutant General George Andrews, to J. C. O'Laughlin, April 30, 1914; both in AGDF 2155177 fw 2151000, Box 7483.

30. Telegram from James A. Scrymser to Adjutant General George Andrews,

May 1, 1914; see also Scrymser's letter to Secretary of War Lindley Garrison, April 27, 1914; both in AGDF 2155106 fw 2151000, Box 7483.

31. Besides those recounted in the text that follows, another incident concerned Fred Boalt who worked for the Newspaper Enterprise Association (NEA). He was disaccredited in July 1914 because of a report in member papers on the questionable conduct of naval officers. A court of inquiry held a hearing on the matter. The report described an incident in which officers subjected prisoners to the rule of flight: prisoners were allowed to run away and if they reached the corner of a building without being shot, they were allowed to go free. The court of inquiry found that the charges in the reporter's dispatch were not true. Secretary of War Garrison characterized the reporter's conduct as "reckless and wanton." See Garrison's statement July 30, 1914, in AGDF 2160640 fs 2151000; see also the cable from General Funston to AGWAR in July 17, 1914, in AGDF 2184608 fw 2151000; letter to Chief of Staff, War Department, July 10, 1914, and letter from the NEA to the President of the United States, July 15, 1914; letter from J. F. Turnulty (Secretary to the President) to Lindley Garrison, Secretary of War, labeled personal, July 16, 1914; and letter from Garrison to J. R. Turnulty, July 16, 1914. All in AGDF 2184608 fw 2151000. Despite the findings of the inquiry, Boalt's story rings true to me, given what I know about the conduct of men in wartime.

32. Cable from General Funston to AGO, May 25, 1914; see also cable from Funston to the Adjutant General, May 19, 1914; both in AGDF 2168498 fw 2151000.

33. See cable from Lindley Garrison to C. S. Albert, Washington bureau of the *World,* May 29, 1914; in AGDF 2168498 fw 2151000.

34. Cable from Garrison to C. S. Albert, May 27, 1914, in AGDF 2168498 fw 2151000.

35. Confidential cables from Garrison to General Funston, May 28, 1914, and May 29, 1914, in AGDF 2168498 fw 2151000.

36. See letters from Garrison to C. S. Albert, May 29, 1914, and to Charles M. Lincoln, the *World*'s editor in New York, May 29, 1914, in AGDF 2168498 fw 2151000.

37. Cable from General Funston to AGO, 25 May 1914, in AGDF 2168498 fw 2151000.

38. By "fictions," I do not mean lies; I mean stories we tell ourselves in order to live meaningfully.

39. Letter from Edgar Sisson to Lindley Garrison, April 25, 1914, in AGDF 2151629 fw 2151000, Box 7483.

40. See letter from Lindley Garrison to the editor of *Collier's,* May 15, 1914, in AGDF, 2151629 fw 2151000, Box 7483.

41. Letter from Mark Sullivan to Lindley Garrison, May 16, 1914, in AGDF, 2151629 fw 2151000, Box 7483.

42. See memoranda from Lindley Garrison to General Wood, May 19, 1914, and from Wood to Garrison, May 19, 1914, in AGDF, 2151629 fw 2151000, Box 7483.

43. Letter from Newton D. Baker to General Frederick Funston, July 1, 1916, in AGDF 2424348 fw 2378010, Box 8140.

44. Telegram signed I. Kelly to the Honorable Newton D. Baker, March 13, 1916, in AGDF 2378926 fw 2378010, Box 8140.

45. Telegram from H. B. Brougham to the Secretary of War, June 24, 1916, in AGDF 2419217 fw 2378010, Box 8140.

46. For an analysis of the language of utopia as one of perfect equilibrium, see my article, "Utopian Elements," on broadcasting in the first half of the twentieth century.

47. Memo from the Judge Advocate General to the Adjutant General, March 25, 1916; see also memo from the Adjutant General to the Judge Advocate General, March 20, 1916; both in AGDF 2419217 fw 2378010, Box 8140.

48. Memorandum for the Chief of Staff, Subject: Censorship on the Mexican Border, from W. W. Macomb, Brigadier General, Chief of War College Division, April 6, 1916, in AGDF 2419217 fw 2378010, Box 8140.

49. Letter from the Adjutant General's Office to C. H. Rogerman, April 3, 1916, in AGDF 2378010, Box 8140.

50. There were exceptions to this general attitude. General Funston, for instance, telegrammed the adjutant general that he considered photographs less harmful to the success of military goals than newspaper correspondents. See telegram dated March 17, 1916, in AGDF 2377883 fw 2378010, Box 8140.

51. For the correspondence regarding motion pictures and photographers, see Arthur Henney to Newton D. Baker, March 15, 1916; Arthur Henney to Major General Hugh L. Scott, March 12, 1916; memo from Newton D. Baker to War Department, March 16, 1916; memo from Major General Scott to the Secretary of War, April 11, 1916; all in AGDF 23 80239 fw 2378010, Box 8140.

52. See memoranda from Major General W. W. Wotherspoon to Adjutant General Andrews, May 2, 1914, in AGDF 2158871 fw 2151000, Box 7483.

53. Memorandum from the Adjutant General to Commanding General, Southern Department, March 22, 1916. To secure this permission, Underwood and Underwood asked each paper using its service to send a telegram of request to the secretary of war. All materials found in AGDF 2377883 fw 2378010, Box 8140.

54. Telegram from General Funston to the Adjutant General in AGDF 2377883 fw 2378010, Box 8140.

55. Letter from Underwood and Underwood's News Photo Service to Newton D. Baker, May 22, 1916, in AGDF, 2377883 fw 2378010, Box 8140.

56. Ibid.

57. Memorandum for the Chief of Staff, Subject: Censorship on the Mexican Border, from W. W. Macomb, Brigadier General, Chief of War College Division, April 6, 1916, in AGDF 2419217 fw 2378010, Box 8140.

58. Memorandum from Brigadier General W. W. Macomb, Chief of the War College Division, to the Army Chief of Staff re: Censorship on the Mexican Border, April 6, 1916, in AGDF 2378926 fw 2378010, Box 8140.

59. Telegram from Clair Kenamore to the Honorable Newton D. Baker, March 20, 1916, in AGDF 2379524 fw 2378010, Box 8140.

60. See telegram from Randolph Marshall, news editor of the *New York Herald*, March 15, 1916; letter from Arthur Henning (Washington Correspondent for the *Chicago Tribune*), March 12, 1916; both in AGDF 2378159 fw 2378010, Box 8140.

61. Randolph Marshall telegram, ibid.

62. Letter from S. T. Hughes to Newton D. Baker, March 16, 1916, in AGDF 2380998 fw 2378010, Box 8140.

63. See the discussion that follows in chapter 3.

Chapter 3: Censorship During the World Wars

1. Mathews, *Reporting the Wars*, 160.
2. Davis, *With the Allies*, 12.
3. Ibid., 11.
4. Ibid., 13.
5. Ibid., 14–16. See also Wythe Williams, *Passed by the Censor*, 120–21, who recounts being imprisoned in the Cherche Midi when caught by the French. He and four others were released on condition they not write anything about their trip for eight days. This restriction included private letters, as well as dispatches meant for publication.
6. Davis, *With the Allies*, 50–52.
7. Letter from Richard Harding Davis to his wife, August 31, 1914; see also C. B. Davis, *Adventures and Letters*, 371.
8. Dunn, *Five Fronts*, 29.
9. Ibid., 28–30.
10. Crozier, *American Reporters on the Western Front*, 97, 99, 103.
11. Ruhl, *Antwerp to Gallipoli*, 128–29.
12. Dunn, *Five Fronts*, 69–70.
13. Crozier, *American Reporters on the Western Front*, 97–98.
14. W. Williams, *Passed by the Censor*, 122.
15. Ibid., 187.
16. Ibid., 245.
17. Ruhl, *Antwerp to Gallipoli*, 128.
18. Dunn, *Five Fronts*, 169–70.
19. Letter from Herbert Corey to Stanley Buckmaster, October 27, 1914. Corey quotes parts of Buckmaster's letter to him in his own response. The letter from Buckmaster is not in the manuscript collection. See Herbert Corey Papers.
20. See Balakian, *Literary Origins of Surrealism*, 7. See especially Paul Fussell's work.
21. Bean, "The Accuracy of the Creel Committee News," *Journalism Quarter*, 263. Bean's article is a defense against charges that Creel's committee was a propaganda agency. See also Mock, *Censorship 1917*, 48.
22. Wiebe, *The Search for Order*.
23. Bean, "The Accuracy of the Creel Committee News," 272, 263.
24. Ibid., 265–66.
25. Ibid., 270.
26. Crozier, *American Reporters on the Western Front*, 123.
27. Memorandum from John J. Pershing to Chief of Staff, War Department, May 23, 1917, AGDF 2605299 fw 2533202, Box 8770.
28. Letter from John J. Pershing to C. H. Dennis, May 23, 1917, AGDF 2623912 fw 2533202, Box 8770.
29. See memorandum from Major General Bliss to Adjutant General, May 23, 1917, AGDF 2623912 fw 2533202, Box 8770.
30. Cable from Pershing to the Adjutant General, June 18, 1917; see also cable from McCain to Pershing, n.d. [June 1917]; both in AGDF 2630931, Box 9056.
31. Cable from Pershing to the Adjutant General, June 9, 1917, AGDF 2630931, Box 9056; see also Pershing cable to Adjutant General June 14, 1917, AGDF

2605299 fw 2533202, Box 8770; for other memoranda regarding Palmer, see Pershing to Adjutant General, June 22, 1917, AGDF 2627204 fw 2533202; and the memos from Newton D. Baker, June 23, 1917, AGDF 2533202, Box 8770.

32. Cable from Pershing to the Adjutant General, June 26, 1917, AGDF 2627204 fw 2533202, Box 8770.

33. See memoranda from Acting Chief of Staff to Adjutant General, June 19, 1917, and from McCain to Pershing, June 20, 1917, AGDF 2627204 fw 2533202, Box 8770.

34. For sample letters, see John Wheeler to Newton D. Baker, May 19, 1917, AGDF 2604193 fw 2533202, Box 8770; Charles D. Albert to Adjutant General, May 23, 1917, AGDF 2604751, Box 8997; O. K. Bovard to Newton D. Baker, May 24, 1917, AGDF 2607724 fw 25332021; Mary Roberts Rinehart to Newton D. Baker, June 2, 1917, AGDF 2618207, Box 9028; Adjutant General to M. R. Rinehart, June 14, 1917, AGDF 2618207, Box 9028; memo from Adjutant General to the Commanding Officer, Madison Barracks, June 14, 1917, AGDF 2618207, Box 9029; Lucian Wheeler to President Wilson, May 5, 1917, AGDF 2599507 fw 2533202, Box 8770.

35. Douglas MacArthur to Adjutant General April 16, 1917, AGDF 2570114 fw 2533202, Box 8770; see also Adjutant General to Chief of Staff, April 13, 1917, and to F. W. Brooker, May 2, 1917, AGDF 2570114 fw 2533202, Box 8770; Frederick W. Brooker to War Department, April 24, 1917, AGDF 2584587 fw 2533202, Box 8770. Brooker was writing on behalf of the newly formed Cinema War News Syndicate.

36. See the flow chart on the organization and distribution of duties for the Intelligence Section, AEF G-2-d 222 6111.

37. See, for example, phone message, January 12, 1918; Urgent memo for the First Army, January 18, 1918; both in AEF GHQ G-2-d E #221, Box 6124.

38. See memo from the Chief of Intelligence Section to the Chief of Staff, October 17, 1917, AEF GHQ G-2-d 221, Box 6127; memorandum to the Chief of Intelligence from Frederick Palmer, Chief of Press Division, AEF GHQ G-2-d 221, Box 6124; memorandum from Frank Page to Lieutenant Colonel Nolan, December 17, 1917, AEF GHQ G-2-d 221, Box 6122, envelope "Magazine-Misc."; see also telephone message concerning coordination with Allies, January 12, 1918, AEF GHQ G-2-d 221, Box 6124.

39. Memorandum for Lieutenant Colonel Nolan, November 15, 1917, AEF GHQ G-2-d Box 6122.

40. Ibid.

41. Unsigned memo to Lieutenant Colonel Nolan, December 24, 1917, AEF GHQ G-2-d Box 6122.

42. Bean, "The Accuracy of the Creel Committee News," 270.

43. Crozier, *American Reporters on the Western Front*, 123.

44. Ibid., 126.

45. Ibid., 213, 159.

46. Larson, "Censorship of Army News during the World War," 319–20. Larson's article is a good summary of the evolution of censorship during the war.

47. General Headquarters, AEF General Order No. 96, Paragraph 1. Quoted in Larson, "Censorship of Army News During the World War," 321.

48. See memorandum for Lt. Col. Nolan, November 15, 1917 AEF GHQ G-2-d, Box 6122.

49. Letter to Frederick Palmer, November 1, 1917, AEF GHQ G-2-d E #222, Box 6111.

50. Memorandum from Francis Wiekes to Lieutenant Watson, January 2, 1918, AEF GHQ G-2-d E #222, Box 6110. See also an earlier unsigned memorandum to Lieutenant Colonel Nolan, November 21, 1917, AEF GHQ G-2-d E #222, Box 6110.

51. Doob, "Propaganda."

52. Letter from Caspar Whitney to Colonel Sweeney, May 29, 1918, AEF GHQ G-2-d E #222, Box 6110.

53. See letter from Lieutenant Colonel Sweeney to Caspar Whitney, May 31, 1918, RG120, AEF GHQ G-2-d E #222, Box 6110.

54. Letter from Caspar Whitney to Lt. Col. Sweeney, June 5, 1918, AEF GHQ G-2-d E #222, Box 6110.

55. Crozier, *American Reporters on the Western Front*, 183.

56. Ibid., 192.

57. Larson, "Censorship of Army News During the World War," 321.

58. Letter from Herbert Corey to his mother, November 21, 1917. Herbert Corey Papers.

59. Ibid.

60. Crozier, *American Reporters on the Western Front*, 183, 192. For other examples, see the telegram to Colonel E. R. McCabe, Censeur Americaine, Neufchateau, [May or June] 1918, signed by Thomas Johnson (*New York Sun*), Herbert Corey and Lincoln Eyre (*New York World*), James P. Howe (AP), Don Martin (*New York Herald*), N. C. Parke (INS), Junius B. Wood (*Chicago Daily News*), Fred Ferguson and Frank Taylor (UP), J. R. Grove (NEA), George Seldes (Marshall Syndicate), and Edwin L. James (*New York Times*), in Herbert Corey Papers. See also Petition to Gerald Morgan, Acting Press Officer, February 21, 1918, in Crozier, *American Reporters on the Western Front*, 197; and letters from Corey to Captain Morgan, June 30, 1918, to Major Bulger, July 30, 1918, to Lieutenant Arthur Delany, Press Section Bureau, August 27, 1918. All in Herbert Corey Papers.

61. Crozier, *American Reporters on the Western Front*, 192.

62. Price, "Governmental Censorship in Wartime," 84 ff; see also letter from Price to Sam Rayburn, Speaker of the House, January 1943, in Byron Price Papers.

63. Byron Price to Sam Rayburn, in Byron Price Papers.

64. Letter of Commendation, December 14, 1918, in Byron Price Papers.

65. Memo from Byron Price to News Editor and Bureau Chiefs, October 22, 1937, in Byron Price Papers.

66. Letter from Herbert Hoover to Byron Price, December 19, 1941, in Byron Price Papers

67. Price, *Notebooks*, 3.5, p. 173; in Byron Price Papers.

68. Ibid., p. 157; for other skirmishes, see note about letters dated March 3, 1941, in Byron Price Papers.

69. Confidential memo to Stephen Early, from Byron Price, March 18, 1942.

70. Price, *Notebooks*, 3.5, p. 81.

71. See ibid., p. 150, for Price's judgment of his relationship to the military.

72. Confidential letter from Byron Price to Kent Cooper, June 9, 1940.

73. Ibid.

74. Price, notes, in Byron Price Papers.

75. See the Byron Price Papers, Box 1. Secret memoranda from Price to Colonel Carlson and Mr. Wolgemuth, April 14, 1945; registered letter from Price to Augustus Giegengack, April 7, 1945; see also the transcript of Jerry Klutz's column appearing in the *Washington Post,* April 5, 1945.

76. Transcript of remarks of Giegengack introduced into the *Congressional Record,* April 3, 1945, in the Byron Price Papers.

77. Secret memorandum from Byron Price for Colonel Carlson and Mr. Wolgemuth, April 14, 1945.

78. See C. J. Smythe, *History of U.S. Censorship in World War II,* 22; and "Communications: The Fourth Front," 94–95.

79. U.S. Office of Censorship. *Code of Wartime Practices for American Broadcasters.*

80. Ibid.

81. Jones, "The Care and Feeding of Correspondents," 51.

82. Thomson, *Blue Pencil Admiral,* 130.

83. Jones, "The Care and Feeding of Correspondents," 51.

84. Thomson, *Blue Pencil Admiral,* 130.

85. Ibid.

86. E. Pyle to J. Pyle, March 11, 1944; see also February 2, 1945, where he remarks on the "frustrating censorship" in the Pacific. In Ernie Pyle Papers.

87. Ibid.

88. E. Pyle to J. Pyle, March 11, 1944. In Ernie Pyle Papers.

89. Trask, "American Intelligence During the Spanish American War," 25. The army did not have as thorough and extensive a process. Although the War Department founded the Military Information Division in 1898, it did not have the beneficial association with a senior war college to help in its planning. See ibid., 27.

90. "Press vs. the Navy," *Newsweek,* February 23, 1942, p. 56. Eventually the conflict was resolved when the navy changed the release date, pushing it up to a time when both morning and evening papers got an even break.

91. Robert Casey to Paul Scott Mowrer, March 17, 1942. In Robert Casey Papers.

92. Ibid.

93. Letter from Casey to Binder, May 23, 1942. In Robert Casey Papers.

94. Casey to Mowrer, March 17, 1942.

95. Jones, "The Care and Feeding of Correspondents," 48.

96. Ibid.

97. Casey to Mowrer, March 17, 1942; Casey to Binder, May 23, 1942,

98. See Pratt, "How the Censors Rigged the News," 97–105; and Sevareid, "Censors in the Saddle," 415–417.

99. Sevareid, "Censors in the Saddle."

Chapter 4: Censorship in Vietnam

1. On credibility problems regarding the body count, see Hammond, *Reporting Vietnam,* 98–103.

2. Ibid., 119ff.

3. See the Disaccreditation or Suspended Correspondents files at the National Archives in Washington, D.C.

4. See, for example, the file on Stuart Reichstein (story detailed on pages 68–69 following).

5. See memo from Lieutenant Colonel James G. Smith to All United States Military Unit Commanders, South Vietnam, in Box 6, Dickey Chapelle Papers.

6. See application samples in accreditation files, e.g., those of R. H. Mitman. In Disaccreditation and Suspended Correspondents files. Unless otherwise stated, subsequent references to accreditation/disacreditation files are also located here.

7. Ibid.

8. Information Advisory and Accreditation Procedures SOP, RG 472, p. 5.

9. Ibid.

10. Ibid. p. 4.

11. Letter from Captain Paul Ceria to James Bryant, November 13, 1971. The outstanding amount was $118.

12. See General William Westmoreland's letter to Admiral John M. Will, n.d. [1968], and other documents in the Shepard file.

13. See the following correspondence in Reichstein's disacreditation file. Letter from Louis Mohle, publisher of the *Post-Register* to the Office of Information, MACV, December 16, 1968; letter from Mohl to Stewart W. Reichstein, June 27, 1969; letter from Charles Renfroe, Secretary, Saigon Post No. 34 to Office of Information, MACV, December 21, 1969; and letter from Robert W. Nolan, Fleet Reserve Association, to Commanding Officer, JUSPAO Press Mission, January 6, 1972. See also "Memorandum for the Record," May 24, 1972, as well as a news clip on currency manipulation, n.d.

14. See memo from the Secretary of Defense to COMUS MACV, May 1972, in Reichstein's disacreditation file.

15. Stuart W. Reichstein to Colonel Cao-Van-Khank, May 4, 1972. Other correspondence indicated that the American Legion did not have permission to use MPCs. In a related case, see the memo indicating that the American Veterans Association was not exempt from duty. Memo from the Permanent Undersecretary of Finance [GVN] to the Director of the Veterans Association. Memo from MACPM-SIDS to the Chief of Staff [ca. May 1972]. In Reichstein's disacreditation file.

16. For another example of currency manipulation, see the file on Edward Hymof, who solicited funds in MPCs for histories of the military. While the military recognized the value of his work, Hymof was ordered to stop disrespecting the ground rules and procedures.

17. See letter from Colonel L. Gorden Hill, Jr., to Dirk Smit. For similar situations, see the files on Avelino Bobadilla and David Silverman.

18. See Cornelius's accreditation/disacreditation files.

19. See the accreditation file for James Bennet.

20. See memo from Colonel C. A. Stanfield to Commanding General, MACV, July 10, 1971, in Ed Rabel's disacreditation file. See also the individual Witness Statement of Colonel Kenwyn Nelson, who was stationed at the 91st Evacuation Hospital, June 23, 1971; and the statements of Major Joyce W. King, Major Patricia

Stemm, Lieutenant Colonel Maxine Douglas, 1st Lieutenant Henry Grambergu—
each dated June 22, 1971.

21. Ibid.

22. See "Memorandum for the Record," signed by Colonel Walter Franzen, June 27, 1971. Ibid.

23. See the deposition of Colonel Lawrence P. Hansen, July 26, 1971. Ibid.

24. Italics added. See memo from Colonel Robert Bryant to Colonel Leonard, July 16, 1971. Ibid.

25. Letter from Colonel Rodger R. Bankson to Harold Ellithorpe, April 3, 1967. In the Harold Ellithorpe accreditation file.

26. Ibid.

27. Ibid.

28. Quoted in a letter from Col. Robert W. Leonard to Peter Jay, bureau chief for the *Post*, February 1, 1971.

29. Letter from Peter A. Jay to Col. Robert W. Leonard, Chief of Information, MACOI, Feb. 1, 1971. See accreditation/disaccreditation file for Jay.

30. Ibid.

31. See "Findings and Recommendations," September 11, 1972, point 4, in Arthur Highbee's file.

32. See Highbee's statements at the board hearing, Sept. 11, 1972, point 2, ibid.

33. See Memorandum for Colonel Barry from Bryant, April 18, 1972, ibid.

34. See Gary Kennedy's file; CBS refused to give him a letter of introduction. NBC, however, gave him a letter testifying that Kennedy was "of sound mind and character." Letter from Ron Steinman to Whom It May Concern, August 22, 1966. The letter did not indicate that NBC was employing him to cover the war.

35. See Rene Briand's and Gary Kennedy's files. Rene Briand accused the GVN of kicking her out of Vietnam because she refused to sleep with an official. The records of women war reporters generally do not indicate that a problem of this sort existed. However, they may not have made sexual harassment complaints.

36. See the letter from Jack Williams to Office of Information, MACV, October 28, 1968, in William Shipley's file.

37. See the draft of a letter to Jack Williamson, ibid.

38. Memo from Colonel W. M. Crooks, Commander (drafted by B. E. Lodge), to Information Officer, ibid.

39. Letter from Elvin Henson to Colonel Wisnac, June 3, 1968.

40. Memo from A. Cots to MACAG, April 22, 1969.

41. Ibid.

42. Ibid. See pt. 5.

43. Letter from Col. Rodger R. Bankson to Eugene V. Risher, May 26, 1967, in Accreditation files, box 2, Daniel Growald files, for example.

44. Ibid. The two reporters identified as uncooperative were William Hall and Robert Kaylor. Steven Van Meter was fired. See the Memorandum for the Record, signed by Major Aaron C. Harey, n.d. According to military sources, Van Meter acted like a "petulant, spoiled teenager and would have fared much better with his staff had he acted gentlemanly." See the incident report in the *Saigon Daily News*, December 6, 1966. See also R. Growald's description of another incident

in November 1966, and the report by Sergeant Soliday and SP4 Michael Chase. In R. Growald files.

45. See R. Growald files.

46. Letter from Jack Klein to Colonel Robert W. Leonard, February 10, 1970, in the James Bennet accreditation file.

47. See statements by Adrian McCullough, July 18, 1971; John P. Krilevich, July 18, 1971; and Thomas Merwin, July 18, 1971, in Henry Colgate's file.

48. See sworn statement by Sgt. Keith Chambers, in the Colgate file.

49. See the "summary of Statements and Information" related to the MACV Ad Hoc Board, August 9, 1971, written by Henry A. Colgate, Mr. Jack Klein, and Mr. Brent Proctor (Bureau chief of the Overseas Media Corporation), ibid.

50. See the memo "To Whom It May Concern," signed by Terry Reynolds, May 26, 1969, and letter from Edward Hymoff, Director of VMH Publishing Co., to MACV-OI, May 29, 1969, in the Terry Reynolds accreditation file.

51. Memo from Captain Richard Morrison to Colonel William M. Crooks, May 26, 1969, and letter from Colonel L. Gordon Hill, Jr., to Terry Reynolds, July 28, 1969, both in the Terry Reynolds accreditation file.

52. Ibid.

53. See memo on the conduct of correspondents, from Colonel George E. Wear to the Commanding General, TFO, August 29, 1967, in the Schell files.

54. For other similar episodes, see the "Memorandum for Record" from Major Patrick H. Dionne, September 10, 1967, and "Memorandum for Record" from Lieutenant Colonel James S. Conklin, September 1, 1967, ibid.

55. Memo from Captain O. A. Gerner, Jr., to the Commanding General, September 19, 1967, ibid.

56. Memo from Colonel J. R. Meacham to the Chief of Information, MACV, September 27, 1967, ibid.

57. See the memo from Major Dionne, ibid.

58. Letter from Otto Zausmer to Orville Schell, May 2, 1967, ibid.

Chapter 5: The Culture of Press Censorship During Wartime

1. See examples of journalists' strategies in chapter 4.

2. Rea, *Facts and Fakes about Cuba*, 37.

3. Memo from AGWAR to all Theater Commanders, April 2, 1944, Adjutant General's Office records, AG000.73-1, Box 4. Documents cited in subsequent notes can also be found in the Adjutant General's Office records.

4. Memo from ETO, United States Army, to AGWAR, August 10, 1944, AG000.74-2, Box 4.

5. Memo from the PRO to AGWAR, June 29, 1944. See also memos from ETOUSA to AGWAR, August 10, 1944, and from AGWAR to ETOUSA, August 10, 1944. All in RG 4xx, AG000.74-2, Box 4. These records indicate that European operations had assigned to it 208 newspaper correspondents, 48 magazine writers, 18 photographers, and 8 news reel operators.

6. Memo from SHAEF Main to 21 Army Group for G-2, December 22, 1944, AG000.7-1, Box 3.

7. Memo from SHAEF Main, signed Eisenhower, to AGWAR, December 4, 1944, AG000.7-1, Box 3.

8. Remarks in a speech to the Dutch Treat Club, May 1966, Tom Tiede Papers, Box 4.

9. Confidential memorandum to Stephen Early, Press Secretary to the President, from Byron Price, January 20, 1942. In Byron Price Papers.

10. Byron Price, Notebooks, 3.6, p. 175.

11. Ibid., p. 176; see also memorandum dated July 30, 1942. Price's advice to the two networks invokes the competition metaphor: "I asked them to keep their shirts on."

12. Price, Notebooks, 3.4, p. 67–68.

13. See memo from AGWAR to ETOUSA, July 10, 1944, AG000.74-2, Box 4.

14. Memo from ETOUSA to AGWAR, July 10, 1944. See also Annex A, Public Relations Plan "Overlord" and 1, Box 3, memo from SHAEF to 21 Army Group, June 9, 1944, both in AG000.7-1, Box 3.

15. Letter from Richard Harding Davis to his mother, January 15, 1897. Richard Harding Davis Papers.

16. Letter from Richard Harding Davis to his mother, January 19, 1897, ibid.

17. Davis to his mother, January 16, 1897, ibid.

18. The best analysis of the military strategy of the insurgents can be found in Foner, *The Spanish-Cuban-American War.* For an account of the scorched island strategy, see Vol. 1, 212–16.

19. Letter from Frances Scovel to her mother, February 10, 1898. In Sylvester Scovel Papers.

20. "Profile of a PIO." In Tom Tiede Papers, Box 5.

21. "Diary," ms. In the H. L. Mencken Papers, p. 17.

22. Ibid., 36.

23. Letter from Richard Tregaskis to Admiral John S. McCain, September 15, 1968. See also letter from Tregaskis to Peter Thomas (1978), which notes the value basis of any contract for a screenplay he might win. Tregaskis Papers (RT1), Box 28. There are two separate collections of Tregaskis's papers. Hereafter, RT1 will refer to the American Heritage collection and RT2 will refer to the collection in Boston.

24. "Profile of a PIO." In Tom Tiede Papers, Box 5.

25. Rea, *Facts and Fakes about Cuba,* 37.

26. See Brown, *The Correspondents War,* 136, 228. A full account of the censor's duties is given in Squires, "Experience of a War Censor."

27. See Moeller's account of photographers in wartime in *Shooting War,* 47.

28. Carnes, *Jimmy Hare,* 13.

29. See Memo from SHAEF to Manning (Mutual), Maynes (Reuters), McGlincy (UP), Leseur (CBS), Duff (BBC), and Marshall (BBC), September 17, 1944. Letter from Laurance Leseur to Colonel E. C. Boehnke, September 26, 1944. On Manning, see Memo from SHAEF Main to AGWAR, November 29, 1944, and Memo from AGWAR to SHAEF Main, December 12, 1944. The thirty-day suspension was only half of what the PRO recommended for the six reporters. See Memo from PR Division, September 4, 1944. All documents can be found in AG000.74-2, Box 4.

30. See Stone, "The A.P. Fifth Paper," 506.

31. Kennan, Cuban Notebook #1, George Kennan Papers.

32. Letter from Fitzhugh Lee to Anthony Chapelle, April 30, 1945. See also memo from Dickie Chapelle to Captain H. B. Miller, April 14, 1945. In Dickey Chapell Papers.

33. See letter from Dickey Chapelle to the Director of Public Relations, May 19, 1945. In Dickie Chapelle Papers.

34. See "Agreement," February 5, 1945. In Dickie Chapelle Papers.

35. Letter from Admiral Sampson to General Gomez, April 30, 1898. In Sylvester Scovel Papers.

36. Letter from Maximo Gomez to Sylvester Scovel, April 30, 1898. In Sylvester Scovel Papers.

37. Letter from Merrill to Sylvester Scovel, December 1, 1898. Some reporters were government employees while they worked for newspapers, e.g., Stephen Bonsal. In Steven Bonsal Papers. Richard Tregaskis tried to get the military to underwrite a book about the Seabees. In Richard Tregaskis Papers (RT1).

38. "Correspondents commended; authorized to wear ribbon." In William Dickinson Papers, Box 9, p. 6.

39. Memo from Dwight D. Eisenhower to All Unit Commanders, American Expeditionary Force, May 11, 1944, RG 472, AG000.7-1, Box 3.

40. Memo from SHAEF Main to AGWAR, November 21, 1944. See also memo from AGWAR to SHAEF Main, November 24, 1944. Both in RG 4xx, AG000.74-2, Box 4.

41. See memo UNITY, signed Eisenhower to AGWAR for combined Chiefs of Staff, May 31, 1944, AG0000.7-1, Box 3.

42. Ibid.

43. Letter from Dickey Chapelle to Hobart Lewis, October 2, 1961. In Dickey Chapelle Papers.

44. Ibid.

45. See notes for a speech to the Pennsylvania Publishers Association, October 14, 1966. Letter from Tom Tiede to George R. Bryan, May 10, 1966. In Tom Tiede Papers, Boxes 4 and 6.

46. Letter from Dickey Chapelle to Howard Calkins, USIS, 1961. In Dickey Chapelle Papers.

47. "Profile of a PIO." In Tom Tiede Papers, Box 5.

48. Letter from Moe to Tom Tiede (1966), ibid. The stories Moe refers to are "18 Trying to Make 19," and "Forgotten Men."

49. Letter from Edward Lansdale to General C. E. LeMay, April 1, 1964. In Dickey Chapelle Papers.

50. Note written to Dickey Chapelle on a copy of a speech that Lansdale gave at the Principia Conference, Vietnam, April 9, 1965. In Dickey Chapelle Papers, Box 8.

51. Letters from Richard Tregaskis to Dick Berlin, January 11, 1965, and to Admiral John McCain [n.d. 1965?]. In Richard Tregaskis Papers (RT1).

52. Letter from Dickey Chapelle to Chet Williams, April 29, 1962. In Dickey Chapelle Papers.

53. Letter from Richard Tregaskis to Richard Berlin, January 17, 1965. In Richard Tregaskis Papers (RT1), Box 3.

54. See the Richard Tregaskis Biography; letter from Richard Tregaskis to Mad-

eline Tregaskis, December 10, 1942 . In Richard Tregaskis Papers (RT1), Boxes 43 and 60.

55. See Memo from PR Division, September 4, 1944, in AG000.74-2, Box 4.

56. See the Richard Tregaskis Biography. In Richard Tregaskis Papers (RT1).

57. Ibid.

58. Thomson, *Blue Pencil Admiral*, 130.

59. Ernie Pyle to J. Pyle, February 21, 1943, Ernie Pyle Papers.

60. Ernie Pyle to J. Pyle, November 11, 1943; but cf November 8, 1943 and June 19, 1943, ibid.

61. Cable from Hal Boyle to George Wells, n.d., Hal Boyle Papers.

62. Ernie Pyle, quoted in Lee Miller, *The Ernie Pyle Story*, 220.

Chapter 6: Experience and Interpretation

1. See Fry's study of romance in *The Secular Scripture*.

2. Capa, *Slightly Out of Focus*, 241.

3. Berlin, *The Roots of Romanticism*, especially chap. 1.

4. Campbell, *The Romantic Ethic*, see particularly 173–201.

5. See Durschmid, *Shooting Wars*, 10.

6. See Paul de Man's account in *Romanticism and Contemporary Criticism*, chap. 1. These essays, gathered and published posthumously, are de Man's lectures for the Gauss Seminar at Princeton. See also Hulme, "Romanticism and Classicism," 35–36, who blames Rousseau for this belief.

7. See Foner, *The Spanish-Cuban-American War*.

8. See George Kennan Papers, Cuban Notebooks, nos. 1 and 2, and Richard Harding Davis Papers, letter to Gus, July 26, 1898, and letter to his mother, January 24, 1897.

9. Brisbane, "The Modern Newspaper in War Time," 550. See also Carnes, *Jimmy Hare*, 60; and "Newspaper Correspondents in War," 538–41.

10. R. H. Davis, "Our Correspondents in Cuba and Puerto Rico," 939, See also "Newspapermen in the War, 455–57.

11. For the details regarding Shafter's difficulties, see Goldhurst, *Pipe, Clay and Drill*, 70–71. For the best historical account of the Spanish-Cuban-American War see Trask, "American Intelligence During the Spanish American War."

12. See letter from Davis to his mother, January 24, 1897. In Richard Harding Davis Papers.

13. Freidel, *Splendid Little War*, 2. Cf. W. R. Hearst, "In the News," July 1, 1940, *The San Francisco Examiner*, a clipping in the William Randolph Hearst Papers.

14. Creelman, *On the Great Highway*, 168–69.

15. De Sola Pinto, "My First War," 67.

16. Mommsen, "Society and War," 531, 538.

17. Geiss, *July 1914*, 10, 20.

18. L. C. F. Turner, *Origins of the First World War*, 110–11, 114–15.

19. Mathews, *Reporting the Wars*, 162–63.

20. Letter from Herbert Corey to his mother, February 18, 1915. In Herbert Corey Papers.

21. Ruhl, *Antwerp to Gallipoli*, 128; Dunn, *Five Fronts*, 160–70.

22. Corey, unpublished memoirs, 35–36. In Herbert Corey Papers.

23. W. Williams, *Passed by the Censor*, 256–57; Corey, unpublished memoirs, 55. In Herbert Corey Papers.

24. Irwin, *Men, Women, and War*, 165, v.

25. Ruhl, *Antwerp to Gallipoli*, 5.

26. W. Williams, *Passed by the Censor*, 252–54.

27. Ruhl, *Antwerp to Gallipoli*, 11.

28. Dunn, *Five Fronts*, 136.

29. Ibid., 188.

30. Ruhl, *Antwerp to Gallipoli*, 46.

31. Davis, *With the Allies*, 28, 31.

32. Ruhl, *Antwerp to Gallipoli*, 115.

33. Mencken, diary ms., p. 71, in Henry Louis Mencken Papers.

34. Dunn, *Five Fronts*, 188.

35. For the Chaplin metaphor, I am indebted to F. M. Forhock, who used it in a different context in "The Edge of Laughter," 243–54.

36. Anna Balakian analyzes surreal poetry in post-war France. See her books, *Literary Origins of Surrealism* and *Surrealism*.

37. Davis, *With the Allies*, 145.

38. Dunn, *Five Fronts*, 132.

39. Williams, *Passed by the Censor*, 194–45; Ruhl, *Antwerp to Gallipoli*, 15.

40. Dunn, *Five Fronts*, 17.

41. Herbert Corey, unpublished memoirs, pp. 168, 158. In Herbert Corey Papers.

42. Ibid., 45.

43. Dunn, *Five Fronts*, 85.

44. Ibid., 17–19.

45. *Ibid.*, 115.

46. Crozier, *American Reporters on the Western Front*, 100.

47. Trumpener, "The Road to Ypres," 460.

48. Crozier, *American Reporters on the Western Front*, 100, 102.

49. Trumpener, "The Road to Ypres," 462.

50. Ibid., 480.

51. Remarque, *All Quiet on the Western Front*, 117–18.

52. Fussell, *The Great War and Modern Memory*, 36–37.

53. Dunn, *Five Fronts*, 16.

54. Brown, *Muddy Boots and Red Socks*.

55. See Arnett, *Live from the Battlefield*, 74–75, 83

56. Letter from David Halberstam to Manny Freedman, July 15, 1963. One instance of writing in code was a brief note Halberstam wrote about Henry Cabot Lodge's decision not to back the current leaders in Saigon, Diem and Nhu. See folder on August-September 1963, Box 3. All documents in David Halberstam Papers.

57. Letter from Nan and Nat G. to David Halberstam, September 15, 1963. Emphasis added. In David Halberstam Papers.

58. Tregaskis, "Vietnam Diary," ms., p. 154. In Richard Tregaskis Papers (RT2).

59. Fitzgerald, "Vietnamese—the People," p. 260. Manuscript in Frances Fitzgerald Papers.

60. Fitzgerald, untitled manuscript In Frances Fitzgerald Papers, Box 9, folder 8.

61. Letter from Dickey Chapelle to Steve, September 28, 1961. In Dickey Chapelle Papers.

62. Letter from Richard Tregaskis to Paul Reynolds, October 18, 1966. In Richard Tregaskis Papers (RT1).

63. Frances Fitzgerald Papers, Box 9, folder 7, p. 5.

64. Letter from William J. Webb [Special Assistant, Public Affairs for Seabees] to Richard Tregaskis, December 17, 1966. For the language he used about the Seabees, see Tregaskis, "Vietnam Diary," manuscript. In Richard Tregaskis Papers (RT2).

65. "TV under Paar" [January 1962], news clip. This is not an isolated instance. In a speech given in 1962, Chapelle said she was having fun in the United States, but she would "rather be back with *my people* in Vietnam." Emphasis added. Both items in the Dickey Chapelle Papers.

66. The man was Ernest Hemingway. Moorehead, *Gellhorn*, 208.

67. Ibid., 218, 221, 223, 225.

68. Ibid., 348.

69. Caputo, "Address at Key West," Phillip Caputo Papers, Box 33, Folder 5.

70. Letter from Richard Tregaskis to Bob Fitzgibbon, editor of *Family Weekly* [1968 or 1969]. In Richard Tregaskis Papers (RT1).

71. Letter from Lance Corporal C. E. Atkins to Tom Tiede, March 7, 1967, in Tom Tiede Papers.

72. See for example a brochure advertising a lecture by Felix Greene, cousin of the English writer Graham Greene, in the Richard Tregaskis Papers (RT2), Box 28.

73. Script for "Highway One," Invasion of Cambodia, Box 1, folder 3, in Dean Brelis Papers.

74. Caputo, "Address at Key West," Phillip Caputo Papers, Box 33, Folder 5.

75. Letter from Richard Tregaskis to Mei-Mei [ca. 1968]; see also Tregaskis to Eddie Sherman, April 21, 1968, and Tregaskis to Francis Ikezaki, April 21, 1968 (in RT1); see also his "Vietnam Diary," ms. pp. 233–55 (in RT2). All documents in Richard Tregaskis Papers.

76. Letter from Richard Tregaskis to Zig Ziegler, August 17, 1967. See letter from Tregaskis to Colston Leigh, August 4, 1967, Box 28. In Tregaskis Papers (RT1).

77. Letter from John Phillips to the editor, *Village Voice* [n.d.], in Frances Fitzgerald Papers, Box 9, Folder 8.

78. Letter from Richard Tregaskis to Sid Goldberg, October 3, 1964. In Tregaskis Papers (RT1).

79. Phillip Caputo Papers, Box 33, pp. 6, 14, 12.

80. See Frances Fitzgerald Papers, Boxes 6 and 9.

81. Ibid., Box 9, Folder 4, on refugees.

82. Ibid., Box 9, Folder 8, p. 24.

83. Ibid., Box 11, Folder 1, p. 2.

84. I do not mean to suggest that the Vietnamese were illiterate so much as to

note that the conventions of Vietnamese culture were those of an oral culture, i.e., conventions resting on tradition, reverence for one's ancestors, and a preference for the interpersonal over written forms of communication.

85. See Frances Fitzgerald Papers, Box 11, folder 1, 4–5.

86. Moorehead, *Gellhorn*, 353.

87. Ibid., 352–56.

88. See Whitney, "Gloria Emerson."

89. Ibid. The best source for Emerson's view of the war is her book *Winners and Losers*.

90. H. L. Mencken, ms. "Diary," 5. In Henry Louis Mencken Papers.

91. Letter from Dean Brelis to his mother, April 26, 1945. In Dean Brelis Papers.

92. Letter from Jack Giannini to Richard Tregaskis, August 22, 1968. In Tregaskis Papers (RT1).

93. Frances Fitzgerald Papers, Box 9, Folder 8, appearing in the May 19, 1966 issue of *Village Voice*, 9 and 12.

94. Frances Fitzgerald, "Vietnam—The People," *Vogue*, 149, no. 9 (May 1967), 174, 260–63.

95. Frances Fitzgerald Papers, Box 9, Folder 8.

96. Tregaskis, *Guadalcanal Diary*, 16.

97. Morris, *Deadline Every Minute*, 240.

98. This number is a little misleading, however. Only two hundred or so covered the conflict at any one time. Most correspondents went over for only four or five weeks, though some reporters covered the war for its duration. See Mott, *American Journalism*, 742.

99. Cited in Geertz, "Common Sense as a Cultural System," 26.

100. See Mander, "The Journalist as Cynic," 91–107.

101. David Halberstam, quoting Normal Mailer, "Introduction," in Mauldin, *Up Front*, viii.

102. Ibid., 16.

103. Ibid.; Sevareid, *Not So Wild a Dream*, 9.

104. Matloff, "American Approach to War," 224–36.

105. *Oklahoma*, February 1944. In 1944 files, Ernie Pyle Papers.

106. Sevareid, from a broadcast quoted in *Not So Wild a Dream*, 495, cf. Casey, *This Is Where I Came In*, 10.

107. Pyle, *Brave Men*, 260–61.

108. Sevareid, *Not So Wild a Dream*, 238.

109. Halberstam, "Introduction," vii-x.

110. "A Reporter's View of Life," manuscript in Paul Scott Mowrer Papers.

111. Transportation, like censorship, was somewhat of a problem in the early days of the war and in certain theaters. See, for example, Rawlings, "The Sweaty Heirs of Richard Harding Davis," 6.

112. See World War II Diary, Robert Casey Papers, 32; Mauldin, *Up Front*, 95; E. Pyle to J. Pyle, January 25 [no year given], Ernie Pyle Papers.

113. Mott, *American Journalism*, 742, 759.

114. Kahn, "The Men behind the By-Lines," 19.

115. E. Pyle to J. Pyle, January 12, 1941.

116. E. Pyle to J. Pyle, February 11, 1944, Ernie Pyle Papers; Miller, *The Ernie Pyle Story*, 30.

117. Robert Sherrod, quoted in Stein, *Under Fire*, 109.

118. Harold Denny of the *New York Times*, quoted in Stein, *Under Fire*, 99.

119. E. Pyle to J. Pyle, May 2, 1943. In Ernie Pyle Papers.

120. Kahn, "The Men behind the By-Lines," 98.

121. Mauldin, *Up Front*, 40–41.

122. E. Pyle, quoted in Miller, *The Ernie Pyle Story*, 274.

123. Geertz, "Common Sense as a Cultural System," 20.

124. Tregaskis, *Guadalcanal Diary*, 146.

125. Byron Price, "Censorship and Common Sense." Address before the annual meeting of the Southern Newspaper Publishers Association, Hot Springs, AR, September 28, 1942. See Advance Release, Office of War Information, in the 1942 files of the Raymond Clapper Papers.

126. Geertz wrongly includes "Literal" as a quality of commonsense imagination. See "Common Sense as a Cultural System," 22ff.

127. In this discussion of common sense, I am drawing somewhat on Cady, *The Light of Common Day*, 5, 10.

128. E. Pyle to J. Pyle, April 14, 1944, cf. May 13, 1943. In Ernie Pyle Papers.

129. E. Pyle, from the notes found on his body and kept at the Ernie Pyle Museum, Albuquerque, NM.

130. Girgus, *The Law of the Heart*, 45.

131. Hal Boyle, "Bob Casey and the Great Gift of Gusto," *New York Times*, January 24, 1945. In 1945 files, Robert Casey Papers.

132. For agreement with this statement see Coblentz, *Newsmen Speak*,190.

133. *American Observer*, December 13, 1943, p. 8. In 1943 files, Raymond Clapper Papers.

134. Roy Howard to Raymond Clapper, February 16, 1942. In the letter Howard upbraids Clapper for a column Clapper wrote that was diametrically opposed to Scripps-Howard's editorial position. Howard's point was that, because of the realistic quality of Clapper's work, Clapper had earned the reputation for accuracy and fair play. Howard went on to say that he could not advantageously oppose Clapper's ideas editorially even when he felt Clapper was wrong. He asked Clapper to keep to a minimum "the number of monkey wrenches you find to toss into our editorial camp." See also Howard to Clapper, March 30, 1943; March 17, 1943, for other assessments of Clapper's work. All documents in Raymond Clapper Papers.

135. Miller, *The Ernie Pyle Story*, 343, 384.

136. For examples, see Ernie Pyle to Paige Cavanaugh, February 12, 1941; June 18, 1942; March 14, 1945; April 23, 1942.

137. E. Pyle to J. Pyle, March 11, 1944 and June 22, 1943; E. Pyle to Paige Cavanaugh, September 17, 1940.

138. From the notes found on Pyle's body, now kept at the museum in Albuquerque, New Mexico.

139. E. Pyle to J. Pyle, August 15, 1943 and September 26, 1942.

140. Capa, *Slightly Out of Focus*, 48.

Chapter 7: *The Occupational Culture of the American War Correspondent*

1. This term is one I adapted from Raymond Williams's work.

2. Dickey Chapelle, however, was able to divest herself of the earlier war's influence, unlike Tregaskis.

3. See Langguth, *Our Vietnam*, 196.

4. Letter from Richard Tregaskis to Paul Reynolds, March 15, 1966, Box 28. In Tregaskis Papers (RT1).

5. See the exchange of letters between Neil Sheehan and his editors in the Neil Sheehan Papers.

6. See, for example, the letter from Bill Dickinson to his family, April 4, 1942. In William B. Dickinson Papers.

7. Ibid.

8. Letter from Hobart Lewis to Dickey Chapelle, August 19, 1963, in Dickey Chapelle Papers, Box 7.

9. Partial letter from June Ornsteen to Tom Tiede, n.d. See also letter from Saul Silverman to Tom Tiede, September 17, 1966. Both letters can be found in Tom Tiede Papers, Box 6.

10. Letter from Mrs. Katherine Brett to Tom Tiede, December 13, 1965, ibid.

11. Ibid.

12. Considine, Column.

13. Copy sent to Marc A. Rose, *Reader's Digest*, June 22, 1945. See Dickey Chapelle Papers.

BIBLIOGRAPHY

Manuscript Collections

Alsop, Joseph Wright. Papers. Library of Congress, Manuscript Division, Washington, DC.

Bonsal, Stephen. Papers. Library of Congress, Manuscript Division, Washington, DC.

Boyle, Hal. Papers. Wisconsin Historical Society, Madison.

Brelis, Dean. Papers. Muger Library, Boston University, Boston.

Caputo, Phillip. Papers. Muger Library, Boston University, Boston.

Casey, Robert. Papers. Newberry Library, Chicago.

Chapelle, Dickey. Papers. Wisconsin Historical Society, Madison.

Clapper, Raymond. Papers. Newberry Library, Chicago.

Corey, Herbert. Papers, Library of Congress, Manuscript Reading Room, Washington, DC.

Davis, Richard Harding. Papers. University of Virginia, Charlottesville.

Dickinson, William B. Papers. American Heritage Center, University of Wyoming, Laramie.

Eaton, W. P. Papers. Aldermann Library, University of Virginia, Charlottesville.

Fitzgerald, Frances. Papers. Muger Library, Boston University, Boston.

Halberstam, David. Papers. Muger Library, Boston University, Boston.

Hearst, William Randolph. Papers. Stanford University Library, Palo Alto, CA.

Kennan, George. Papers. Library of Congress, Manuscript Division, Washington, DC.

Knickerbocker, Hubert Renfro. Papers. Columbia University Libraries, New York.

Kuhn, Ferdinand. Papers. Columbia University Libraries, New York.

Mencken, Henry Louis. Papers. Library of Congress, Manuscript Division, Washington, DC.

Morrison, Allan Malcolm. Papers. New York Public Library, Schomburg Center for Research in Black Culture, New York.

Mowrer, Paul Scott. Papers. Newberry Library, Chicago.

Pacifica Foundation. Records. Wisconsin State Historical Society, Madison.

Price, Byron. Papers. Wisconsin State Historical Society, Madison.

Pyle, Ernie. Papers. Lilly Library, Indiana University, Bloomington.

Scovel, Sylvester. Papers. Missouri Historical Society, St. Louis.

Sheehan, Neil. Papers, Library of Congress, Manuscript Division, Washington DC.

Tiede, Tom. Papers. Muger Library, Boston University, Boston.
Tregaskis, Richard. Papers. American Heritage Center, University of Wyoming, Laramie [RT1].
Tregaskis, Richard. Papers. Muger Library, Boston University, Boston [RT2].
Warner, Albert Lyman. Papers. Wisconsin State Historical Society, Madison.
Watkins, Armitage. Papers on the U.S. Office of War Information. Columbia University Libraries, New York.

Government Documents Collections

Adjutant General's Document File. Records from 1895 through 1919. National Archives, Washington, DC. Abbreviated in notes as AGDF.
Adjutant General's Office. Records from 1939–1945. National Archives, Washington, DC. Abbreviated in notes as AGO.
Disaccreditation or Suspended Correspondents [Vietnam]. National Archives, Washington, DC.
Historical Summaries [of AFRTS]. National Archives, Washington, DC.
Information Advisory and Accreditation Procedures SOP. National Archives, Washington, DC.

Primary and Secondary Publications

Albrecht-Carrie, Rene. *The Meaning of the First World War.* Englewood-Cliffs, NJ: Prentice Hall, 1965.
Anderson, Benedict. *Imagined Communities: Reflections on the Origin and Spread of Nationalism.* Revised edition. New York and London: Verso, 1991.
Arnett, Peter. *Live from the Battlefield: From Vietnam to Baghdad, 35 Years in the World's War Zones.* New York: Simon and Shuster, 1994.
Baker, Ray Stannard. "How the News of the War Is Reported." *McClure's Magazine* 11 (September 1898): 491–95.
Balakian, Anna. *Literary Origins of Surrealism.* New York: New York University Press, 1947.
———. *Surrealism.* New York: E.P. Dutton, 1970.
Baldasty, Gerald. *The Commercialization of News in the Nineteenth Century.* Madison: University of Wisconsin Press, 1992.
Barnhurst, Kevin G., and John Nerone. *The Form of News.* New York: Guilford Press, 2001.
Barton, Fred. "Ambassador to Mr. Average." *Coronet* 13 (June 1943): 125–29.
Bean, Walter P. "The Accuracy of the Creel Committee News, 1917–1919: An Examination of Cases." *Journalism Quarterly* (July 1941): 263–72.
Berlin, Isaiah. *The Roots of Romanticism.* Princeton: Princeton University Press, 1999.
Bigart, Homer. *Forward Positions: The War Correspondence of Homer Bigart.* Fayetteville: University of Arkansas Press, 1992.
Blondheim, Menahem. *News Over the Wires: The Telegraph and the Flow of Public Information in America, 1844–1897.* Cambridge, MA: Harvard University Press, 1994.

———. "'Public Sentiment Is Everything': The Union's Public Communications Strategy and the Bogus Proclamation of 1864." *The Journal of American History* 89, no. 3. Available at http://tinyurl.com/yfbvwgz (accessed November 30, 2009).

Boemeke, Manfred F. Roger Chickering, and Stig Forster, ed. *Anticipating Total War: The German and American Experiences, 1871–1914.* Cambridge: Cambridge University Press, 1999.

Boyle, Hal. "Bob Casey and the Great Gift of Gusto." *New York Times* 61 (January 24, 1945).

Breen, T. H. *The Marketplace of Revolution: How Consumer Politics Shaped American Independence.* New York: Oxford University Press, 2004.

Brisbane, Arthur. "The Modern Newspaper in War Time." *Cosmopolitan* 25 (September 1898): 541–57.

———. "Newspaper Correspondents in War." *Review of Reviews* 9 (November 1898): 5.

Broun, Heywood. *Our Army at the Front.* New York: Charles Scribner's, 1919.

Brown, Charles. *The Correspondent's War.* New York: Charles Scribner's, 1967.

Browne, Malcolm. *Muddy Boots and Red Socks: A Reporter's Life.* New York: Times Books, 1993.

Cady, Edwin H. *The Light of Common Day: Realism in American Fiction.* Bloomington: Indiana University Press, 1971.

Cairns, John. "Some Recent Historians and the Strange Defeat of 1940." *Journal of Modern History* 46 (March 1974): 60–95.

Campbell, Colin. *The Romantic Ethic and the Spirit of Modern Capitalism.* London: Basil Blackwell, 1987.

Campbell, W. Joseph. *The Year That Defined American Journalism: 1897 and the Clash of Paradigms.* New York: Routledge, 2006.

Capa, Robert. *Slightly Out of Focus.* New York: Henry Holt, 1947.

Carnes, Cecil. *Jimmy Hare: News Photographer, Half a Century with a Camera.* New York: McMillan, 1940.

Carey, James. *Communications as Culture: Essays on Media and Society.* Boston: Unwin Hyman, 1989.

Casey, Ralph. "Propaganda and Public Opinion," 429–77. In *War in the Twentieth Century.* Edited by Willard Waller. New York: Random House, 1940.

Casey, Robert J. *This Is Where I Came In.* New York: Bobbs-Merrill, 1945.

Canoff, David, and Doan Van Toai, comp. and ed. *Vietnam: A Portrait of Its People at War.* London and New York: I.B. Tauris Publishers, 1996.

Cobb, Irvin. *The Glory of the Coming.* New York: Doran, 1918.

Coblentz, Edmond. *Newsmen Speak.* Los Angeles: University of California Press, 1954.

"Communications: The Fourth Front." *Fortune* 20 (November 1939): 90–96.

"Complaint from Paris." *Newsweek* 22 (September 11, 1944): 86.

Considine, Robert. Column. *New York Journal American.* November 8, 1965.

Cooke, John Byrne. *Reporting the War: Freedom of the Press from the American Revolution to the War on Terrorism.* New York: Palgrave Macmillan, 2007.

Creelman, James. *On the Great Highway.* Boston: Lothrop Publishing, 1901.

Crozier, Emmet. *American Reporters on the Western Front, 1914–1918.* New York: Oxford University Press, 1959.

Culbert, David H. "This Is London: Edward R. Morrow, Radio News, and American Aid to Britain." *Journal of Popular Culture* 10 (Summer 1976): 28–37.
Davis, Charles B. *Adventures and Letters of Richard Harding Davis.* New York: Charles Scribner's, 1917.
Davis, Richard Harding. *Cuba in Wartime.* New York: Charles Scribner's, 1897.
———. *Notes of a War Correspondent.* New York: Charles Scribner's, 1910.
———. "Our Correspondents in Cuba and Puerto Rico." *Harper's Monthly* 98 (May 1899): 938–48.
———. *With the Allies.* New York: Charles Scribner's, 1918.
De Man, Paul. *Romanticism and Contemporary Criticism.* Edited by E. S. Burt, Kevin Newmark, and Andrzej Warminski. Baltimore: Johns Hopkins University Press, 1993.
Desmond, Robert. *The Information Process: World News Reporting to the Twentieth Century.* Iowa City: University of Iowa Press, 1977.
De Sola Pinto, Vivian. "My First War: Memoirs of a Spectacled Subaltern," 67–84 in George A. Panichas, *Promise of Greatness: The War of 1914–1918.* New York: John Day, 1968.
Dewey, John. *Experience and Nature.* New York: Dover, 1958.
Doctorow, E. L. *Ragtime.* New York: Random House, 1975.
Doob, Lawrence. "Propaganda." *International Encyclopedia of Communication.* Vol. 3. New York: Oxford University Press, 1989.
Downey, Fairfax. *Richard Harding Davis Papers: His Day.* New York: Charles Scribner's, 1933.
Dunn, Robert. *Five Fronts.* New York: Dodd, Mead and Co., 1915.
Durschmid, Erik. *Shooting Wars: My Life as a War Cameraman from Cuba to Iraq.* New York: Pharos Books, 1990.
Dyson, A. E. *The Crazy Fabric.* New York: St. Martins Press, 1965.
Ellis, John. *The Social History of the Machine Gun.* New York: Pantheon, 1975.
Emerson, Gloria. *Winners and Losers: Battles, Retreats, Gains, Losses, and Ruins from a Long War.* New York: Random House, 1976.
Emery, Michael. *On the Front Lines: Following America's Foreign Correspondents across the Twentieth Century.* Journalism History Series. Edited by Sanford J. Ungar. Washington, DC: American University Press, 1995.
Emery, Michael, Edwin Emery, and Nancy L. Roberts. *The Press and America: An Interpretive History of the Mass Media.* Boston: Allyn and Bacon, 2000.
The Encyclopedia of Military History. Revised Edition. New York: Harper and Row, 1977.
Esper, George (and the Associated Press). *The Eyewitness History of the Vietnam War.* New York: Villard Books, 1983.
Fligstein, Neil. "Who Served in the Military, 1940–1973." *Armed Forces and Society* 6 (Winter 1980): 297–312.
Flint, Grover. *Marching with Gomez.* New York: Lamsom Wolffe, 1898.
Foner, Phillip S. *The Spanish-Cuban-American War and the Birth of American Imperialism, 1895–1902.* 2 Vols. New York: Monthly Review Press, 1972.
Forhock, F. M. "The Edge of Laughter: Some Modern Fiction and the Grotesque," 243–54. In *Veins of Humor.* Edited by Harry Levin. Cambridge, MA: Harvard University Press, 1972.

Freidel, Frank. *The Splendid Little War.* Boston: Little, Brown, 1958.
Frye, Northrop. *The Great Code: The Bible and Literature.* New York: Harcourt, Brace, Jovanovich, 1982.
———. *The Secular Scripture: A Study of the Structure of Romance.* Cambridge, MA: Harvard University Press, 1976.
Fussell, Paul. *The Great War and Modern Memory.* New York: Oxford University Press, 2000.
Geertz, Clifford. "Common Sense as a Cultural System." *Antioch Review* 33 (Spring 1975): 5–26.
———. *The Interpretation of Cultures: Selected Essays.* New York: Basic Books, 1973.
Geiss, Immanuel, ed. *July 1914: The Outbreak of the First World War.* New York: Scribner's, 1967.
Gellner, Ernest. *Nations and Nationalism.* Ithaca, NY: Cornell University Press, 1983.
Girgus, Sam B. *The Law of the Heart.* Austin: University of Texas Press, 1979.
Gleckner, Robert F., and Gerald E. Enscoe. *Romanticism: Points of View.* Detroit, MI: Wayne State University Press, 1975.
Goldhurst, Richard. *Pipe, Clay and Drill: John Pershing: The Classic American Soldier.* New York: Faber and Faber, 1977.
Grattan, Hartley C. *Why We Fought.* New York: Vanguard, 1929.
Greene, Graham. *The Quiet American.* London: W. Heinemann and the Bodley Head, 1973.
Greenfeld, Liah. *Nationalism: Five Roads to Modernity.* Boston: Harvard University Press, 1993.
Habermas, Jurgen. *The Structural Transformation of the Public Sphere: An Inquiry into a Category of Bourgeois Society.* Boston: MIT Press, 1991.
Halberstam, David. *The Best and the Brightest.* With an introduction by John McCain. New York: Modern Library Edition, 2001.
———. "Introduction." In *Up Front,* by Bill Mauldin. New York: Norton, 1944.
Hallin, Daniel C. *The Uncensored War: The Media and Vietnam.* Berkeley: University of California Press, 1989.
Hammond, William. *Reporting Vietnam: Media and Military at War.* Lawrence: University Press of Kansas, 1998.
Hecht, Ben. *New York Times Book Review* 61 (July 29, 1945): 5.
Hemment, John C. *Cannon and Camera.* New York: Appelton, 1898.
Herr, Michael. *Dispatches.* New York: Knopf, 1977.
Higham, John. "The Redefinition of America in the Twentieth Century," 301–26. In *German and American Nationalism.* Edited by Hartmut Lehmann and Hermann Wellenreuther. New York: Oxford University Press, 1999.
Holbrook, Stuart. *Lost Men of American History.* New York: Macmillan, 1946.
Howard, Michael. *War in European History.* London: Oxford University Press, 1976.
Hulme, T. E. "Romanticism and Classicism." In *Romanticism: Points of View.* Edited by Robert F. Gleckner and Gerald E. Enscoe. Detroit, MI: Wayne State University Press, 1975.
International Encyclopedia of Communication. New York: Oxford University Press, 1989.

Irwin, Will. *Men, Women, and War.* New York: Appleton and Company, 1915.
———. *A Reporter at Armageddon: Letters from the Front and Behind the Lines of the Great War.* New York: Appelton, 1918.
Jamieson, Fredric. *The Political Unconscious.* Ithaca, NY: Cornell University Press, 1981.
Jones, Edgar L. "The Care and Feeding of Correspondents." *Atlantic Monthly* 176 (October 1945): 46–51.
"Joseph Pulitzer and the New Journalism." *Chatauquan* 65 (January 1912): 156–58.
Jowet, Garth, and Victoria O'Donnell. *Propaganda and Persuasion.* Second edition. Newburry Park: Sage, 1991; Fourth edition (Beverly Hills: Sage, 2006).
Kahn, E. J. "The Men behind the By-Lines." *Saturday Evening Post* 216 (September 11, 1943): 19, 96, 98.
Keegan, John. *The Face of Battle.* New York: Viking Press, 1976.
Kennan, George. *Campaigning in Cuba.* New York: Century, 1899.
Kersh, Rogan. *Dreams of a More Perfect Union.* Ithaca, NY: Cornell University Press, 2001.
Kirstein, Lincoln. *Rhymes of a PFC.* New York: New Directions, 1964.
Knightley, Phillip. *The First Casuality.* Baltimore: Johns Hopkins University Press, [1975] 2004.
Koistinen, Paul A. C. *Planning War, Pursuing Peace: The Political Economy of American War, 1920–1939.* Lawrence: University Press of Kansas, 1998.
Lam, Quang Thi. *The Twenty-Five Year Century: A South Vietnamese General Remembers the Indochina War to the Fall of Saigon.* Denton: University of North Texas Press, 2001.
Landers, James. *The Weekly War: Newsmagazines and Vietnam.* Columbia: University of Missouri Press, 2004.
Langguth, A. J. *Our Vietnam: The War 1954–1975.* New York: Simon and Shuster, 2000.
Lardner, John. "Occupational Risks of a War Correspondent." *Newsweek* (December 6, 1943): 20.
Larson, Cedric. "American Army Newspapers in the World War." *Journalism Quarterly* 17 (June 1940): 121–32.
———. "Censorship of Army News during the World War, 1919–1918." *Journalism Quarterly* 17 (December 1940): 313–23.
Mander, Mary S. "American War Correspondents During World War II: Common Sense as a View of the World." *American Journalism* 1 (Summer 1983): 17–30.
———. *Framing Friction: Media and Social Conflict.* Champaign: University of Illinois Press, 1999.
———. "The Journalist as Cynic." *Antioch Review* 38 (Winter 1980): 91–107.
———. "Pen and Sword: Problems of Reporting the Spanish-American War." *Journalism History* 9:1 (Spring 1982): 2–9, 28.
———. "Utopian Elements in the Discourse on Broadcasting." *Journal of Communications Inquiry* 12, no. 2 (Summer 1988), 71–88.
Martelli, George. "The Propagandist's Propaganda." *Encounter* 42 (March 1974): 47–52.
Mathews, Joseph. *Reporting the Wars.* Minneapolis: University of Minnesota Press, 1957.

Matloff, Maurice. "American Approach to War," 224–36. In *The Theory and Practice of War*. Edited by Michael Howard. Bloomington: Indiana University Press, 1965.

Mauldin, Bill. *Up Front*. New York: Norton, 1944.

Merlin, M. Giovanna. "The Socio-Economic Background and War Mortality During Vietnam's Wars." *Demography* 37, no. 1 (February 2000): 1–15.

Meyrowitz, Joshua. *The Impact of Electronic Media on Social Behavior*. New York: Oxford University Press, 1985.

Middlebrook, Martin. *First Day on the Somme: July 1, 1916*. New York: W.W. Norton, 1972.

Miller, Lee. *The Ernie Pyle Story*. New York: Viking, 1950.

Millis, Walter. *Road to War: America 1914–1918*. Boston: Houghton Mifflin, 1935.

Mock, James R. *Censorship 1917*. Princeton, NJ: L. Milford, 1941.

Moeller, Susan D. *Shooting War: Photography and the American Experience of Combat*. New York: Basic Books, 1989.

Mommsen, W. J. "Society and War: Two New Analyses of World War I." *Journal of Modern History* 47, no 3 (September 1975): 530–38.

Moorehead, Caroline. *Gellhorn: A Twentieth-Century Life*. New York: Henry Holt, 2003.

Morris, Joe Alex. *Deadline Every Minute*. Garden City, NY: Doubleday, 1957.

Mott, Frank Luther. *American Journalism*. New York: Macmillan, 1947.

Munson, Eve, and Catherine A. Warren, ed. *James Carey: A Critical Reader*. Minneapolis: University of Minnesota Press, 1997.

Nafziger, Ralph. "World War Correspondents and Censorship of the Belligerents." *Journalism Quarterly* 14 (September 1937): 226–43.

Nerone, John. *The Culture of the Press in the Early Republic*. New York: Garland, 1989.

———. "The Mythology of the Penny Press." *Critical Studies in Mass Communication* 4, no. 4 (December 1987): 376–404.

"Newspaper Correspondents in War." *Review of Reviews* 9 (November 1898): 538–41.

"Newspapermen in the War." *Literary Digest* 17, no. 915 (October 15, 1898): 455–57.

Newton, Adam Zachary. *Narrative Ethics*. Boston: Harvard University Press, 1995.

Norris, Frank. "With Lawton at El Caney." *Century Magazine* 58 (June 1899): 304–9.

O'Keefe, Kevin. *A Thousand Deadlines: New York City Press and American Neutrality, 1917*. The Hague: Nijhoff, 1972.

The Oxford Companion to American Military History. Edited by John Whiteclay Chambers II. New York: Oxford University Press, 1999.

Panichas, George A. *Promise of Greatness: The War of 1914–1918*. New York: John Day, 1968.

Patterson, Annabel. *Censorship and Interpretation*. Madison: University of Wisconsin Press, 1984.

Peterson, H. C. *Propaganda for War: The Campaign Against American Neutrality, 1914–1917*. Norman: University of Oklahoma Press, 1939.

Pratt, Fletcher. "How the Censors Rigged the News." *Harper's Magazine* 192 (February 1946): 97–105.
"Press vs. the Navy." *Newsweek* 19 (February 23, 1942): 56.
Price, Byron. "Government Censorship in Wartime." *The American Political Science Review* 36, no. 5 (October 1942): 837–49.
Prochnau, William. *Once Upon a Distant War.* New York: Times Books, 1995.
"Pros and Cons of Embedded Journalism." Available at http://www.pbs.org/ newshour/extra/features/jan-june03/embed_3-27.html (accessed November 23, 2009).
Pyle, Ernie. *Brave Men.* New York: Holt, 1943.
Rawlings, C. A. "The Sweaty Heirs of Richard Harding Davis." *Saturday Evening Post* 216 (April 29, 1944): 6.
Rea, George Bronson. *Facts and Fakes about Cuba.* New York: George Monroe's Sons, 1897.
———. "The Night of the Explosion in Havana." *Harper's Weekly* 96 (March 5, 1898): 222.
Remak, Joachim. *The Origins of World War I, 1871–1914.* Second edition. Fort Worth, TX: Harcourt, Brace and Company, 1995.
Remarque, Erich Maria. *All Quiet on the Western Front.* Greenwich, CT: Fawcett Publications, 1928.
Report on the Office of Censorship. Washington, DC: U.S. Government Printing Office, 1946.
Ruhl, Arthur. *Antwerp to Gallipoli: A Year of War on Many Fronts.* New York: C. Scribner's Sons, 1916.
Schudson, Michael. *Discovering the News: A Social History of American Newspapers.* New York: Basic Books, 1978.
———. *Origins of the Ideal of Objectivity in the Professions: Studies in the History of American Journalism and American Law, 1830–1940.* New York: Garland, 1990.
Segal, David R. "How Equal Is Equity?" *Society* 18, no. 3 (1981): 31–33.
Seitz, Donald C. "Stephen Crane: War Correspondent." *Bookman* 76 (February 1933): 137–40.
Sevareid, Eric. "Censors in the Saddle." *Nation* 160 (April 14, 1945): 415–17.
———. *Not So Wild a Dream.* New York: Atheneum, 1976.
Sheehan, Neil. *A Bright Shining Lie: John Paul Vann and America in Vietnam.* New York: Vintage Books, 1989.
———. *After the War Was Over.* New York: Random House, 1992.
Sherrod, Robert. "Best Covered Story." *Time* 43 (December 13, 1943): 76.
Smith, Jeffrey A. *War and Press Freedom: The Problem of Prerogative of Power.* New York: Oxford University Press, 1999.
Smythe, C. J. *History of U.S. Censorship in World War II.* Master's Thesis. Urbana: University of Illinois, 1951.
Smythe, Donald. *Guerrilla Warrior: The Early Life of John J. Pershing.* New York: Scribner's, 1973.
Sommers, Martin. "The War to Get War News." *Saturday Evening Post* 216 (March 25, 1944).
Spears, John R. "Afloat for News on Wartime." *Scribner's Magazine* 11 (October 1898): 501–4.

Spencer, Graham. *The Media and Peace: From Vietnam to the War on Terror.* London: Palgrave Macmillan, 2005.

Sproule, J. Michael. *Propaganda and Democracy: The American Experience of Media and Mass Persuasion.* Cambridge, UK: Cambridge University Press, 1997.

Squires, Grant. "Experience of a War Censor." *Atlantic Monthly* 83 (March 1899): 425–32.

Stein, M.L. *Under Fire: The Story of American War Correspondents.* New York: Massner, 1968.

Stone, Melville. "The A.P. Fifth Paper: Its Work in War." *Century Magazine* 70 (August 1905): 504–10.

Sweeney, Michael S. *The Military and the Press: An Uneasy Truce.* Evanston, IL: Northwestern University Press, 2006.

Tallman, Gary C., and Joseph P. McKerns. "'Press Mess:' David Halberstam, the Buddhist Crisis, and the U.S. Policy in Vietnam, 1963." *Journalism and Communication Monographs* 2, no. 3 (Fall 2000): 109–55.

Tensill, C. C. *America Goes to War.* Boston: Houghton Mifflin, 1938.

Thomson, George P. *Blue Pencil Admiral: The Inside Story of Press Censorship.* London: Sampsom, Low, Marston, n.d.

Trask, David. "American Intelligence During the Spanish American War." In *Crucible of Empire: The Spanish American War and Its Aftermath.* Edited by James C. Bradford. Annapolis, MD: U.S. Naval Institute, 1993.

Tregaskis, Richard. *Guadalcanal Diary.* New York: Random House, 1947.

Trumpener, Ulrich. "The Road to Ypres: Beginnings of Gas Warfare in World War I." *Journal of Modern History* 47 (September 1975): 460–80.

Turner, Frederick Jackson. *History, Frontier, and Section.* Santa Fe: University of New Mexico Press, 1993.

Turner, L. C. F. *Origins of the First World War.* New York: W.W. Norton, 1970.

U.S. Office of Censorship. *Code of Wartime Practices for American Broadcasters.* Washington, DC: U.S. Government Printing Office, 1943.

Unseem, Michael. "Conscription and Class." *Society* 18, no. 3 (1981).

Van, Tien Dung. *Our Great Spring Victory: An Account of the Liberation of South Vietnam.* New York and London: Monthly Review Press, 1977.

Waller, Willard, ed. *War in the Twentieth Century.* New York: Dryden Press, 1940.

The War of 1898 and U.S. Interventions, 1898–1934: An Encyclopedia. Edited by Benjamin R. Beede. New York: Garland, 1994.

"War Reporters Fume at Cable Cartel's Workings as Big Story of the Tunisian Campaign Breaks." *Newsweek* 21 (April 12, 1943): 72, 74.

Whitney, Craig R. "Gloria Emerson, Chronicler of War's Damage, Dies at 75." *New York Times.* Available at http://tinyurl.com/yk6rh74; accessed December 16, 2009.

Wiebe, Robert. *The Search for Order.* New York: Hill and Wang, 1967.

Williams, Raymond. *Culture and Society, 1780–1950.* New York: Columbia University Press, 1983.

———. *The Long Revolution.* New York: Columbia University Press, 1961.

———. *Sociology of Culture,* New York: Schocken Books, 1982.

Williams, Wythe. *Passed by the Censor: The Experience of an American News-paper Man in France.* New York: E.P. Dutton, 1916.

Worcester, David. *The Art of Satire.* New York: Russell and Russell, 1960.

Ziff, Larzer. *The American 1890s; Life and Times of a Lost Generation.* New York: Viking Press, 1966.

Zobrist, Benedict K. "How Victor Lawson's Newspapers Covered the Cuban War of 1898." *Journalism Quarterly* 38 (Summer 1961): 323–31.

INDEX

MARY S. MANDER is Professor Emerita in the
College of Communications at the Pennsylvania
State University. She edited *Framing Friction: Media
and Social Conflict* as well as *Communication
in Transition.*

The University of Illinois Press
is a founding member of the
Association of American University Presses.

University of Illinois Press
1325 South Oak Street
Champaign, IL 61820-6903
www.press.uillinois.edu

Printed and bound by CPI Group (UK) Ltd, Croydon, CR0 4YY

16/04/2025

14658439-0001